Keeping and Breeding Snakes

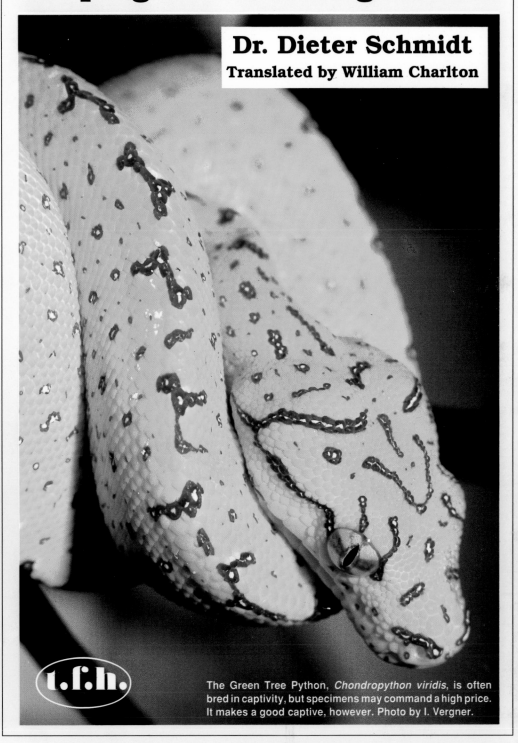

Dr. Dieter Schmidt
Translated by William Charlton

The Green Tree Python, *Chondropython viridis*, is often bred in captivity, but specimens may command a high price. It makes a good captive, however. Photo by I. Vergner.

Table of Contents

"We must . . . give the propagation of our charges clear precedence over mere 'keeping' and cooperate in this, because it will soon become essential to do so, especially in the terrarium hobby."

—H. G. Petzold

Foreword

"The keeping of pet animals is an educational factor that must be taken seriously. It is becoming increasingly important as urbanized humanity becomes estranged from nature." These words of the famous animal-behavior researcher Konrad Lorenz touch on the complicated relations of nature, culture, and society in these times of progressive expansion of the artificial environment and the reduction of the natural living spaces of plants and animals. Increasing urbanization and the growing longing for nature are leading people more and more to invite plants and animals into their homes. The time spent with these creatures, and the responsibility and resulting increase in knowledge associated with it, serve the personal development of the individual. The care of plants and animals in the home thus would be very commendable—but only as long as it is a question of "domesticated" plants and animals. The growing interest in the keeping of pet animals, as can be observed most of all in many industrialized countries, does not stop with the reptiles and amphibians either. In most cases, though less so of late, these animals are obtained by collecting wild animals; their commercial propagation is the exception, occurring mostly with the various species of

Described only within the last fifty years, the handsome Gray-banded Kingsnake, Lampropeltis alterna, has quickly become a hobbyist's favorite. Photo by K. H. Switak.

Captive-breeding efforts have produced some of the most attractive, not to mention unusual, color and pattern varieties. Corn Snakes, *Elaphe guttata guttata,* for example, are normally blotched, but this specimen was selectively bred for striping. Photo by Patrick H. Briggs, courtesy Lloyd Lemke.

Elaphe, Lampropeltis, and some boas and pythons. Inadequate knowledge and lack of information about the needs of these animals often lead to wrong keeping practices and high losses. The living "commodity" is consumed.

The increasing threat to many species because of worldwide destruction of their natural biotopes has prompted organizations of hobbyists in different countries to make the propagation of the species already present in terraria (and the limited importation for propagation of species that seem suitable) the goal of their activities. This general change in attitude has been achieved with dedicated hobbyists. The care and propagation of species particularly suitable for keeping in the terrarium have increasingly become the focus of their efforts. In the meantime, the result has been a wealth of experiences and successes.

We would like to thank all the hobbyists who contributed to the development of this work, either through their direct support or the experiences they provided. Our thanks also go to the publisher, who supported us in producing the manuscript and made possible its publication.

Schönow
Dieter Schmidt, Dr. Sci.

RELATIONS OF THE ENVIRONMENTAL FACTORS IN THE TERRARIUM TO ONE ANOTHER AND TO THE ANIMAL

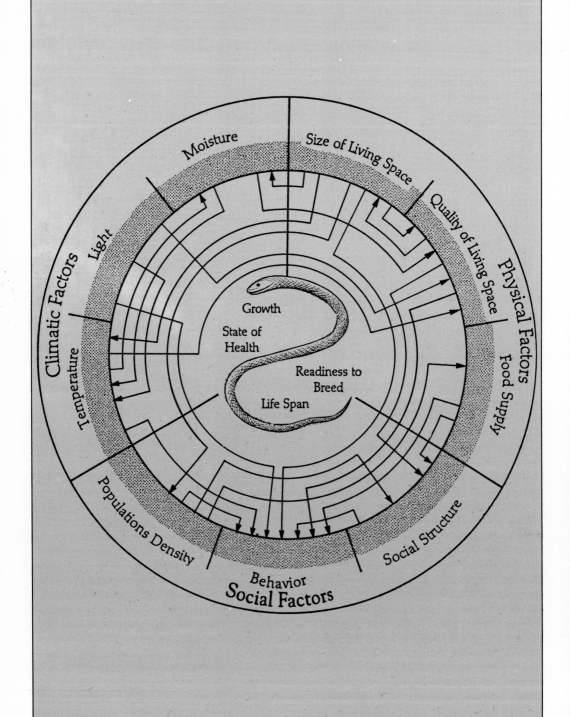

Living Space: The Terrarium

The terrarium as a living space for snakes is an ecological system whose influential factors are largely determined by the hobbyist and which are interrelated in many ways. A perfect imitation of the natural environmental conditions of the animals is impossible in the terrarium, and unnecessary.

SNAKE TERRARIA AND THEIR FURNISHINGS

The terrarium—its construction, its furnishing, and its technical equipment—demands close attention if we are to provide for the appropriate care of its inhabitants. The dimensions of the terrarium must suit the size and habits of the snakes as well as the number of specimens it will hold. For smaller species, such as garter snakes (*Thamnophis*), a terrarium 50 cm long, 30 cm wide, and 30 cm (20 X 12 X 12 in) high is adequate. Larger rat snakes (*Elaphe*) need housing with dimensions of at least 100 cm X 50 cm X 100 to 200 cm (40 X 20 X 40-80 in). In larger terraria, a differentiated microclimate is easier to achieve than in smaller facilities. Furthermore, the dimensions of the cage should suit the habits of the snake, whether it is an arboreal, terrestrial, or aquatic species.

In the wild, the size of a snake's living space is largely determined by the availability of food. Pronounced territorial behavior with the formation of territories is unknown in snakes. This explains why snakes do well even in relatively small terraria.

Depending on their location, indoor terraria usually have rectangular or—when, for example, the use of a corner of a room seems advantageous—triangular or pentagonal bases, vertical sides and rear walls, and in most cases vertical fronts. Terraria built into a window or bay require special insulation on the outside against heat. Greenhouse terraria, heated or unheated for the summer season, are expensive and need a suitable garden, preferably adjacent to the house.

An affordable alternative to the indoor or outdoor terrarium is the open-air terrarium on the balcony or terrace or in the garden. With suitable construction—extensive surfaces of netting to permit the unimpeded entry of sunlight and to prevent overheating, the cage set up in a location protected from wind—this hybrid of the indoor and outdoor cage has considerable advantages over an outdoor terrarium for keeping snakes. Outdoor terraria, regardless of how well built they are, are scarcely recommended for keeping snakes and are not well suited for breeding snakes.

An artificial biotope must be created for the snakes in the terrarium, in which they feel safe and can engage in their natural habits: movement, rest, sleep, feeding, and reproduction. To this end, favorable conditions of light, temperature, humidity, and ventilation must be provided. But the hobbyist also places demands on the terrarium. It should be possible for him to build and furnish it affordably given his technical knowledge and abilities—purchased terraria usually are quite expensive and do not always meet all expectations. The hobbyist will want to observe the habits of his charges as much as possible. The terrarium must be readily accessible and easy to clean and disinfect. It must close tightly to prevent the animals from escaping.

Possibly the most important demand placed on the terrarium is that it be nice to look at; when set up in a room, it should improve its livability. This is not always easy to achieve with terraria that will be used to breed and rear snakes. A breeding terrarium cannot be a show terrarium, but compromises between function and appearance are possible.

Building with wood is an old method of terrarium construction. Wood can be worked easily and without too much specialized knowledge and is affordable. Wood, however, has a big disadvantage: Even with the most careful protective measures, it is unsuitable for moist terraria. The construction of a terrarium of steel or aluminum

angle irons requires an expert or at least expert preparatory work. Angle irons also need to be well protected from the effects of moisture and are very heavy. Framing materials of hard plastic, which were used for a long time in terrarium construction, seldom are used today. All-glass technology, taken from aquarium construction, has become prevalent, at least for small and medium terraria. Cemented glass terraria block little   of the view and are easy to clean. Although acrylic plastic is expensive, it is better than window glass. A terrarium with a volume of about a cubic meter (3.5 cubic ft) needs 8- to 10-millimeter-thick (0.3-0.4 in) glass and weighs a total of about 100 kilograms (220 pounds). For terraria with a volume of about 0.1 cubic meters (0.35 cubic ft), a glass thickness of

Small plastic containers are ideal for housing very small snakes, quarantining ill specimens, temporarily housing snakes during cleaning, or holding snakes during transport. Such containers are available at most pet shops. Photo courtesy of Hagen.

Many snakes like to climb, and it behooves the keeper of such serpents to provide a branch or two. Beware, though, that wood is difficult to keep clean; most branches probably will have to be discarded and replaced. Photo of an Aesculapian False Coral Snake, *Erythrolamprus aesculapi*, by W. Wuster.

up to 5 millimeters (0.2 in) will do. Cutting the panes of glass to exact specifications is not for everyone. Any hobbyist, however, can smooth the edges of the glass with a corundum stone, clean the glass with a degreasing product, and glue the terrarium with one of the acetic-acid-based silicone cements available on the market. For ventilating the glued glass terrarium, the use of plastic mesh glued between strips of glass, over holes bored in the glass, or over installed hard-plastic elements is suitable.

Removable panes that run in a U- or double-U-shaped track enclose the front of the terrarium. Double-U tracks permit the terrarium to be opened even when there is no room above or to the side for the front pane. There is always a small crack between the two sliding panes, however, that can never be sealed satisfactorily and which, particularly with livebearing snake species, provides the newborn offspring a means of escape. Trap doors with glued-on hinges are also possible with all-glass cementing technology but need lots of space.

Bottom heating, installed water basins, potted plants, and ventilation conduits require a double terrarium bottom. The same is true in medium to large terraria for the installation of lighting and irradiation elements in a roof structure separated from the interior of the terrarium by metal gauze. Suitable blinds or shutters prevent the light from shining directly in the eyes of the observer.

The quality of the living space is important to the inhabitants of the terrarium. Their artificial habitat not only must meet their morphological and ecological requirements, but their psychological ones as well. Included here are suitable hiding places, basking surfaces, climbing branches, and bathing facilities. Planting the snake terrarium usually is a concession to the observer, but can be essential for certain arboreal snake species. It also helps to raise the humidity in moist terraria.

Even before the actual furnishing of the terrarium, the construction of the rear wall must be completed. Rock structures are too heavy and often produce hiding places inaccessible to the hobbyist. Rear walls made of pieces of bark glued together are hard to clean, and even if the cracks are carefully sealed with wood putty of matching color they offer undesirable hollow spaces in terraria with small snakes. Rear walls of mixtures of loam and plaster of Paris look quite natural. They have the disadvantages of soaking up water, not being very durable,

There are many subs　　s a keeper can use with captive snakes　　n ideal substrate is both safe for the anim　　s and easy for the keeper to work with. Photo courtesy of Four Paws.

The best type of setup for neonates is one that focuses on simplicity; the main priority is getting the snakes eating, not how nice the tank looks. Photo of hatching Desert-Horned Vipers, *Cerastes cerastes*, by K. H. Switak.

and being hard to clean. Rear walls of plastic are durable and easy to clean, but are shiny and do not look natural.

I have found a type of rear wall that is easy to build, does not weigh much, acts as an insulator, can be made to look very natural, and also is easy to wash and disinfect. Irregular pieces of a foam plastic glued to the rear wall of the terrarium form the base structure. At the same time basking surfaces and niches for plants can be built in. Then follows the application and modeling of an about 1-cm (0.4-in) layer of cement, sand, and latex. After a few days this layer will have hardened and can be painted with a thin paste of latex, cement, and paint as desired. By using different shades of color, it is possible to make the imitation rocks look natural. A similar rear-wall construction is possible with floor leveling compound.

The substrate is of particular importance for burrowing snake species and as a moisture reservoir in moist terraria. Washed sand, for example, is a natural hiding place for Desert Horned-Vipers (*Cerastes cerastes*). Sand boas (*Eryx*) also like to burrow in sand. Peat and sand mixtures are suitable for various types of moist terraria. For most snake species that live in dry terraria, a layer of loose, dry forest moss several centimeters thick is adequate. Droppings and food remains are easy to remove along with it.

Many snakes, even terrestrial species, like to climb. A sturdy climbing branch offers the opportunity to climb, hide, and rest. Artificial climbing branches with a skeleton of wire mesh and covered with a layer of plastic, cement, or plaster of Paris are very durable and can be built in any desired form. They do not rot, are easy to clean, and can even include a heating cable or serve as the covering for a lamp. Many arboreal snake species prefer thin climbing branches overgrown with climbing plants. For predominantly terrestrial snakes, as well as the common water snakes, a decorative, half-rotted pine stump has proved effective as the focal point of the terrarium. In small,

dry terraria, fairly thin, gnarled dead vines look very attractive.

Most snakes prefer hiding places that provide close contact with the animal's back. Besides hollow spaces under flat rocks, curved pieces of bark are readily accepted hiding places even for fairly large snakes. Lockable boxes that double as hiding places are recommended for keeping both large nonvenomous and venomous snakes.

The type and size of water bowl depend on the length and habits of the snakes. Water bowls should have smooth, easy-to-clean sides and, if they cannot be drained, should be easy to remove from the terrarium. Although sunken bowls look more natural, they are soon soiled by the substrate pushed into them by the snakes. Regular water changes are indispensable when caring for snakes. Because many snakes deposit their excrement in water, filtering the water or even biological self-cleaning is not adequate with fairly large, planted water bowls.

Plants in the snake terrarium mainly have decorative value, but only if they have not been damaged or dug up by the animals. Plants should be kept in pots or in plant tubs placed in the substrate or set in the rear wall of the terrarium so they can be replaced regularly. A planting that corresponds to the vegetation found in the snakes' native biotope is of significance only for esthetic reasons in the biotope terrarium. Plastic plants are a compromise; prejudices against them stem from unnatural-looking imitations. Plastic plants can be "planted" decoratively in holes in the terrarium rear wall or in stumps. Plastic plants, which can be disinfected, also easily meet the hygienic demands of the breeding terrarium. A particularly hygienic terrarium with minimal furnishings and without plants is necessary for the quarantine of newly purchased snakes or for the care of visibly sick animals. A substrate of newspaper is low in germs and permits the complete removal of droppings. A substrate of wood shavings, which keepers of giant snakes like to use, also has proved effective in the quarantine terrarium.

Snake Food: Feeding Snakes

A diet of good quality and sufficient quantity is as important as optimal keeping conditions for snakes. The metabolism of poikilothermic (coldblooded) snakes is not nearly as intensive as that of warmblooded birds or mammals. Snakes can be real fasting artists. In order to keep them for years in the terrarium and breed them successfully, however, a varied and nutritious diet is necessary.

Time and again we read sensational accounts of the periods of time in which large snakes in particular do not feed. Refusal of food over periods of one to two years has been described for many species. (Numbering among the "record holders" is a Reticulated Python, *Python reticulatus*, that fasted for three years.) In passing judgment on these occurrences, the relatively large amounts of food that are ingested while feeding usually are overlooked. It has been calculated for large pythons that close to 400 times the daily energy requirement can be taken in at one meal. Starving snakes also become emaciated very slowly. An experiment showed, for example, that several Florida Kingsnakes, *Lampropeltis getula floridana*, lost an average of only 6.3 percent of body mass after 17 weeks of starvation.

Usually scarcely noticed, because it is not always that obvious in the terrarium, is the fact that—like reproduction—metabolism also is subject to a natural annual rhythm. Included in this rhythm are pauses in feeding before the molt, during mating season, and in late stages of pregnancy. Newly purchased snakes should be fed as soon as possible. Stressful situations caused by capture and shipment, changed environmental conditions in the terrarium, unfamiliar food supply, or illnesses that have turned up in the meantime influence normal metabolism and the first intake of food. The hobbyist has three ways to keep snakes that refuse food from starving. First, it is advisable to offer the snakes an environment as similar as possible to what they were used to and to give them species-typical prey repeatedly. The snakes should be shielded from all distur-

bances; the presence of curious strangers is especially disturbing. If this does not help, the environmental conditions—temperature, humidity, lighting—should be changed and a continuous state of stimulation should be achieved by offering the most diverse foods. Finally, forced-feeding is the last resort.

Specialization on a particular food is not only species-typical in snakes, but often varies from individual to individual and sometimes changes. For example, the only animals of a fairly large assortment that a male Corn Snake, *Elaphe guttata*, would eat were one-day-old chicks and sparrows, including dead ones; rodents of all kinds and all sizes were offered again and again but were refused. A purchased adult Common Garter Snake, *Thamnophis sirtalis*, ate frogs exclusively, which presented considerable problems because native frogs are protected in Germany and thus not available. One day the lone animal was placed with a group of other garter snakes and from then on took—because of food envy?—fish, even cut up, from a dish.

If a species-specific or individual preference for particular prey exists, it is possible that white mice are refused, but gray or black ones are taken readily. Smell certainly plays an important role when, for example, laboratory mice are ignored but a vole, field mouse, or young rat is taken immediately.

It must be kept in mind that young snakes often prefer a diet different from that preferred by adults. Also frequently overlooked is the fact that nocturnal snake species often cannot be induced to accept food offered during the day. Their keeper should remember the old rule of the terrarium hobby, that aggressive food animals should be removed from the terrarium at night so that the snakes, which become more sluggish due to the cooler temperatures, are not injured by them. If you must leave a mouse in overnight, a little food in the terrarium for the hungry gnawer lessens the danger considerably.

Based on observations in the wild, changes in the preferred diet also are known to occur from season to season. For example, the

A lighted hood with a fliptop lid has two appealing features—it makes feedings easy (although you may have to modify the lid in order for it to be more secure), and the light casts an attractive glow into the enclosure. Photo courtesy of Hagen.

Broad-banded Copperhead, *Agkistrodon contortrix laticinctus*, from North America feeds on frogs in early spring, on young birds in late spring, and on small rodents in summer, before switching to frogs again in the fall.

The frequency of food intake depends on the period of digestion. The interval from ingestion to defecation depends on the temperature of the terrarium, the type of food, and the amount of food eaten; higher temperatures speed up digestion substantially, fish are digested faster than mammals or birds, and full satiation lasts longer than comparatively small meals. Each hobbyist will therefore have to accumulate experience by making observations of his own snakes.

One feeding every two weeks suffices for large snakes; juveniles feed once or twice a week. Water and garter snakes, such as members of the genera *Natrix*, *Nerodia*, and *Thamnophis*, can be offered food every two to three days.

Finally, the manner of presenting food plays a role: moving prey usually is preferred, since it stimulates natural reflexes—dead prey probably is taken in the wild only in exceptional cases. Some snakes refuse live food for a long time after an unexpected mouse bite.

In general, many snakes in the terrarium soon become accustomed to dead prey animals, particularly when they are moved in front of them with forceps or tongs. Moreover, the prey does not even always have to be freshly killed or freshly thawed. Young snakes often take dead food animals as the first food without problems.

Offering too many food animals at one time is to be avoided. Several food animals may be killed reflexively, but ultimately only

Scenic sheeting not only gives a tank the illusion of greater depth, but can add visual spice to an otherwise dull setup. Check your local pet shop; they may carry a variety of scenes. Photo courtesy Creative Surprizes.

Artificial plants have certain advantages over live plants, one of them being that artificial plants require little care. They are also reusable. Photo courtesy of Hagen.

Note the cage essentials in this setup—a branch for climbing, a water trough, a sensible substrate (in this case sphagnum), and a series of ventilation holes. Photo by D. Schmidt.

one animal is eaten. Once the capturing or swallowing reflex is triggered, it also is possible that too much food or too large pieces of food will be swallowed. In extreme cases the lining of the enormously distended esophagus will not stand the strain and will split. Such injuries, which by the way also occur in the careless force-feeding of young snakes, usually heal without complications. The combination of very warm temperatures in the terrarium and ample food intake can cause the food to decompose more rapidly than it can be digested. The resulting gases that form can cause the snake's body to swell up, and after one or two days the entire, not exactly pleasant-smelling, stomach contents may be regurgitated. Such physical exertion can have serious consequences with weakened animals.

Freezing food animals is a very convenient method for having the right food available at all times. It is essential that freezing takes place very rapidly at a temperature no higher than -18°C (0°F) and that the food does not become warm, much less thaw and be refrozen a second time during the several months of storage. In this way, food fishes, mammals (particularly the baby or pinkie mice needed for rearing baby snakes), and sporadically available day-old chicks can be kept in stock.

The food animals are killed most easily and without bloodshed with a cellulose pad soaked in ether in a tightly closed container. Then they are packed in reasonable portions either directly in airtight plastic bags or in packets of aluminum foil, several of which can be frozen and stored in a sealed plastic bag. Before feeding, the food portion must be warmed to body temperature.

Force-feeding to save an already emaciated snake from starvation is always a last resort. It neither agrees much with the snake nor is it especially safe for the hobbyist when it is a question of large or venomous snakes. Folds of skin, so-called hunger folds, and the clear protrusion of the backbone in otherwise round-backed species are clear symptoms that the snake's state of nutrition has become precarious and that force-feeding is indicated.

To force-feed larger snakes you need an assistant who grasps the snake behind the head and carefully stretches the front part of the body. With giant snakes you need an additional helper for each meter (yard) of body length. The mouth is forced open gently with the aid of a wooden spatula or the like. With blunt forceps the prey animal then is pushed deep into the snake's gullet. A rounded, smooth rod then can be used to push the food further in. The next step is an external massage. With very weak snakes only small bites of easily digested food should be given. Force-feeding does not require the use of species-typical prey. Fish and strips of meat are much easier to feed than mice. With long-term force-feeding, however, plain fish or mammal flesh must be enriched with calcium and multivitamin preparations (A, D3, E, C, and with fish eaters also vitamin B complex).

The feeding of a food paste through a funnel is a relatively easy and gentle method. The most diverse recipes for this food paste have been devised, calling for such ingredients as egg yolk, scrambled eggs, ground meat, warm milk, fructose, and prepared food mixtures (baby foods).

The most nutritious possible diet, which can be offered with a syringe through a funnel or plastic cannula, is a standard food paste consisting of ground beef heart, poultry liver, dried or fresh daphnia or fairy shrimp, minerals, and vitamins. This food paste is not too liquid to administer.

Snakes that specialize on reptiles—lizards and snakes—present special problems in feeding. Not all species accept a substitute diet, so they must be force-fed. The most familiar snake eaters include the King Cobra (*Ophiophagus hannah*), the Banded Krait (*Bungarus fasciatus*), the Mussurana (*Clelia clelia*), the Black-headed Python (*Aspidites melanocephalus*), and several kingsnakes of the genus, *Lampropeltis*. The last two, however, also take other food animals. The rearing of lizards and snakes specifically for the purpose of feeding is not worthwhile, which does not rule out the feeding of runts or deformed animals (not sick ones!) in individual cases. Beware of being too optimistic about switching lizard- or snake-eating snakes to mice or of force-feeding them their whole lives. It is better to refrain from keeping species that must feed on other snakes or on lizards.

That snakes, particularly the reptile-eating species, have been observed eating their shed skins may well be explained by chance and not by a specific behavior, as, for example, in geckos. The eating of plant matter, such as pieces of sweet fruit by garter snakes (*Thamnophis*), also is likely only an aberrant reaction under terrarium conditions. Vegetable matter is of no significance in the diet of snakes and is not known to be taken in the wild or even to be digested.

The keeper must not forget the importance of water. Snakes are suction drinkers that drink with the mouth slightly open, but they also can take in water with a closed mouth through the groove provided in the rostral scale for the tongue. The sucking effect is supported by side-to-side chewing movements of the jaws. Water quality apparently is tested by sense of smell, for it can be observed time and again that snakes soon show up and drink greedily when the water bowl is filled with fresh water. Many tropical species, particularly arboreal snakes, take their water from droplets.

Climate in the Terrarium

Our charges have a considerable ability to adapt to their environment. Nonetheless, specific climatic factors contribute substantially to maintenance of health, readiness to breed, and a long life span. Even if the provenance of a snake is known, as a rule only data from climatic charts or climatic diagrams are available to us; these data describe the characteristic succession of typical weather conditions—simply the climate (macroclimate) of an area. Ignored are the mesoclimate and the microclimate, which is the climate that is so important for keeping animals. The microclimate of the layers of air near the ground—and many snake species live in this zone—differs from the macroclimate in general through less air movement and greater temperature variations. Climatic charts and climatic diagrams, even when the elevation is considered, can only be rough criteria for the climatic factors to be reproduced in the terrarium.

No hobbyist can be expected to monitor and control continuously the climatic factors in the terrarium. For this reason it is important from the start to use technology to measure and regulate the climate. For reasons of safety and technological proficiency, the hobbyist will not be able to get by without experts in the planning and installation of the equipment necessary to produce a favorable climate in the terrarium.

Naturally we do not want to introduce mechanization and automation at any price, but before we start we should consider the following. We should:

1) limit ourselves to sensible and absolutely necessary measures;

2) choose simple and manageable solutions;

3) demand high reliability and functional safety of the components and groups of components;

4) ensure that the components and devices can be repaired or interchanged;

5) stockpile or be able to purchase spare parts, even after a number of years;

6) have the option of manual switching or emergency operation in case of defects.

LIGHT

Both the animals and plants in the terrarium need light. The intensity of illumination, the period of illumination, and the color of the light are subject to seasonal and daily variations.

The intensity of illumination of natural daylight is impossible to duplicate in the terrarium. In summer at noon under a clear sky, light intensities of up to 100,000 lux have been measured; in winter under the same conditions 10,000 lux are still present, while barely 300 lux penetrate a distance of only 2 meters (6.6 ft) from a window. A light bulb produces 20 to 40 lux. It is obvious that plants are highly dependent on the period of illumination, but few empirical data exist for animals, especially for snakes. It is certain, however, that besides other climatic factors, day length plays an important role in reproductive periodicity. The seasonal changes in day length are in part functions of geographic latitude. An average daily period of illumination of 12 to 14 hours is adequate in the terrarium.

Scarcely any data are available on the importance of light color in snake care. Long-wave yellow, red, and infrared radiation, however, penetrates the body and warms it. The blue region of the spectrum, on the other hand, is beneficial for plant growth. The significance of ultraviolet radiation for snakes is controversial. It can stimulate the metabolism and can reduce the growth of germs. As measurements have shown, the ultraviolet permeability of the skin of a Boa Constrictor (*Boa constrictor*) is only 1% and that of a racer (*Coluber* sp.) is only 0.3% (human skin, in contrast, is 33%).

The best source of light for a terrarium is doubtless unfiltered sunlight. It can only be used in the outdoor terrarium and to a limited extent in the greenhouse terrarium or in the immediate vicinity of a window. On the one hand, however, the hours of sunshine in northern latitudes are insufficient for sun-loving species, and on the other the terrarium can quickly overheat, which can

Full-spectrum lighting is not necessarily essential to the survival of captive snakes, but many keepers claim to get better breeding results after exposing their stock to it. It is certainly something to consider. Photo courtesy Hagen.

trum. High-pressure mercury-vapor lamps and similar specialized lamps produce a very large amount of light, but can only be used in larger terraria. Like fluorescent tubes, lamps of this kind need an adapter to operate. The warmth produced by these adapters can be used to heat the terrarium substrate. Since the danger of burning always exists when lighting devices heat up, wire guards should protect against touching, or the bulb can be built into a separate box. Unprotected electrical cords must be avoided, since gnawers among the food animals like to chew on cables.

If the lighting is not regulated manually, it is controlled most easily with the aid of a timer. When purchasing a timer, make sure it has a reserve gear that maintains the daily rhythm during brief power outages. Also beneficial are timers with several switch circuits that can be used to control other devices (heaters, misters, and the like). A rheostat can be used in outdoor and greenhouse terraria to turn on artificial light sources for supplemental light. Twilight effects in the morning and evening hours can be produced with lights, but are a technical frivolity in the care of snakes.

TEMPERATURE

As poikilothermic animals, snakes are dependent to a high degree on the ambient

lead to the death of its occupants. Thus the snake keeper cannot get by without artificial sources of light even with nocturnal and crepuscular snakes.

An incandescent bulb and reflector is the cheapest and easiest to install light source. The heat it simultaneously produces can be used to warm the terrarium, but can be troublesome at higher wattages. Fluorescent tubes, on the other hand, produce substantially less heat. There are special fluorescent tubes for promoting plant growth, as well as those with a component of ultraviolet light; they can also be used for continuous operation, if necessary coupled with lamps producing radiation from other regions of the spec-

Providing a snake with the correct photoperiod (day/night cycle) is very important—a captive snake's behavior is affected by the length of its days and nights. Photo courtesy of Energy Savers.

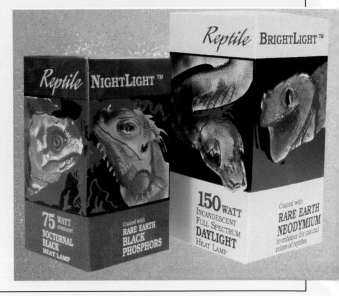

temperature for their vital functions. Temperatures below the freezing point are fatal, as are temperatures substantially above 40°C (104°F). In general, too low temperatures lead to colds, too high to heat stroke. Between these extremes lie the regions of torpor, which occurs, depending on the provenance of the snakes, at between 4 and about 10°C (39-50°F) in hibernation; the activation temperature; and the preferred temperature. The activation temperature is essentially equivalent to moderate keeping temperatures. Examples of the activation temperature given in the literature include 26°C (79°F) for the Common Garter Snake (*Thamnophis sirtalis*), 28°C (82°F) for the American Rat Snake (*Elaphe obsoleta*), and 30°C (86°F) for the Boa Constrictor (*Boa constrictor*) and a few rattlesnakes (*Crotalus*). The preferred temperatures for many species in the terrarium were determined experimentally with rectal temperature probes; for example, the preferred temperature is 32.9°C (92°F) for the Northern Adder (*Vipera berus*), 33.3°C (93°F) for the

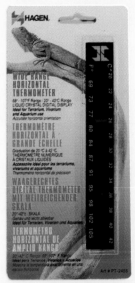

A wide-range thermometer can be a useful tool in the terrarium. Photo courtesy of Hagen.

ANNUAL RHYTHM OF DAY LENGTH AS A FUNCTION OF LATITUDE.

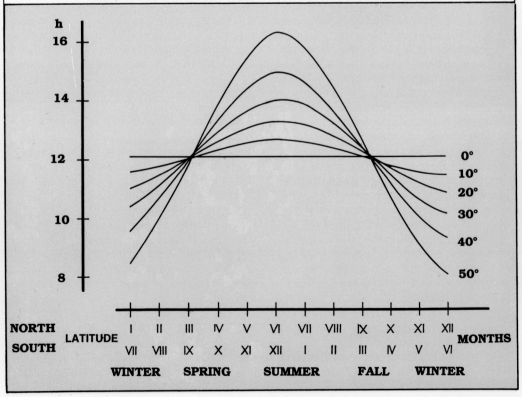

Dice Snake (*Natrix tessellata*), 34.3°C (94°F) for the Ringed Snake (*Natrix natrix*), 35°C (95°F) for the Smooth Snake (*Coronella austriaca*), 36.7°C (98°F) for the Asp Viper (*Vipera aspis*), and 40.1°C (104°F) for the Javelin Sand Boa (*Eryx jaculus*).

The preferred temperatures determined without considering other climatic factors usually are much too high for the terrarium and can at most serve as rough estimates for the temperature under a radiation source. The numerous influential factors make it impossible to give keeping temperatures for individual species. Depending on the climatic zone, however, median air temperatures in the terrarium of from 25 to 33°C (77-93°F) can be considered as favorable. In general, a nighttime temperature drop of about 5 to 10°C (9-18°F) can be expected, 2 to 4°C (3-7°F) with animals that live on the forest floor or in tropical rainforest. Extreme temperatures are better tolerated at low humidity.

When considering the temperatures in the terrarium, we must distinguish between heat from the substrate, air, and radiation; to some extent, the snakes should be able to choose between these sources.

A simple glass thermometer (measuring range from 0 to 50°C, 32 to 120°F) is suitable for checking the temperature in the terrarium; minimum-maximum thermometers additionally make it possible to determine the highest and lowest temperature since the last time the thermometer was set. To monitor continuously the elapsed temperature in terrarium installations, the purchase of a temperature recorder (thermograph) is recommended. The thermograph can also be coupled with a humidity recorder (hygrograph) to form a thermohygrograph, which records the precise progression of changes in temperature and humidity over the course of a week.

Electricity is the best energy source for heating terraria. Electric heating is easy to install and regulate, dependable, clean in operation, and largely maintenance-free. Although the operating costs are relatively high, the purchase price is low.

Incandescent or mercury-vapor lamps with reflectors, as well as infrared-light or infra-red-dark radiators, give off radiated heat and influence air temperature in addition to providing illumination. All are suitable as electrical heating devices. Infrared radiators, however, to a greater extent than the other light sources, tend to produce "roasting" dry heat. Low-power (40–to 100-watt) infrared-dark radiators with normal light bulb sockets and glass, porcelain, or ceramic housings are very easy to use and also are suitable for smaller terraria.

Substrate heating can be provided by heating plates or mats under the terrarium; heating cables with lead, aluminum, or plastic coatings; and—especially for the smallest terraria—low-power aquarium glass heaters. Most can operate dry, placed inside an earthenware pipe, a hollow tile, or a "rock" fashioned of cement. Heating plates and mats usually are moisture-sensitive and cannot stand any condensation; one side must therefore be able to radiate freely.

The same is true of the ballasts of fluorescent tubes and mercury-vapor lamps, which must be installed outside the terrarium or in a special heating tunnel. Heating cables can be run through the substrate or even through the water basin. The radius of curvature must not be less than that recommended by the manufacturer. They should be plugged in outside the terrarium and rodents must be prevented from gnawing at them. Electric air heaters are scarcely suitable for continuous operation, and then at most for terrarium rooms or greenhouse terraria.

Expensive hot-water heating is an alternative to electric heating. It is suitable only for large terrarium installations and even then is recommended only if hot water is used to heat the rest of the house.

Contact thermometers with mercury or bimetallic relays or electronic thermostats make it easy to regulate electric heating in the terrarium. A certain sluggishness of the switching devices is not troublesome. Various possibilities for regulating hot-water heating also exist.

MOISTURE

Without water, life in the terrarium is impossible. Besides the potable water in drinking and bathing vessels or in droplets after spraying, the moisture in the substrate and air plays an important role.

As the temperature falls at night, the humidity in the terrarium becomes higher than during the day. For snakes from desert or plains regions, a slight moistening of one section of the substrate is adequate. In the rainforest terrarium, the humidity during the day should range between 60 and 90% and should be even higher at night; regular spraying is necessary. For most species of snakes, fairly dry keeping conditions—relative humidity from 50 to 60%—are appropriate. In this way the growth of undesirable germs is minimized and the use of special moist egg-laying sites is promoted. A simple hygrometer is adequate for determining the relative humidity.

In terraria with fairly large water bowls, heating the water generally is sufficient to raise the humidity. Electric humidifiers and special misting devices are worthwhile only in large terraria or terrarium installations. Ventilating the terrarium not only removes stagnant air and prevents condensation, it regulates humidity. Ventilating the terrarium by means of a lower louver and an upper ventilation flap lets the rising warm air escape naturally. With a small ventilator, movement of the air can be achieved by the high- or low-pressure principle, which also can be used to raise the humidity if the air flowing in passes across a heated water vessel or a moist, porous substrate. For small terraria, an aquarium air pump is sufficient for turning over and humidifying the air. The humidifying and irrigating devices can be controlled by a hygrostat; by connecting this device to a timer, it also is possible to take into account the natural daily variations in humidity.

SOCIAL FACTORS IN THE TERRARIUM

Little is known about social behavior in snakes. Furthermore, social behavior in the terrarium can scarcely correspond to that in the wild. Interrelations between two snakes lie on the lowest biosocial level in the wild: snakes usually are solitary animals. The gathering of several individuals usually is brought about by influences of an inanimate nature. These often are climatic factors, as when, for example, a sunning site protected from wind or a hiding place that appears to be suited for hibernation leads to a fairly large gathering (aggregation). Aggregations of snakes on the basis of specific attractive substances—chemical substances that usually serve for sexual attraction—also are only temporary in nature, but already stand on a somewhat higher social level than those interrelations caused by climatic factors. "Presocial" interrelations on the basis of, among other things, specific mating requirements, are scarcely present in snakes.

Conditions in the terrarium are completely different. The forced coexistence of several snakes in the smallest of spaces unavoidably leads to unnatural social influences. Population density thus plays an important role in the terrarium. Two or three males and three or four females represents the upper population limit in a terrarium of appropriate size and quality of furnishings and with respect to favorable conditions for mate selection as well. It is best to keep compatible pairs without other conspecifics, to avoid disturbance and to increase the chances of successful propagation. When a number of snakes live in a terrarium, they often congregate in a tangle at favorite basking sites or in hiding places. This sort of body contact doubtless also expresses the snakes' preference for hiding places that provide body pressure. Two snakes in the wild are only rarely encountered in close body contact, at least outside the breeding season or hibernation.

Overpopulation of the terrarium causes more than problems of hygiene. Animals with asynchronous functional cycles usually disturb one another: resting animals are disturbed by active ones, satiated snakes by hungry ones, and those not in breeding condition by those that are ready to breed.

Whether snakes of different species should be kept together in the terrarium can be decided only by considering the most diverse factors, such as the demands on the microclimate, on the terrarium conditions, on the food supply, on the feeding habits (predators), and on the daily and seasonal rhythms of activity.

Hygiene

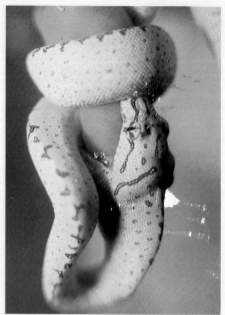

You probably will find that most young snakes are very eager feeders. Here, a young Green Tree Python, *Chondropython viridis*, is taking pinkie. Photo by I. Vergner.

If you want to get good breeding results from your snakes, then it is essential that you keep them in peak health. This Great Plains Rat Snake, *Elaphe guttata emoryi*, for example, is an excellent specimen and thus a prime candidate for propagation. Photo by M. Kantz.

A basic condition for maintaining a healthy, long-lived, and ready-to-breed stock of terrarium animals is the fulfillment of essential hygienic demands. This begins before stocking the first terrarium, using preventive methods that are intended to guard against subsequent outbreaks of disease, decreases in vitality, and other problems. These preventive measures include:

1) construction of the terrarium (type of construction, size, shape, glass thickness, provisions for ventilation, ease of servicing and cleaning);

2) location of the terrarium (taking into account external climatic factors—direct sunlight, room temperature, draft, among others—by setting up the terrarium properly and using technical measures);

3) technical furnishing of the terrarium (installation of equipment for lighting and irradiation, heating, ventilation, humidifying, and if possible automatic control devices);

4) furnishing of the terrarium (ease of cleaning and disinfection through practical rear wall and substrate construc-

Regular feedings and feedings involving as varied a diet as possible are keys to good snake health. Although you might not want to offer lovebirds to your snakes, as someone has done for this Angolan Python, *Python anchietae*, the point is, if a snake is willing to take a variety of items, you should provide them. Photo by K. H. Switak.

tion, suitable hiding places and climbing facilities, practical planting);

5) stocking with healthy animals (acquiring captive-bred animals from stocks that are unobjectionable from a veterinary and hygienic point of view leads to the fewest problems);

6) basic knowledge of the terrarium hobby and the effort to increase this knowledge through the use of your own experiences, the study of specialist journals and books, contact with other terrarists, taking part in specialist meetings, and not least through membership in an organization devoted to the terrarium hobby.

A further complex of preventive measures for keeping our charges healthy is concerned with the upkeep of the terrarium and the care of its inhabitants (prophylaxis). Here the knowledge of the requirements of the species to be kept plays an important role. Only in this way can optimal environmental conditions be ensured, including the physiological and psychological requirements of appropriate keeping conditions, food supply, care, and exclusion or elimination of all disruptive factors from the environment, including pathogens. In addition to order and cleanliness, remember that punctuality, dependability, a feeling of responsibility, self-initiative, and calmness and prudence when handling snakes also are basic requirements for the proper care of the animals.

Keeping our charges healthy is possible only with the most scrupulous cleanliness. Therefore every terrarium must be a hygienic terrarium. A sterile keeping environment, a terrarium free of the resting or reproductive forms of living microorganisms and parasites and in which renewed infestation is prevented, can exist only under laboratory conditions, not in the terraria of hobbyists. The occasionally used concept of the "semi-sterile terrarium" is preposterous. If what is meant by this term is a terrarium low in germs, with minimal furnishings and a substrate (sand, peat, wood shavings, paper) that can be quickly replaced completely, without plants and with ease of disinfection, then the spe-

cific hygienic conditions should be spelled out. Terraria of this kind are especially well suited for the quarantine of newly purchased snakes and the care of sick animals.

As a general principle, a daily inspection of the terraria and their inhabitants is advisable. This does not mean that only the general condition of the terrarium equipment and the terrarium climate should be checked. It is more important that all excrement, food remains, and shed skins, among other things, are removed and fresh, clean drinking and bathing water is provided. Plants must be watered and dead or damaged plant parts removed. To remove droppings and the like, a broad spatula or a small shovel—long-handled with snakes that bite—works quite well. A "hygienic" substrate is preferable to a thick layer of soil. In rainforest terraria, in particular, the removal of excrement requires great care. Long metal or plastic forceps or, better yet, long-handled tongs find many uses. It is very practical if the water basin can be removed for cleaning. Plastic containers work better than ceramic bowls, even if the latter look more natural. A stiff brush for cleaning dishes is very practical for scrubbing the water bowl. It eventually will prove necessary to remove the calcium rings in the water bowl; mineral deposits are removed most easily and thoroughly with dilute hydrochloric acid, but the corrosive action and caustic smell of this material must be taken into account. Terrarium glass should be cleaned for more than esthetic reasons. Dust and fingerprints are to be removed from the outside, and water spots, tracks made by crawling snakes, and excrement from the inside. A sponge, warm water, and a clean, dry towel do good service here. If the glass is not too dirty, a glass cleaner, but not a spray, can be used.

To prevent the transmission of germs from one terrarium to another, separate utensils often are recommended for each terrarium. When tending a fairly large number of terraria housed in a large space, however, this hardly is possible

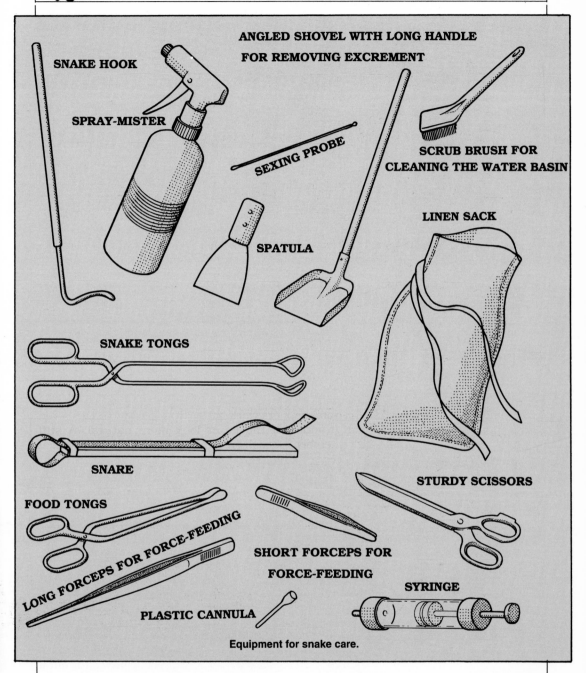

SNAKE HOOK

ANGLED SHOVEL WITH LONG HANDLE
FOR REMOVING EXCREMENT

SPRAY-MISTER

SEXING PROBE

SCRUB BRUSH FOR
CLEANING THE WATER BASIN

SPATULA

LINEN SACK

SNAKE TONGS

SNARE

STURDY SCISSORS

FOOD TONGS

LONG FORCEPS FOR FORCE-FEEDING

SHORT FORCEPS FOR
FORCE-FEEDING

SYRINGE

PLASTIC CANNULA

Equipment for snake care.

and not very promising. It seems more important to clean and disinfect all utensils thoroughly after use. This is quite easily accomplished by putting the soiled spatula, shovel, forceps, and so forth in disinfectant in a plastic trash can with a lid. This solution will have to be replaced at intervals of one to two weeks. Obviously, soiled cleaning towels should either be boiled or replaced after use.

A terrarium must be cleaned thoroughly at least three or four times a year. While their homes are being cleaned, snakes are most easily stored in sacks in a warm and draft-free place. Everything must be removed from the terrarium and first dried, then cleaned in water. To eradicate pathogens of all kinds, a broad-spectrum disinfectant is sprayed on or spread with a wash cloth. Follow manufacturer's instructions for the disinfectant being used. The prescribed concentration and period of action—usually at least four hours—must be followed, otherwise the degree of effectiveness will be unsatisfactory. In the most diverse products, the most important active disinfecting compounds are phenol and its derivatives (3 to 5% solution), formaldehyde (2 to 5%), and quaternary ammonium compounds (0.2 to 0.4%). Disinfectants containing peracetic acid can also be used with animals present (0.2 to 0.4% solution)—a 1% solution for terrarium disinfection—and therefore are particularly recommended.

After the terrarium has been disinfected, it should be rinsed out thoroughly with water one more time to remove all traces of disinfectant.

Objects used to furnish the terrarium that you do not want to do without, like climbing branches, shelter boxes, water basins, and rocks, are disinfected in the same way. The substrate, pieces of bark, and preferably the plants as well are replaced.

Gassing (bug bombs) is an effective, not too expensive method of disinfection, particularly for the disinfection of entire terrarium installations. It requires specialized knowledge, however, and should be left to the expert.

The daily cleaning of terraria of venomous snakes and large, aggressive snakes demands special precautionary measures. Therefore, on principle, a terrarium for venomous snakes must be equipped with shelter boxes of adequate size that can be locked securely. Also practical is the use of bipartite terraria that can be divided by a pane of glass or the like and permit safe handling in the snake-free section. For peaceful, nonaggressive venomous snakes, a plastic

A healthy snake's scales will be as clean (free of blisters, cuts, and other lesions) as those on this beautiful albino California Kingsnake, *Lampropeltis getula californiae*. Note also how clear the eyes are. Photo by Jim Merli.

Finding the exact food required by your snake may be difficult. Eastern Hognose Snakes, *Heterodon platirhinos*, for example, generally only eat toads. Photo by William B. Allen, Jr.

This is a Texas Coral Snake, *Micrurus fulvius tenere*, eating a Gray-banded Kingsnake, *Lampropeltis alterna*. Coral snakes are not only highly venomous, but notorious snake-eaters as well. Such snakes are not recommended for captivity. Photo by Paul Freed.

facial shield, leather gloves, and long-handled utensils also can minimize the danger.

Infectious diseases of snakes that are communicable and infectious to humans, so-called zoonoses, are not known (salmonellosis, common food poisoning, being a possible exception). Nonetheless, the basic principles of hygiene always must be observed. One of these principles is that after every contact with the animals and with the terrarium and its furnishings, the hands must be washed thoroughly. An additional disinfection of the hands after handling sick or dead animals also is advisable. When possible, for reasons of hygiene and to make work easier, a sink should be installed in the terrarium room.

For temporary storage, for transport and shipment of dead snakes for posting (dissection) at a scientific or veterinary institution, and for shipment of stools (feces) for testing, suitable air- and water-tight containers such as plastic bags are to be used.

Accidents or injuries require appropriate first aid. Bites from aggressive snakes can never be ruled out. If there is no serious flesh wound, by and large there will be no problems. Even heavily bleeding wounds heal in a short time if secondary infection is avoided. The treatment of venomous snake bites, including those of rear-fangs, requires facts and knowledge that cannot be further discussed here. Keepers of venomous snakes also must be able to recognize special behaviors on the part of their snakes if they wish to avoid bites.

"Environmental protection" means protecting others from the possible consequences of your pets. The first commandment is to make the terraria and as far as possible the room in which the terraria are located escape-proof. Many a harmless snake has caused outsiders to panic, to say nothing of the real danger to bystanders from escaped venomous snakes. The same applies to escaped rats, mice, and other food animals. Do not forget the burdening of the environment through unpleasant smells—whether by mice droppings that are not removed fast enough, a regurgitated prey animal, or a dead food animal lying in an inaccessible corner that has begun to decompose. All waste is to be eliminated hygienically—-burning it would be the ideal solution where allowed by law.

Purchase and Transport

The hobbyist who acquires snakes with the intention of breeding them as a rule will know precisely which species to purchase and which sex of a particular species is needed. Information already will have been obtained from the literature or from experienced friends about the requirements of the animals of interest. Personally collecting specimens is doubtless a favored method of acquiring snakes, and there is the additional benefit of becoming familiar with their natural environment. When collecting is done conscientiously and is limited to your own needs in unthreatened populations, it will scarcely be detrimental to the species. It goes without saying, however, that the conservation laws of the country in question and the provisions of CITES and other international agreements when crossing borders must be known and observed. The purchase of a snake from a dealer is a matter of trust. Though most dealers in imported specimens are honest and try to carry the best possible specimens, wild-caught snakes often are ill, emaciated, damaged, and/or severely stressed. You should never accept uncritically the seller's information on the species (identifications often are wrong or incomplete), living requirements (often poorly known for wild-caught snakes of less common species), and condition of the animal. The animal must be submitted to a thorough examination, in the course of which the following questions are to be considered:

1) What is the snake's general state of nutrition? Is it severely emaciated? Is it active? Does it try to wriggle out of the hand or even to bite?
2) Did the snake shed well? Are remnants of old skin still present, particularly on the eyes or the tip of the tail? Do individual scales protrude (possibly caused by mite infestation)? Are open wounds or growths under the skin present?
3) Are the eyes clear? (Cloudiness of the eyes before shedding is normal.)
4) Is the snake's mouth closed? Is the inside of the mouth free of deposits, bloody spots, and mucus?
5) Is the tip of the snout cut and inflamed?
6) Are sounds of breathing audible? (The hissing of some species is typical.) If mucus is present in the mouth, pneumonia should be suspected.
7) Is the area around the cloaca clean or is it encrusted?

You usually will be able to place complete trust in the purchase of snakes from a well-known breeder. The inspection of his terrarium installation and the breeding animals and the free exchange of his experiences with the animals in question are advantages whose value cannot be overestimated. You have the guarantee of purchasing healthy snakes and perhaps a chance of obtaining them somewhat cheaper than on the retail market. However, you will usually have to make the effort to rear the young snakes you have purchased. A breeder usually will not sell older animals, unless he has surplus specimens of one sex or you can offer him in exchange a different species in which he is interested. That breeders prefer to sell young snakes is just due to the lack of enough time, space, and food to rear a large number of juveniles conveniently and economically.

Snakes are packed in linen sacks of appropriate size that are deeper than wide. Only animals of the same size and not aggressive toward one another should be transported together in one sack. Be careful with venomous snakes, which can bite through most sacks! For this reason opaque cloth sacks are more practical for venomous snakes than are transparent sacks. If it is long enough, the mouth of the sack is twisted and knotted or tied shut at the top with a string. In so doing care must be taken that a snake is not tied up, too.

The temperature conditions must be given consideration on longer trips. During a trip by car in the summer, snakes placed in the rear window soon overheat. In the winter a foam plastic container, if necessary equipped with a hot-water bottle, does good service. Young nonvenomous snakes are most likely to survive transport in winter in a small sack hung around the neck under the outer garments.

Shipping snakes by express or air carrier (snakes cannot be legally sent by mail in many countries) requires more preparation. Snakes should only be shipped with an empty digestive tract. After packing the snakes in sturdy linen sacks, these should be marked with the scientific name of the species and the number of individuals they contain. Special notices are required for venomous snakes. An insulated container is recommended in both summer and winter. A sturdy carton, better yet a light box, ensures undamaged arrival. Do not forget to include a sufficient number of small ventilation holes or larger ones covered with wire mesh. Inscriptions on the transport box such as **"Caution: Live animals, keep at temperatures of about xx°"** or **"Caution, venomous snakes!"** must also be included. When transporting snakes across borders, in addition to papers for shipping, certification for species regulated under CITES or which are subject to national conservation laws will occasionally be necessary, and customs and veterinary documents must be included. Accurate, complete documentation of any species protected under endangered species laws is vital if you wish to prevent legal problems later on. Always be sure you understand all relevant laws before ordering or shipping snakes across state and national boundaries—the laws may be exceeding complicated and you may need specialized legal advice.

On fast shipments normally there is no danger that the animals will dry out. Adding a little damp moss or a moist sponge, however, is recommended with young snakes. The shipping bags must in no case be wet or they will become impermeable to air.

Snakes cooled to low temperatures must gradually be brought to normal terrarium temperatures again. The new arrival will be subjected to the least stress if it is left to crawl out of the opened sack on its own.

To prevent the spread of disease, it is recommended that new arrivals be placed in quarantine. The quarantine period generally is four weeks, which is not long enough, however, in the case of amoebic dysentery. Bacteriologic and parasitologic examinations of freshly collected droppings or at least of swabs of the cloaca must be left to the spe-cialist. Mite infestation is easy to control, however, and the treatment can be carried out immediately.

On longer shipments and those with intermediate stops, a preventive dose of vitamins may be advised because it will speed initial food intake.

Now a few words on the keeping of venomous snakes and giant snakes in captivity. Opinions on whether these animals should be kept in the home terrarium differ widely, ranging from complete rejection to almost thoughtless, irresponsible approval. But what is the basis for the great interest of the majority of zoo and serpentarium visitors in venomous snakes and especially large specimens of giant snakes?

Doubtless the attraction to the unusual and sensational plays a role here. The "grave danger" just behind the glass certainly causes a prickling sensation in the observer. If this craving is the main motive for keeping such snakes in the terrarium, and if keeping them serves only to satisfy vanity and the desire to show off, then it should be rejected.

On the other hand, why should these snakes with their especially interesting behaviors not be equally entitled to be kept and bred by hobbyists in the same way as "harmless" snakes—of course while taking into consideration a number of essential precautions? Public opinion with its negative observations and attacks against the keeping of venomous snakes is more the result of unconscious fear and basic dislike for snakes than of a feeling of responsibility. A total ban on the keeping of venomous snakes and giant snakes is just as senseless as unqualified approval or even promotion of these branches of the terrarium hobby.

Basically, the keeping of dangerous snakes should be the exception, and the only motivation for doing so should be a deep, scientifically oriented interest in their habits. Knowledge and years of experience with harmless snakes are essential prerequisites for the hobbyist. That part of the animal trade that continues to thoughtlessly sell giant snakes that grow to large size and, in some countries, even sells venomous snakes to beginners, also must not shirk its responsibility.

Documentation

In order to document satisfactorily the keeping and propagation of the terrarium animal, it must be possible to identify precisely the individual animal during its whole life. This problem crops up when several snakes of one species are kept in one terrarium. The hobbyist who owns only a few animals will in most cases be able to recognize them individually and may even give them names. To identify the individual animal in a fairly large stock, individual recognition by the keeper is no longer adequate. His absence alone makes it impossible for a helper to document important occurrences, because the individual snake will not be recognized precisely. The following simple code is recommended for naming. **Eoq/80-B,** for example, means that the snake is a Yellow Rat Snake, *Elaphe obsoleta quadrivittata*, that was born or purchased in 1980; it is the second (B) snake of the year. This coding system can be expanded or modified to meet the hobbyist's individual needs.

The most diverse methods of marking have been tried with varying degrees of success. In some cases the ventral scales were marked with a hot branding iron or markings were made on the back with a freeze-brand iron. After about two years these sorts of markings were no longer distinguishable. Snakes were marked for life by electrical tattooing of the belly scales when they were still light in color. Employed successfully on many occasions was the notching of scales on the underside of the tail according to a particular code. Infected wounds, regeneration of the scales, and the difficulty of notching the scales of small, young specimens make this method only conditionally recommendable for terrarium animals.

Photographing the animals is probably the optimal solution, preferably the head from above and from the side, the middle section, as well as the cloacal region and the tail. Plain, unmarked snakes, however, obviously do not adapt well to this method.

In many cases it is sufficient to sketch the markings in the head-neck region, which

Yellow Rat Snake (male, 2 yrs. old)
Chart for 1993

Feeding	11/2	11/9	11/21	12/1	12/6			
Shedding	10/20	12/24						
Breeding	5/21	5/30						
Defecation	11/5	11/12	11/29					
Cleaning	11/10	11/20	11/30	12/10	12/20			
Misc.	Regurgitated meal 6/9				Laid 14 eggs 7/28			

Good keepers maintain careful records of all of their snakes' activities.

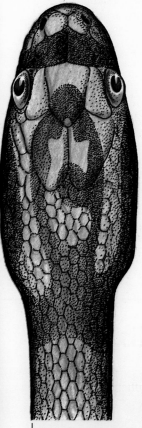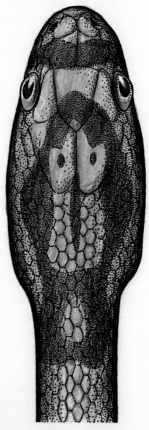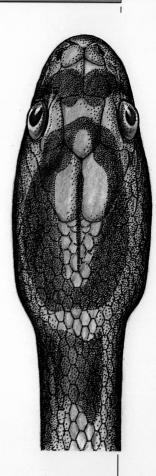

Three head patterns of the Corn Snake, *Elaphe guttata guttata*.

in many species are unique in almost every individual. The distribution of spots, for example, in patterned rat snake species differs from individual to individual and does not change. Unfortunately, some of these snakes lose all their markings in old age. With the Boa Constrictor, sketching the tail markings has proved useful for identification. A drawing of the pattern of spots on the head and neck region becomes superfluous if during the molt the sloughed skin is cut off behind the neck, cut lengthwise on the underside, and mounted right side up. Snakes that are plain on top sometimes have patterned belly scales—such markings also can be sketched. Finally, individual characters, such as shape of the nostrils, damaged rostral scales, missing tips of tails, and the like, can be used to identify an individual.

Gluing a small colored and numbered plastic disk, such as is used by beekeepers, to the head of the snake with transparent nail polish is a useful way to temporarily mark individuals until the next molt. A permanent and unmistakable method is the injection of a microelectronic transponder just a few millimeters long under the skin or into a muscle. The transponder transmits a digital code that can be read on a recording device from a distance. Though still expensive, the use of transponders to permanently identify rare or special snakes holds the greatest promise for the future. The method already is being used extensively in horses, dogs and cats, and birds.

For documentation to be really useful, it must be filled out conscientiously, punctually, completely, and accurately. In addition to provenance, lineage, age, sex, keeping conditions (hibernation and the like), food intake, physical development, and breeding results, it also should include information on the state of health and on treatments for illness.

The use of a file card is definitely preferable to making entries in a notebook. The individual record cards can be changed, removed when an animal dies, or sorted according to particular criteria. A typical record card contains all the essential data from the life of the snake in question. Only through the documentation of such data can patterns be recognized, new experiences and findings substantiated, and generalizations occasionally be made. Additionally, whatever information can be kept on a file card also can be kept in a computer, which allows even more potential for readily recording data of all types and comparing them as required.

Innumerable experiences of successful snake keepers and breeders have been lost because the person in question did not take notes and so did not pass on his knowledge. An academic degree in biology is by no means a prerequisite to noting a fact of interest and importance to other hobbyists and even to the academic world. The biological knowledge gained in the terrarium cannot necessarily be used to predict the habits of the animals in the wild without substantial human influence. Some questions, such as that of behavior in the population, can only be answered through herpetological field research. On the other hand, many observations can only be made in the terrarium. This is especially true of reproductive biology. For this reason it is essential that as many known factors as possible of the inanimate and living environment are included in the recording of observations of reproductive biology. For just this reason, scrupulous and accurate documentation is indispensable.

Pre-Mating Considerations

THE REPRODUCTIVE ORGANS

Like all typical reptiles, snakes basically have separate sexes: that is, there are males and females. (But the exception proves the rule—in the Island Lancehead, *Bothrops insularis*, there are pseudohermaphrodites, intersexes. Through a genetic defect, besides fertile females, infertile "females" also occur that exhibit more or less well-developed male reproductive organs.) Because of the elongated body form of snakes, the reproductive organs are arranged asymmetrically in the body: the right ovary and the right testis are located farther to the front than the left. In the blindsnakes of the family Typhlopidae only the right ovary is developed normally; the left ovary, including its oviduct, is completely absent.

The gonads of male and female snakes, in addition to producing a number of highly effective sex hormones, above all produce the germ cells: sperm and egg cells (oocytes).

Sex hormones play an important role in the internal regulation of reproduction. On the basis of their chemical structure these are steroid hormones, which are produced and secreted in the ovaries and testes and control the differentiation of sex in the embryo, the expression of secondary sex characteristics, as well as the maturation of egg cells and sperm. Under their control are the cyclical changes in the female reproductive organs, the maintenance of pregnancy, and the initiation of egg-laying or birth. In short, they regulate the entire reproductive behavior of the animals.

The process of sperm production (spermiogenesis) takes place in the seminiferous tubules of the oblong testes. The fully developed sperm are produced in several stages of development. They initially are stored in the epididymis located alongside the testis, but in part also in the sperm duct (ductus deferens), and are transported through the latter to the cloaca during copulation.

In the process of egg maturation (oogenesis) that takes place in the oblong-oval ovaries, the egg cells (oocytes) develop in small, specialized vesicles (follicles). They are finally released at ovulation and are captured by a conical enlargement (infundibulum) of the oviduct. The oviducts are very thin-walled and by means of contractions are able to transport the eggs in the direction of the cloaca. In addition, the oviducts possess mucus-secreting glands as well as glands that are responsible for the formation of the egg shell. In the livebearing snakes, a large part of the oviduct is thick-walled and muscular; it serves to hold the developing fetuses. This muscular enlargement is often called the uterus. It would be more accurate, however, to call it an "egg holder." The two oviducts usually open separately in the cloaca, but in some species they join in a common excretory duct. Following ovulation the remainder of each follicle develops into a yellowish body (corpus luteum) that produces hormones to maintain pregnancy and survives for a fairly long time. In snakes its function has not yet been fully explained, since its experimental removal does not have a noticeable effect on the further development of the embryos.

Like all members of the order Squamata, snakes possess a double male copulatory organ. (More technically, there is a single median penis that is split almost to the base, each half functioning as an independent structure. Each half is a hemipenis.) Males have two hemipenes, of which only one, the one that happens to be closest to the female's cloaca, is inserted during copulation. Through the interplay of blood vessels and muscles, the hemipenis becomes erect; in the resting state it is retracted as a blind pouch in the underside of the tail. The hemipenes, which when erect are everted like the fingers of a glove, can be simple, bilobed, or even bifurcated, depending on the species of snake. The surface may in part be covered with bony hooks or tubercles, and a deep sperm groove (sulcus spermaticus) that may extend to the tip of the hemipenis is present. The form of the hemipenis, its surface structure, and the course of the unbranched, forked, or two-branched sperm groove often are species-specific and sometimes are used to help answer taxonomic questions. The shape of the hemipenis is adapted to the female cloaca, in which the hemipenis is so firmly anchored during copulation that a forced separation of the two animals can lead to injuries. This species-specific adaptation usually is considered to be a barrier to copulation between different species. After ejaculation, the swelling of the hemipenis subsides as the collected blood flows out, and the organ is retracted by muscles in the tail.

Some blindsnakes of the family Typhlopidae have hemipene structures that differ considerably from typical snake hemipenes. They have massive hemipenes that presumably function like those of turtles or crocodilians. For that matter, the typhlopids differ considerably from all other living snakes in many aspects of their soft anatomy and osteology and are considered by some specialists to be lizards or some type of lizard—snake intermediate. (Snakes evolved from lizards, of course.)

Also located in the posterior part of the trunk, in addition to the reproductive organs, are paired fat bodies, the contents of which are used during the reproductive period to meet the elevated nutrient requirements.

SEX DETERMINATION

An essential prerequisite for the systematic propagation of terrarium animals is the sure determination of the sex of living animals. Because external primary sex characters are not present in snakes, the simplest method of sex determination is the examination of secondary sex characters. Sex-specific color characters, body proportions, and ornamentation occur quite frequently in lizards, but in snakes we usually look for them in vain. However, there are other indications: Male snakes often have fewer belly scales (ventrals) and more undertail scales (subcaudals) than females of the same species. Their body is thus relatively shorter and their tail—in order to hold the retracted hemipenes—is relatively longer than in females. These characters alone usually do not permit accurate sex determination because the individual overlap between the sexes is too great. Other morphological criteria that can be used include the relatively broader base of the tail and the gradually tapering tail of male snakes in comparison to females. In females, on the other hand, the tail is often clearly and abruptly set off from the body.

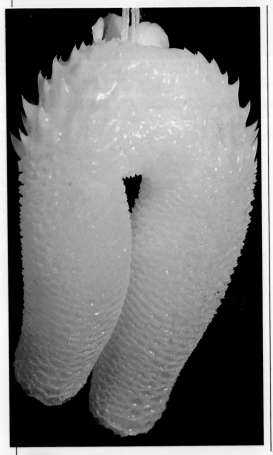

The hemipenes of a Western Rattlesnake, *Crotalus viridis*. Hemipenes are found on male snakes and lizards, are paired, and are located inside the base of the tail behind the cloaca. Photo by John Visser.

A little-known criterion is the occurrence of sex-specific keeled scales in a few species. For example, in a high percentage of sexually mature male Indigo Snakes (*Drymarchon corais*), a smooth-scaled snake of the New World, weakly keeled dorsal scales have been observed. These keeled scales can occur in one to five scale rows on the middle of the back in older animals. They usually begin one-fourth to one-third the body length behind the head and gradually become weaker toward the rear. Such keeled scales occurring only in males also have been observed in other smooth-scaled snakes. Even species with keeled scales, such as some *Nerodia* and *Thamnophis*, exhibit distinctively keeled scales or even knobs over the base of the tail in adult males. Some male aquatic snakes have small fleshy papillae on the scales of the underside of the head that appear at sexual maturity and may play a part in courtship.

In some snakes, like the North American water and garter snakes of the genera *Nerodia* and *Thamnophis*, clear differences in size between the sexes can be observed in most species. A sure sex determination is possible

Some hemipenes are forked, like those on this Mole Snake, *Pseudaspis cana*. Note also the spiny quality of the organ. This helps hold it in place during copulation. Photo by John Visser.

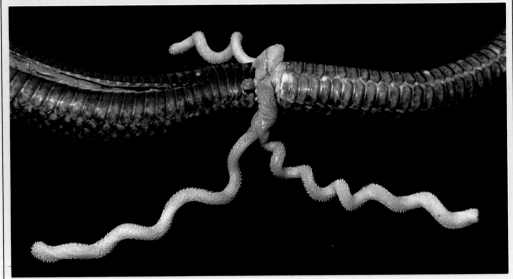

Urinary/reproductive apparatus of a Ringed Snake, *Natrix natrix*.

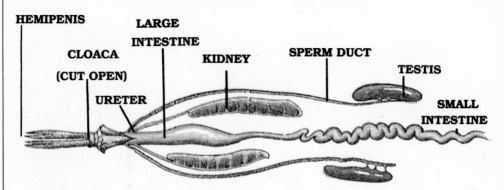

HEMIPENIS — LARGE INTESTINE — CLOACA (CUT OPEN) — KIDNEY — SPERM DUCT — TESTIS — URETER — SMALL INTESTINE

MALE

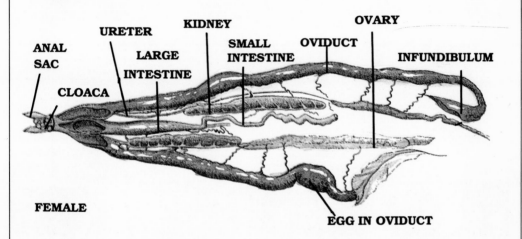

ANAL SAC — URETER — KIDNEY — OVARY — CLOACA — LARGE INTESTINE — SMALL INTESTINE — OVIDUCT — INFUNDIBULUM

FEMALE

EGG IN OVIDUCT

Copulatory organs of a male Timber Rattlesnake, *Crotalus horridus*.

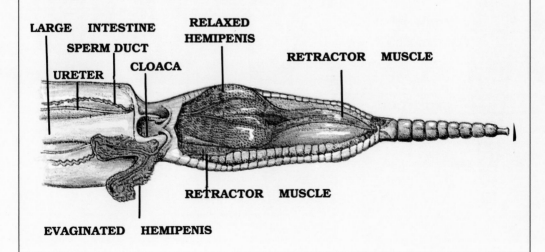

LARGE INTESTINE — RELAXED HEMIPENIS — SPERM DUCT — RETRACTOR MUSCLE — URETER — CLOACA

RETRACTOR MUSCLE

EVAGINATED HEMIPENIS

Schematized basic structural types of the snake hemipenis.

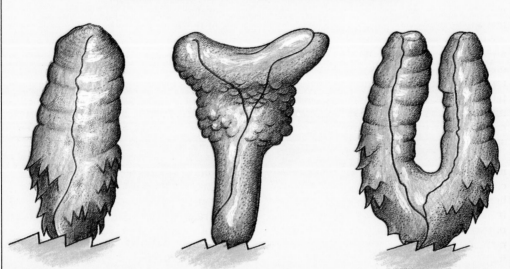

only with captive-bred animals of the same age and that have been reared under the same conditions. Females then display a multiple of the body circumference and live weight of males. Differences in size of this kind between the sexes also occur in other species. For example, male Reticulated Pythons, *Python reticulatus*, grow scarcely longer than 4.5 meters (15 ft), but females can grow almost 2 meters (6.6 ft) longer than the longest male.

The anal spurs—externally visible rem-

Sexual Differences

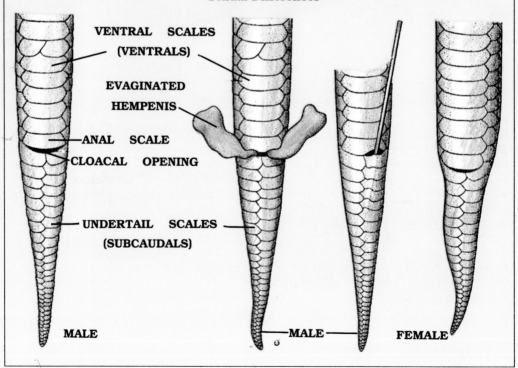

VENTRAL   SCALES
(VENTRALS)

EVAGINATED
HEMPENIS

ANAL   SCALE
CLOACAL   OPENING

UNDERTAIL   SCALES
(SUBCAUDALS)

MALE   MALE   FEMALE

nants of the hind legs that are present in most boas and pythons, *Cylindrophis*, and a few other primitive groups of snakes—often are used for sex determination. Although the anal spurs of males are more strongly developed, there are individual differences, and they sometimes are present in females. Statistical studies have shown that young female Boa Constrictors less than 1 meter (3.3 ft) in length do not have detectable anal spurs.

Sex-linked coloration is known in only a few snake species, above all the *Vipera* species. For example, gray and less frequently light brown to yellowish shades predominate in male Long-nosed Vipers (*Vipera ammodytes*), and the markings are prominent. Female Long-nosed Vipers, on the other hand, exhibit brown to red ground colors and

Particularly conspicuous are the sex-specific protuberances on the snouts of members of the tree snake genus *Langaha* from Madagascar. These snakes, however, are of little significance in the terrarium hobby, though they recently have been imported in numbers and possibly may be bred in captivity.

More technical methods of sex determination in snakes often are very time-consuming and require expensive laboratory equipment, so they are scarcely suitable for routine sex determination in terrarium animals. The only fairly practical technique is x-ray examination in an animal clinic. With the aid of x-ray photographs, in many species the ossified hooks of the hemipenes are detectable, which makes it possible to identify the male sex. Adult males of giant snakes such as *Boa*

Vestiges of the pelvis with the projecting anal spurs in an African Rock-Python, *Python sebae*.

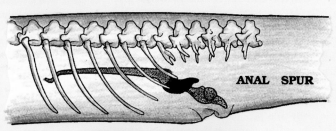

ANAL SPUR

AFRICAN ROCK-PYTHON

duller markings. Male Northern Adders (*Vipera berus*) are primarily gray in various gradations, and females have predominantly yellowish to red and brown ground colors, although there are also gray females as well as black specimens in each sex. In Northern Adders the dorsal markings of the male are more prominent than those of the female.

The sex-specific coloration of the Smooth Snake (*Coronella austriaca*) is reversed. The males usually have brown or rufus ground colors; females, on the other hand, are more gray or brownish black. The bellies are brownish or gray, respectively. The posterior half of the tail of the female Sand Viper (*Cerastes vipera*) from the Sahara is black; in contrast, that of the male is not.

constrictor and *Python molurus* do not exhibit ossified penis hooks, but they have larger vestiges of the pelvis and hind legs than do females. In contrast to this, the evidence of calcified egg shells or the skeletons of fetuses would indicate that the snake is a female. The x-ray method is particularly recommended in poisonous snakes for reasons of safety, because the radiographs can be taken through the transport sack.

Sex determination on the basis of the number of red blood corpuscles, the concentration of the male sex hormone testosterone in the blood, and the endoscopic examination of the internal reproductive organs are reserved for scientific institutions because they are complicated and very expensive to

Anal spur of a large snake. Photo by K-P. Lehmann.

perform, as well as being commercially un-available.

Which method of sex determination is generally recommended to the hobbyist? On the basis of the anatomic structure of the male copulatory organ, direct proof of the sex can be obtained by establishing the presence of the hemipenes, which when not in use are retracted in the direction of the tip of the tail. The skin of these invaginated pouches is also sloughed and occasionally remains attached to the shed skin of a male. A special ball-tipped probe, the gauge of which must be appropriate for the size of the snake to be examined, can be carefully inserted into one hemipenis at a time in the tailward direction. To perform this procedure, a smaller snake will be placed on its back with the left hand

In some species, sex can be determined simply by looking at the coloration. The male of these two young Caucasus Vipers, *Vipera kaznakovi*, for example, is the darker one in the foreground. Photo by L. Trutnau.

This is a radiograph of an Amur Rat Snake, *Elaphe schrencki*, showing the animal's ossified penile hooks. One of the images is slightly obscured by the vertebrae. Photo by L. Sassenburg.

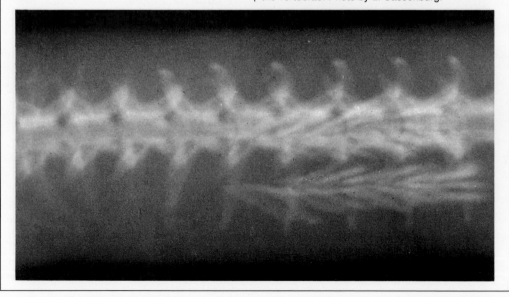

Sex Determination with a probe.

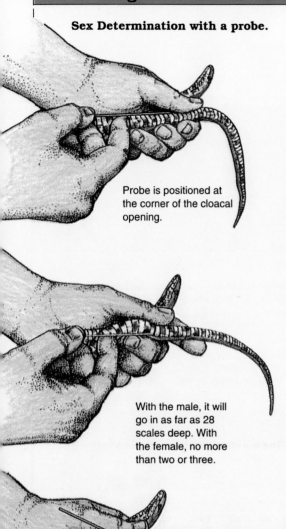

Probe is positioned at the corner of the cloacal opening.

With the male, it will go in as far as 28 scales deep. With the female, no more than two or three.

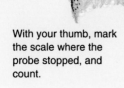

With your thumb, mark the scale where the probe stopped, and count.

(assuming the prober is right-handed) holding the rear part of the body. Then the probe is carefully inserted tailward into the visible opening in one of the corners of the cloaca and is pushed into a hemipenis. The distance the probe can be inserted—this is visible externally—depends on the species. In typical colubrids such as rat snakes and kingsnakes, for example, if it slides in as far as the fourth to twenty-eighth undertail (subcaudal) scale, a hemipenis is present and the snake is a male. The interior space can be probed to this extent only in males. In females of a few species, such as *Boa constrictor*, the probe can penetrate to about the third undertail scale. This should be kept in mind! Experience in interpreting the extent to which the probe slides in is essential in correctly sexing snakes. In females of some groups the scent glands at the base of the tail can be mistaken for hemipenes.

With careful handling of the probe, which can be lubricated with mineral oil or some other neutral substance, and with some practice, the sex of the snake can be determined with fair certainty using this method. The danger of injury for the animal is slight—in contrast to the method sometimes practiced of exposing the hemipenes by pressing with the thumbs on the underside of the base of the tail. An assistant, who holds the struggling snake in the proper position prior to the procedure, is necessary for probing larger snakes. For reasons of hygiene, the disinfection of the probe before and after each examination is recommended. It is best not to probe very young snakes. Under certain circumstances the retraction of the pouches of the hemipenes, which are evaginated in the fetal state, is not yet complete in young snakes, and the hollow spaces are not detectable. In such cases (especially immediately after birth or hatching) the hemipenes may be visible externally for a matter of several hours or even days.

SEXUAL MATURITY

The systematic efforts of the hobbyist to propagate snakes in the terrarium require that they be sexually mature. Sexual maturity is reached when germ cells capable of being fertilized (sperm or egg cells) can be

Karotype of a male and a female Mainland Tiger Snake, *Notechis scutatus*. The sex chromosomes (Z, W) are heteromorphic in the female.

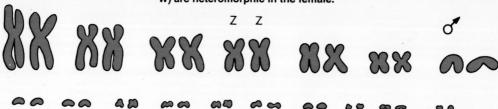

Z Z   ♂

2n = 34

Z W   ♀

Section of the exuvium of a Boa Constrictor, *Boa constrictor*, with sloughings of the hemipenes and anal spurs.

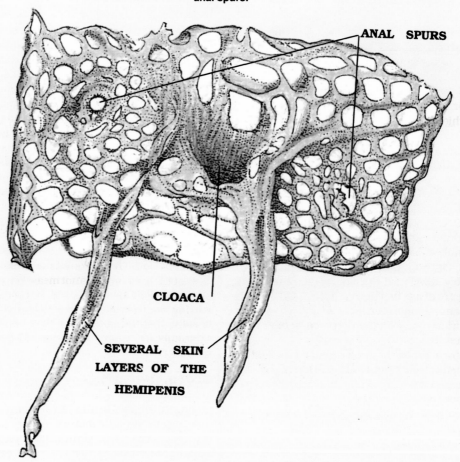

ANAL SPURS

CLOACA

SEVERAL SKIN
LAYERS OF THE
HEMIPENIS

released and the reproductive organs thus are functional. Sexual behaviors need not occur synchronously, but are—because the hobbyist cannot prove directly the presence of mature germ cells—important clues when present.

In addition to sexual maturity, reproductive maturity is also significant for the further development of the growing snake and for the first pregnancy. By reproductive maturity is meant an individual development of the body that brings the sexually mature animal to the act of reproduction. The onset of reproductive maturity under terrarium conditions as a rule takes place later than that of sexual maturity. This has nothing to do with the fact that captive snakes grow faster—both in length and mass—than wild snakes as a result of intensive feeding at above-average temperatures and exhibit certain manifestations of domestication with respect to reproduction. Sexual maturity occurs earlier and reproductive rates can be higher than under natural conditions.

At the same time, the age of the snake and the onset of sexual maturity are not unambiguous criteria for the time of their first use for breeding. Numerous cases are known in which, for example, *Elaphe*, *Nerodia*, and *Thamnophis* species became pregnant at less than one year of age when their natural rhythm of life was ignored and they were fed continuously. For example, captive-bred Western Garter Snakes (*Thamnophis elegans*) after eight months reached a length of 53 to 59 cm (21-24 in)—the average length of adults—and became pregnant. With giant snakes, especially the Boa Constrictor (*Boa constrictor*), the successful breeding of suitably developed specimens at scarcely two years of age has been reported. On the other hand, the age of sexual maturity given for the African Rock-Python (*Python sebae*) in the literature is 10 to 15 years for wild snakes in Africa, probably an average age for wild specimens of most giant snakes. The way in which sexual maturity can be reached with the increasing "domestication" of a species after years of propagation under favorable terrarium conditions is shown by the Common Garter Snake (*Thamnophis sirtalis*), where age at maturity is reduced from 27 months to less than ten months over five generations.

Unfortunately, because of the lack of precise data on age, body length, and sexual maturity, and also because of the great individual variation in these values, no general remarks about the attainment of reproductive maturity in snakes can be made. It is significant that age plays only a secondary role and that the stage of maturity of the snakes determined by a particular body size is decisive.

ONSET OF SEXUAL MATURITY IN CAPTIVE-BRED FEMALE EASTERN GARTER SNAKES, *THAMNOPHIS SIRTALIS SIRTALIS*.

Generation	Age in Months
F_1	27
F_2	23
F_3	$11^1/_2$
F_4	13
F_5	$9^1/_2$

Although the body size of a snake is chiefly expressed in its body length, a body mass proportionate to the length should be taken into consideration. Unusually thin snakes can be long enough, old enough, and sexually mature, but can still have problems in reproduction. Poorly developed germ cells, difficulties in hatching or at birth, and a low number of young are aspects of low body mass. Often the mother snake is so weak after laying the eggs or giving birth to the young that she cannot recover and dies. Just because the body of the snake is suitably developed, however, does not mean that young snakes should be "fattened." Too intensive rearing could lead to extreme growth and obesity, and functional disturbances of the reproductive organs could be the consequence.

PERIODICITY OF REPRODUCTION

In most of our earth's climatic zones, the course of a year is characterized by the seasons with their typical changes in weather. All organisms adapt to this rhythm of the seasons, the changes in temperature, light (in particular the relation of light to dark periods), and the food supply. In regions with tropical climates with slight seasonal changes in temperature, the annual rhythm is characterized by differences in rainfall.

Reproduction in snakes is subject to a natural periodicity and is controlled by both internal and external influences. Little is known about the existence and significance of such rhythms, and ignoring them in the terrarium often is a decisive impediment to the propagation of terrarium dwellers. The reason why these rhythms are so difficult to study

Any of the boids (boas and pythons) can be tricky to breed in captivity; you should, at the very least, have an intimate understanding of their natural reproductive habits before you try propagating them in your home. Photo of an African Rock-Python, *Python sebae*, by Paul Freed.

in the living animal is that the reproductive cycle is expressed externally only in reproductive behavior; the actual cyclic changes in the morphology, histology, and physiology of the reproductive organs are concealed from the hobbyist. To this is added that the periodicity of reproduction of male and female snakes differs.

Although the annual rhythm of repro-

duction for many snake species, particularly in the temperate zones, runs through one reproductive period a year, there are many transitions between this so-called monocyclic reproduction through bicyclic to polycyclic rhythms. Different cycles occur even within a species. For example, though populations of southern areas of occurrence may be bicyclic, individuals from northern re-

ANNUAL CYCLE OF THE LEOPARD RAT SNAKE, *ELAPHE SITULA*.

HIBERNATION	ACTIVE LIFE		HIBERNATION
	MATING	EGG-LAYING HATCHING	
		ESTIVATION	

J	F	M	A	M	J	J	A	S	O	N	D

REPRODUCTIVE CYCLE OF THE WESTERN RATTLESNAKE, *CROTALUS VIRIDIS*, IN NORTHERN IDAHO.

	Apr.	May	June	July	Aug.	Sept.	Oct.
Birth						————	
Pregnancy			————————————————				
Ovulation		——					
Egg maturation	————————					- - - - -	
Mating	——						
Sperm in Spermatic Duct	————————————————————————————————						- - -
MONTH	Apr.	May	June	July	Aug.	Sept.	Oct.

gions might reproduce only once a year or only every second or third year. The assumption that snakes from tropical regions behave acyclically (without cycles) probably is not true in most cases.

Four categories have been distinguished in the male sexual cycle: continuous sperm formation, sperm formation in summer, sperm formation before mating, and mixed forms. For many North American and European colubrid species, the following annual rhythm has been observed in male snakes:

1) spermiogenesis begins in April and continues to November; it is most intense in the fall;
2) the sperm reach the epididymis, where they are stored during the coming winter and spring;
3) the testes shrink in winter;
4) with the start of spring matings, the sperm travel though the spermatic duct and some are ejaculated;
5) the epididymis do not fill up again with sperm until late summer;
6) when a fall mating takes place, the one-year-old sperm remaining in the spermatic duct are used.

In one study of Western (Prairie) Rattlesnakes (*Crotalus viridis*), most sperm was found in the sperm-conducting ducts from March to October. Ovulation took place from mid-May to mid-June, and the birth period of this livebearing species was limited to a relatively short period.

The control of reproductive periodicity also plays a decisive role in the reproduction of snakes in the terrarium. Environmental factors act on the hypothalamus, a part of the middle brain, from which appropriate information is transmitted hormonally through the pituitary gland (hypophysis) to the gonads.

A hardy and very beautiful creature, the Western Rattlesnake, *Crotalus viridis*, can be found in a wide variety of habitats and will take a great number of food items, including mammals, birds, lizards, snakes, and amphibians. Photo by R. T. Zappalorti.

An important task for the hobbyist who wants to stimulate his snakes to breed is to promote these factors as much as possible. Big problems can arise because the provenance of the snakes often is not known or the climatic conditions of the snake's homeland are not known with certainty. No weather atlas or vague description of the homeland of these snakes is of any use here. Even the collecting of the snakes by the hobbyist himself provides little knowledge, unless he has the opportunity to experience the climatic conditions over a period of at least a year. Another problem arises when individuals of a single species being used in a breeding program come from different parts of the range of the species. The lack of synchronization of their reproductive periodicity can make propagation in the terrarium impossible.

Fortunately, reproduction often is successful even under the most diverse terrarium conditions. Does this call into question the specific factors that influence reproduction? Does this mean that observations in the terrarium cannot be carried over to conditions in the wild, or that they even must be considered to be wrong? Neither is true. The successful propagation "in spite of everything" merely proves the great adaptability of the animals and makes it possible to influence individual factors randomly in planned experiments and to study their effects.

Among the climatic environmental factors, temperature assumes a primary role. Reproduction of snakes in the terrarium often has succeeded after overwintering at cool temperatures. In experiments with Common Garter Snakes (*Thamnophis sirtalis*), it was demonstrated that low temperatures and darkness stimulated the growth of the ovarian follicles and the readiness to breed in females. Starting in the fall, two groups of experimental animals were kept in a 12-hour light-dark rhythm for 20 weeks at 4°C (39°F) and 17°C (63°F), respectively. In each group the ovaries remained the same size and exhibited no differences. In a third group of female snakes, which simultaneously had been exposed to the same rhythm of illumination at warm temperatures, the ovaries degenerated completely. This degeneration persisted the whole year. The males were overwintered at cool temperatures and were then acclimated for a few days at 30°C (86°F). A mating test limited to 30 seconds between a hormonally stimulated female (0.4 microgram 17 beta-estradiol per day for five days) and a male that seemed to be ready to breed demonstrated the positive influence of cool overwintering. This experiment was carried out under conditions of constant lighting.

The changed lighting conditions during overwintering often are ignored. Terrarium experiments with Corn Snakes (*Elaphe guttata*) showed how the lengthening of the daily light period alone stimulated mating activity in the spring.

In the tropical rainforest, where changes in temperature and day length are relatively slight in the course of a year, the alternation of dryness and high humidity plays a poorly known and under-appreciated role.

The size and quality of the living space and, closely related to this, the social factor of population density can disrupt the initiation of reproduction. With snakes, which in contrast to many lizard species do not exhibit a pronounced social hierarchy with territorial behavior, a terrarium that is too small and holds a large number of animals can lead to aggressive behavior, the suppression of the sexual activity of weaker animals, and obstruction of mating. It can be assumed that, as has been observed in other reptiles, the presence of sexually active male snakes stimulates the ovarian functions in females. A uniform distribution of pheromones and constant unrest in the terrarium, however, can lead to disturbed relations between the sexes.

Because the availability of food is subject to seasonal variation in the wild, diet also influences sexual events. Even so, a generally good state of nutrition by itself is not enough to ensure optimal pregnancy and the viability of young snakes.

As experiments with Western (Prairie) Rattlesnakes (*Crotalus viridis*) showed, the size of the fatty bodies in the snake's body is an important criterion for the frequency of reproduction in females. During pregnancy, when snakes take in little or no food, the fatty bodies are broken down to meet the body's energy needs and do not start to grow again until the fall.

TYPES OF REPRODUCTIVE PERIODICITY IN SNAKES

Type	Main period of reproduction	Preparation for period of reproduction	Main cue for reproduction	Day length in reproductive period (hours)	Selected species
A	Spring to early summer	Hibernation (cold and dark)	Temperature elevation	12	Garter and Ribbon Snakes (Thamnophis) Rattlesnakes (Crotalus) Eurasian vipers (Vipera)
B	Spring to early summer	Shortened period of illumination	Slight temperature reduction (rest period)	16	Rat snakes (Elaphe) Kingsnakes (Lampropeltis) Other snakes of temperate and subtropical zones.
C	Fall to winter	Customary high temperatures; period of illumination of about 12 hours	Shortening of the period of illumination; slight reduction in temperature	8	Boas (Boinae) Pythons (Pythoninae) Indigo snakes (Drymarchon)
D	Independent of season	None	None or unknown (moisture?)	12	Cobras (Naja) King Cobras (Ophiophagus) Rat snakes (Elaphe) from tropical regions

Terrarium conditions, which usually do not correspond to actualities in the wild, can intentionally or unintentionally lead to a shifting of the natural periodicity of reproduction or to the disappearance of reproductive rhythm. In snakes from temperate climates that hibernate at low temperatures and in darkness, the natural rhythm normally is retained. An indication of favorable keeping conditions, in particular an ample food supply, is the production of a second clutch in late summer by various species after the regular reproductive period in the spring; the offspring would scarcely be able to reach maturity under the natural climatic conditions of their homeland, because the juveniles would hardly survive the oncoming winter without the chance to build up their energy reserves.

North American rat snakes (Elaphe) in the author's terraria laid their clutches regularly in the time from mid-May to early July after an eight-week hibernation from December to February. A large percentage of the females, however, then produced a second, although usually somewhat smaller, clutch from late July to late August. The interval from the first to the second clutch was 50 to 71 days.

Numerous reports demonstrate that snakes from warm regions, which do not hibernate, maintain their natural reproductive rhythm for several years in the terrarium. For example, Egyptian Cobras (Naja haje) always mated in February and March and their youngsters hatched in July. A deliberate displacement of the reproductive rhythm by half a year can be beneficial when we want snakes from the temperate zones of

NATURAL TIME OF EGGLAYING OR THE BIRTH OF YOUNG SNAKES FOR SELECTED SNAKE
SPECIES AND MAIN AREAS OF OCCURRENCE.

Egg-laying or birth of young snakes (*)	Specific example	Main area of occurence
January—February	Black Forest Cobra *(Pseudohaje goldi)*	W, Central, SW Africa.
January—April	Australian Water Snake *(Tropidonophis mairi)*	New Guinea; N, NE Australia; Molucca.
February—March	Mainland Tiger Snake *(Notechis scutatus)**	Australia (Victoria, New South Wales).
February—April	Common Puff-Adder *(Bitis arietans)**	S Morocco; S Arabia; Central, S Africa.
March—April	Rough-scaled Bush Viper *(Atheris squamiger)**	Western Central Africa
March—May	Ball Python *(Python regius)*	W, Central Africa
March—December	Long-nosed Tree Snake *(Ahaetulla nasuta)*	SE Asia.
April	Reticulated Python *(Python reticulatus)* African Rock-Python *(Python sebae)*	SE Asia. Africa south of the Sahara.
April—May	Mountain Patchnose Snake *(Salvadora grahamiae)* Herald Snake *(Crotaphopeltis hotamboeia)*	USA (western states); NE Mexico. tropical Africa (not rainforest).
May—June	Glossy Snake *(Arizona elegans)* Asian Rock-Python *(Python molurus)*	USA (midwest, California): NW Mexico. S, SE Asia.
May-June	Corn Snake *(Elaphe guttata)*	Central, E, SE USA; NE Mexico.
May—August	Boa Constrictor *(Boa constrictor)**	Antilles; Argentina, S Mexico.
May—August	Green Tree Python *(Chondropython viridis)** Southern Water Snake *(Nerodia fasciata)**	New Guinea; N Australia. Central USA.
June	American Racer *(Coluber constrictor)*	S Canada; USA; Mexico.
June—July	Aesculapian Rat Snake *(Elaphe longissima)* American Rat Snake *(Elaphe obsoleta)* Sand-Boa *(Eryx miliaris)* Headband Dwarf Snake *(Eirenis modestus)* Viperine Water Snake *(Natrix maura)*	S. Europe, Asia Minor. NE Canada; USA; NE Mexico. central Asia to W Mongolia. Near East to Persia. W, SW Europe, NW Africa.

June—August	Steppes Rat Snake *(Elaphe dione)*	Ukraine to Korea; NE China.
	Amur Rat Snake *(Elaphe schrencki)*	E Soviet Union; NE China; Korea.
June—August	Common King Snake *(Lampropeltis getula)*	E USA; Mexico.
	Dice Snake *(Natrix tessellata)*	central Europe to central Asia.
June—November	Brown Water Snake *(Nerodia taxispilota)**	SE USA.
July—August	Desert Horned Viper *(Cerastes cerastes)*	N Africa; Israel; Arabia.
July—August	Four-lined Rat Snake *(Elaphe quatuorlineata)*	SE Europe, W Asia.
July—August	Common Garter Snake *(Thamnophis sirtalis)**	S Canada; USA; N Mexico.
July—November	Eastern Ribbon Snake *(Thamnophis sauritus)**	SE USA.
August—September	Smooth Snake *(Coronella austriaca)**	Central, S Europe; Asia Minor; Caucusus.
September	Fischer's Slender Boa *(Epicrates striatus)**	Haiti, Bahamas.
September—October	Javelin Sand-Boa *(Eryx jaculus)**	SE Europe; SW Asia; N Africa.
September—October	Long-nosed Viper *(Vipera ammodytes)**	SE Europe; W Asia.
September—April	Australian Water Python *(Liasis mackloti fuscus)*	New Guinea; Timor.
October	Kenyan Sand-Boa *(Eryx colubrinus)**	N, E Africa.
November—December	Horned Bush Viper *(Atheris superciliaris)**	E, SE Africa.
December—January	Cape Cobra *(Naja nivea)*	S, SW Africa.
December—February	Green Bush Snake *(Philothammus irregularis)*	Africa other than the north.

the southern hemisphere to reproduce in northern latitudes.

Valid information on reproductive periodicity in the terrarium can be obtained only under the same environmental conditions after several years of observations and preferably over several generations. Even then the results apply only to the terrarium installation in question.

The diversity of reproductive types in snakes makes inferences for terrarium practice difficult. An attempt was made to classify typical groups of reproductive periodicity, taking into consideration the cycles of each sex. This resulted in four basic groups. Within the first two groups (types A and B) another division could be made with respect to the cycles of spermiogenesis in the species with

SNAKE SPECIES WITH SEVERAL EGGLAYINGS PER YEAR IN THE WILD

Time of Egg-laying	Species	Main area of occurrence
Twice a year (April—May and December—January)	African Egg-eating Snake *(Dasypeltis scabra)*	S Arabia; E, Central, S Africa.
Twice a year (various times)	Dhaman *(Ptyas mucosus)*	Soviet Union; China; S, SE Asia
Several times distributed through the year	Fish Snake *(Xenochrophis piscator)*	Pakistan; China; SE Asia.
	Banded Cat-eyed Snake *(Leptodeira annulata)*	Mexico to Argentina.

CLIMATIC ZONES AND TIME OF LAYING EGGS OR GIVING BIRTH TO YOUNG

Climatic zone	time
1. Temperate zone	Short, strictly limited; usually in the spring; one clutch or litter.
2. Subtropical zone	Longer, but still limited; from spring to summer; several clutches or litters are possible.
3. Tropical zone of tradewinds and high pressure areas	Considerably extended; limited by the seasonal principal rainy period; the annual course of temperature change has a less limiting effect.
4. Tropical zone (zone of monsoons, equatorial zone)	Clutches or litters usually distributed throughout the year.
5. Special cases (arid regions with occasional rainfall)	Relatively short, dependent on the occurrence of rainfall; often only one clutch or litter; with insufficient rainfall, resorption of the eggs or embryos in the mother's body.

It is crucial that a snake's system be completely cleaned out before it goes into hibernation. Here, this is being accomplished by soaking the snake, in this case a young Gaboon Viper, *Bitis gabonica*, in a tub of warm water. Photo by Jim Merli.

maximum sperm production in the spring before mating and in those with spermiogenesis starting in late summer with the storage of sperm until spring mating. Other subdivisions and exceptions are to be expected, of course.

The problems discussed so far make it clear that the hobbyist must be as familiar as possible with the natural factors that influence the snake in its homeland. It also is essential to know the timing of these factors and to duplicate these factors in the terrarium, of course while allowing for the external climate, that is, our seasons. Although snakes are highly adaptable to less than favorable conditions in the terrarium and may have long life spans in captivity, routinely successful propagation is more demanding.

DORMANCY

With the change of seasons in the temperate northern and southern hemispheres, and also in tropical zones, there are times in which the snakes do not find favorable living conditions. Either the ambient temperatures in winter do not give the reptiles, which are dependent on an external supply of heat, a chance to be active, or high temperatures and extreme dryness make a period of summer dormancy seem sensible. In tropical regions in which the alternation of extreme dryness and heavy monsoons or equatorial rainfall determine the seasons, snakes enter a more or less pronounced period of summer dormancy (estivation). Food intake and intensity of movement are strongly curtailed, and cooler hiding places, which must not dry out completely, are sought. In the terrarium this estivation of snakes is less conspicuous, and it is sufficient to allow dryness to prevail while holding the temperature constant. The start of the rainy season has a stimulating effect on reproduction in the wild. By moistening the substrate and providing frequent intense spraying, the natural conditions are simulated and the mating drive is initiated.

Far more important for snakes from temperate zones is providing winter dormancy (hibernation). The lowered temperatures, combined with the shortening of day length or total darkness, are requirements for the stimulation of reproductive activity in spring. Old, weak, and sick animals do not survive the stress of this forced dormancy, which sometimes lasts several months. Consequently, under terrarium conditions sickly animals and those in poor condition, as well as very young animals that have not been able to lay down sufficient fat reserves, should not be overwintered at cold temperatures. The onset of hibernation, however, is not determined only by the drop in temperature. An internal biorhythm undoubtedly plays a role in snakes, but it is not as pronounced as in mammals, in which it is better to speak of a "winter sleep." The internal influence can be observed when snakes from temperate zones are kept at warm temperatures in winter and are offered food regularly. As a rule, activity will be reduced and food will be refused for weeks or months in winter.

The duration of hibernation depends on the latitude and altitude of a snake's range. Snakes from northern Europe or Canada hibernate for six to eight months, those from central Europe and the northern United States about five to seven months. Even in subtropical regions, where the average winter temperatures fall to only 10 to 12°C (50-54°F), a hibernation lasting several weeks occurs.

If we wish to systematically breed snakes, we should not ignore the stimulating effect of hibernation. It corresponds to the natural rhythm of life of these animals and contributes to a longer life expectancy. Possible losses that occur during or shortly after the end of hibernation normally affect, as long as there are no gross errors on the part of the hobbyist, only feeble individuals.

Hibernation can begin when the snakes no longer feed with the same appetite as before and start to limit their activity. The food supply is curtailed but normal terrarium temperatures are maintained at first. The period of illumination is reduced to eight hours. Be certain that all the animals have evacuated their bowels, otherwise any food still in the digestive tract would decompose during hibernation and under certain circumstances would lead to death only after the conclusion of torpor. Next the temperature should be lowered slowly over a period of about two weeks and the lighting switched off. If the terraria are in a room that can be kept cool in winter, it is easiest to leave the animals in their usual terraria. Plants must of course be removed. Make sure that there are enough hiding places available for the animals, which must never dry out completely during hibernation. By gradually reducing the temperature—most easily accomplished by regulating electric heating by means of a thermostat—the room temperature can be reduced gradually to 8 to 10°C (46-50°F) with snakes from southern latitudes or 4 to 6°C (39-43°F) with animals from northern latitudes. Furnace heat is not suitable for this kind of overwintering. The terrarium with the snakes could be moved to a cool room with the appropriate temperatures. A drop in temperature to the freezing point absolutely must be avoided; subfreezing temperatures are fatal.

In some houses, cool, not-too-damp basements offer good overwintering facilities. Such conditions do not prevail in centrally heated homes. Attics are usually unsuitable as overwintering sites because of the danger of freezing. If the "apartment hobbyist" has no good friends who can offer his animals a place to overwinter, a way out must be found. One effective solution is to overwinter the snakes in an insulated container on the balcony. By heating the container slightly and regulating the temperature with a thermostat, subfreezing temperatures are avoided. Warm spells in winter, however, must be taken into account. Overwintering in a refrigerator seems to be an optimal solution, as long as the danger of drying out and the occasional need for ventilation are addressed. This overwintering method has proved its worth especially with amphibians, but there has been little experience with snakes.

Whenever the animals cannot stay in their terrarium, it is necessary to transfer them to a special overwintering box. Suitable for this purpose is a small terrarium or better yet a tight-closing wooden box with ventilation holes covered with galvanized wire mesh or the like. Rats and mice must be kept out. Good insulation of the overwintering box is very beneficial so that brief temperature fluctuations cannot affect the animals.

Suitable substrates include not too wet moss, leaves, leaf mold, and wood shavings. The material must never dry out completely. If hibernating snakes are kept too wet, blister diseases ("snake smallpox") can be the result. Moldy substrate must be replaced. Hiding places such as pieces of bark, flat rocks,

Excelsior (another word for wood shavings) is a good substrate to use with hibernating snakes. They can burrow into it easily enough and it can obtained at most any pet shop. Photo by Isabelle Francais, courtesy of Bill and Marcia Brant.

Some snakes are remarkably delicate and will be highly sensitive to the trials of hibernation, while others, like the garter and ribbon snakes, genus Thamnophis, are quite hardy and will do well even if temperatures fluctuate every now and then. It behooves you to find out which kind of snake you have before you "put it down." Photo by John Iverson.

flowerpots, and the like, which apply a certain amount of pressure to the backs of the snakes, are preferred. The snakes often rest coiled together in these hiding places. In the wild, thousands of Common Garter Snakes (*Thamnophis sirtalis*), for example, can be found together in the most favorable hibernation dens.

A weekly inspection of the overwintering container must be carried out without disturbing the snakes. Snakes that have not taken shelter when exposed to suitably low temperatures could be ill. These individuals must not be allowed to hibernate. If the snakes are unusually active, the temperatures are too high (above 10°C, 50°F), and the snakes must be given the opportunity to drink. Regardless of the length of the natural hibernation, in general six to eight weeks in addition to the time needed to cool and rewarm the snakes slowly are sufficient in the terrarium. Even shorter periods of dormancy of only four weeks, which are usually tolerated well even by weaker animals, promote reproductive periodicity. Long overwintering periods may reduce the cost of lighting, heating, and food, but empty terraria in

the home are not particularly attractive either.

After the hibernation period is complete, gradually raise the temperature again and allow light to enter. A completely cooled terrarium room, individual terraria, or overwintering boxes can be rewarmed very slowly (about 2°C, 3-4°F, per day) by regulating the temperature with a thermostat. After the temperature reaches 18 to 20°C (65-68°F), the terrarium lighting is turned on briefly. Snakes that have hibernated in a special overwintering container are put back in their thoroughly cleaned and disinfected terrarium. Bathing the animal in lukewarm water is recommended because the snake drinks the water, which makes the mucous membrane of the digestive tract functional again so it can effectively digest the first meal. Snakes usually drink on their own at the end of hibernation and bathe in preparation of an approaching molt. Food is offered a few days after rewarming. Sometimes it is refused; a molt or even the initial reproductive activities—the search for mates and attempted copulations—take precedence. Such behaviors show

These two male California Mountain Kingsnakes, *Lampropeltis zonata*, are engaged in a ritual pre-mating combat, which, as herpetologists are now discovering, is an act common with many snake species. Photo by L. Trutnau.

Ritual fighting in Long-nosed Vipers, *Vipera ammodytes*.

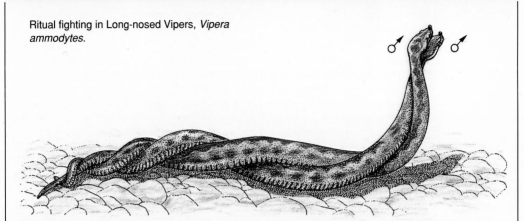

♂↗   ♂↗

that our efforts to provide the snakes with favorable conditions for the approaching period of reproduction were successful.

FINDING AND CHOOSING MATES

To positively influence the sexes' readiness to breed, knowledge of reproductive behavior is required. In snakes, in particular, there often is the problem that a male does not want to mate with the available female despite the hobbyist's best efforts. This means that testing must be done, and the surest success often is achieved when a group of several males and females can be kept together.

Reproductive behavior includes sexual behavior in the strictest sense (mating behavior, copulation) as well as the care of the eggs and young. It is important to fulfill the following functions:

1) identifying the characters of the mates, such as the species, sex, age, and readiness to breed (sex determination);

2) overcoming the individual distance (attracting the sexes);

3) synchronizing the physiological processes and events until mating is completed.

This usually is the full extent of reproductive behavior in snakes. Mate bonding is virtually nonexistent. Only the Asian Cobra (*Naja naja*) exhibits a kind of pair

Long-nosed Viper. *Vipera ammodytes*. Photo by W. Wuster.

formation. In the spring, the Long-nosed Viper (*Vipera ammodytes*) usually is encountered in pairs in hiding places or at basking sites in its homeland, thus forming a temporary mating partnership. Care behavior exists only in the brood care of a few species; at best it is possible to speak of brood provision—actions like seeking out a site for egg-laying with an apparently favorable temperature and moisture content—that ends after the eggs are laid. (There are exceptions to this, especially some pythons, in females of various species that stay with their eggs during all or part of development.)

Before we discuss the behaviors that lead up to copulation, let's discuss the "jousting behavior" or male combat rituals of some snakes. Misinterpreted initially, this behavior rarely is observed under terrarium conditions. It was first described in several European colubrids (*Elaphe longissima, Coluber najadum, Malpolon monspessulanus*) and was thought to be "courtship behavior" or a "wedding dance" leading up to mating. Subsequently the American herpetologist C. E. Shaw was able to prove through terrarium observations of rattlesnakes that it was a question of a ritual behavior between male animals, more appropriately called "ritual combat." These fights proceed in a ritualized fashion without leading to serious injuries (except in rare cases). The concept of ritual combat—at first used only for jousting in an upright position—now has been extended to jousting in the horizontal position with entwined bodies.

The reasons for ritual combat in snakes are unclear. In other reptile species, especially lizards, territorial defense plays a role. Although snakes are somewhat sedentary, territorial behavior has not been demonstrated so far. Homosexual tendencies can also be ruled out, although in overpopulated terraria male snakes—stimulated by the simultaneous presence of females in estrus—sometimes make sexual advances toward other males. The most likely explanation is that ritual fights are struggles between rivals for the favor of females. Even though it usually is expressly stated that no female was nearby in observations of ritual combat in the wild, in principle it cannot be ruled out that the "bone of contention" simply was overlooked by the observer. The defense of a small area around the female by males has been described in the Sinaloan Milksnake (*Lampropeltis triangulum sinaloae*), and fighting can occur in this instance. This behavior was not observed when several males were kept together without females. Unequivocally demonstrated—at least in the terrarium—is that stimulation by food can trigger ritual fights in males without the presence of females. These fights cannot be ruled out as an expression of social dominance, efforts to win a more favorable position in the hierarchy, although this has not been unequivocally demonstrated in snakes.

Ritual fights have been observed in most families of snakes. Only isolated observations exist for giant snakes: the rearing up and mutual pushing away of Rainbow Boas (*Epicrates cenchria*) and the entwining of the rear part of the body in the Madagascar Tree-Boa (*Sanzinia madagascariensis*). In these fights the anal spurs scratch vigorously against the scales of the opponent. Typical for snakes is an almost complete entwining of both animals. In the Aesculapian Rat Snake (*Elaphe longissima*) a rearing of the front part of the body into a lyre-shaped posture has been reported.

A form of ritual fighting similar to that found in colubrids is known in elapids and some of the vipers, including the Northern Viper (*Vipera berus*). Puff Adders (*Bitis arietans*) crawl jerkily along the rival, while the snake on the bottom raises the front part of its body and tries to throw the rival off by suddenly recoiling the front of the body.

Ritual fighting in pitvipers has been analyzed especially thoroughly. In *Agkistrodon piscivorus*, the semi-aquatic North American Cottonmouth, ritual fights even were observed in the water. The fangs are not used during jousting, and the rattles of rattlesnakes also remain silent.

Although it can be generally assumed that the male snake is the more active mate, stimulating actions also come from the female. Here olfactory stimuli, which are analyzed with the Jacobson's organ, play an important role. Visual recognition of the mate is insignificant in snakes, since distinct sec-

Ritual fighting in Red Diamond Rattlesnakes, *Crotalus ruber*.

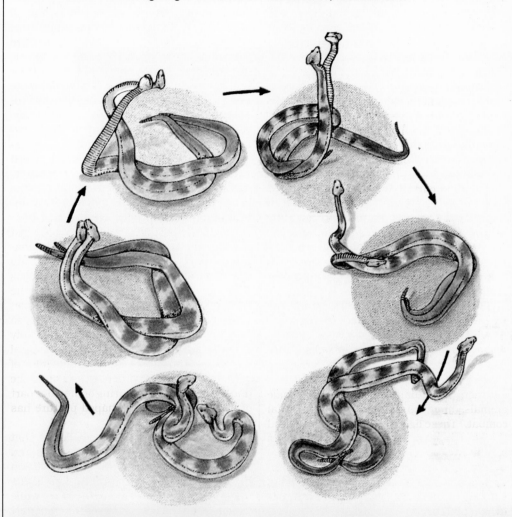

ondary sex characters typically are not present. Decisive for the sexual attraction of males by females are chemical aromatic substances, sex pheromones, which are released by the female during estrus. It is not clear if the pheromones are released from the female anal glands. Excretions from the cutaneous glands (nuchodorsal glands) located under the scales of the nape or back also may play a role in some water snakes. The release of sex pheromones can reflect the seasonal changes of the reproductive activity of the species in question, as was demonstrated by experiments with Common Garter Snakes (*Thamnophis sirtalis*). Males of this species

react to artificially laid pheromone trails chiefly in the months from April to June, not at all in July, and to a reduced extent from August to October.

The strict specificity of these pheromones is significant. In experiments, males of *Thamnophis sirtalis* and *T. butleri*, species occurring in the same range, chose trails with traces of pheromone from females of their own species more often than trails without pheromone or with pheromones of the other species. Male Plains Garter Snakes of the subspecies *Thamnophis radix radix* from Illinois and *T. r. haydeni* from Colorado recognized and preferred traces from the females of their own subspecies. These findings from terrarium experiments on the specificity of the action of pheromones could prove helpful in the study of the taxonomic relationships between snakes.

Also interesting in this connection is the recent discovery that some male garter snakes release a pheromone similar to that of the ready-to-mate female. In the mass matings occasionally observed at the completion of hibernation in these species, these males ward off other male rivals with these pheromones and thereby improve their chances of reaching females and thus successfully mating. Females in turn prefer the "fragrant" males by up to 70% over the normal males. It is still unclear, however, why all male snakes do not choose this apparently quite successful reproductive strategy.

The pheromones deposited on scent trails by the female are detected in the most minute concentrations by males of the same species and are followed by means of rapid flicking of the tongue. In experiments with giant snakes, masking of this scent by spraying the female with strong perfume, artificially coloring the female to mislead the sense of sight, or covering the males' eyes did not reduce successful mate-finding ability by the males. Only when the male's Jacobson's organ was rendered inoperable or the entire body of the female was covered with petroleum jelly did the males abandon mating attempts.

The attractive effect of sex pheromones can lead to the gathering of several to many breeding snakes of the same species (an aggregation). The sex pheromones also stimulate the reproductive drive of both sexes. Because male and female snakes live together in captivity in the most confined space, eventually scent trails are distributed throughout the terrarium. Nonetheless, it is not hard to find mates in this comparatively tiny area. It also is clear that when the sexes are put together after long separation, rapid and intense sexual stimulation results.

The gorgeous Sinaloan Milk Snake, *Lampropeltis triangulum sinaloae*, is one of the most commonly bred snakes in modern herpetoculture. It is a hardy animal that does remarkably well in captivity. Photo by B. Kahl.

Mating

Following the recognition and attraction of the mate, the animals approach each other. The at first seemingly passive female snake is extensively chased and touched by the male—a whole group of suitors may even be present. Tactile stimuli often are characteristic of the species in question. Often the male crawls over the female's back. At the same time he rubs the underside of his head on his mate's back. The sense of touch plays an important role in this stage of sexual stimulation. Many species react with the tactile organs on the scales of their lips and chin. Organs of touch also are present in the cloacal region. The tails entwine. In large species of colubrids, typical undulating movements of one or both mates can be observed. The entwining of the tails, often accompanied by the pressing together of the cloacas, follows a partial or complete entwining of the female by the male.

In various vipers and pitvipers, abrupt thrusts by the male against the female's back are part of the mating ceremony. In some colubrids, in particular in the genera *Elaphe*, *Coluber*, and *Coronella*, an interesting behavior, the biting of the nape, can be observed. It doubtless permits the male to hold fast to the writhing female, but it also serves as sexual stimulation. Without injuring the female seriously, the ready-to-breed male to some

In this photo of a pair of anerytrhistic Corn Snakes, *Elaphe guttata guttata*, mating, you can clearly see the male's hemipenis inserted in the female. Photo by V. Nagele.

extent first bites randomly, but later usually deliberately bites the nape region of the female. The anal spurs of male giant snakes have a similar stimulating function, and they simultaneously help the male to hold fast to the female.

The courtship phase as a rule is the longest in the entire mating behavior. If the female has not yet been stimulated

Mating of *Coluber* sp.

sufficiently, males court her favor for days or weeks. Finally copulation takes place. By pressing the cloacas together laterally or after lifting the female's tail from below, a hemipenis is inserted into the female's cloaca (intromission). The hemipenis is swollen and anchors itself in the cloaca, often supported by characteristic hooks.

In the Brown Water Snake (*Nerodia taxispilota*), various garter snakes (*Thamnophis*), and the Rough Earth Snake (*Virginia striatula*), as well as the Southern Black Racer (*Coluber constrictor priapus*), it was observed at the conclusion of ejaculation that a rapidly hardening gelatinous plug, secreted by the male's kidneys, was deposited in the female's cloaca and blocked the openings of the oviducts. The length of time this plug remained intact was temperature-dependent. Under controlled terrarium conditions, an apparently enzymatic dissolution of the plug was observed within two days at 21°C (70°F) and after two weeks at 4°C (39°F). At the same time, ready-to-mate males were able to distinguish clearly between females with and without a mating plug because of the pheromone signal released by the female. It remains unclear, however, how repeated copulations of a female snake with several males in succession are possible.

Copulation often lasts a long time, up to several hours. The anchoring of the hemipenis in the cloaca is so intense that when disturbed the often physically stronger female carries the male away with her. As far as possible, disturbances should be avoided during this decisive phase of reproduction. This applies not only to the keeper and visitors, but also to other inhabitants of the terrarium, in particular conspecific and sexually interested males. Disturbances of this kind often are grounds for breaking off copulation. Even without visible cause, the duration of copulation is highly variable in the same and related species.

As in all reptiles, during copulation the release of the ejaculate occurs in the outermost part of the female reproductive tract. Intense contractions of the lower reproductive tract carry the sperm very rapidly into the oviducts. Most, if not all, snakes ovulate one week after mating at the earliest, often later. The sperm are therefore stored for several weeks or months in the lumen or the folds of the oviducts. They concentrate in small groups, and their heads are sometimes in loose contact with the cells of the superficial tissue of the reproductive duct. When mating takes place in the fall, the sperm are stored for seven to eight months. Then the sperm are held in specialized vesicles or sacs in the oviducts called

Detail of the breeding of Sinaloan Milk Snakes, *Lampropeltis triangulum sinaloae*. During copulation, some snakes may lie together for hours. The keeper who wants to watch his or her snakes mating may be in for a long wait. Photo by L. Trutnau.

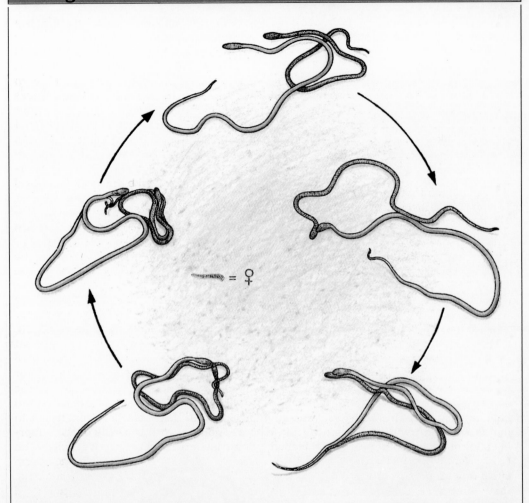

Courtship of the Collared Dwarf Snake, *Eirenis collaris*.

DURATION OF COPULATION OF A FEW SNAKE SPECIES

Species	Duration
Blood Python (*Python curtus*)	9 . . . 13 hrs
Green Anaconda (*Eunectes murinus*)	25 . . . 110 min
Striped Keelback (*Amphiesma stolata*)	3 . . . 4 hrs
American Rat Snake (*Elaphe obsoleta*)	10 . . . 40 min
Eastern Green Mamba (*Dendroaspis angusticeps*)	15 . . . 17 hrs
Western Diamondback Rattlesnake and Red Diamond Rattlesnake (*Crotalos atrox, C. ruber*)	8 . . . 10, max. 22³/₄ hrs

seminal receptacles. The sperm reach a high concentration in these storage organs. The cells lining the oviducts have 5- to 10-micrometer-long cilia (kinocilia) that actively assist the second stage of sperm migration in the oviducts. The movement of sperm proceeds with a series of endocrine changes in the oviducts, so it can be assumed that a chemical stimulation in a particular stage of the sexual cycle is decisive for the movement of sperm. It cannot be ruled out that the sperm must undergo further maturation in storage (capacitation) in the female reproductive tract to become fully viable.

The possibility of long-term survival of sperm in the female reproductive organs—together with the possibility of delayed development of the embryo—is one of the mechanisms by which snakes can make the time of birth of young or laying of eggs independent of the sexual cycle of the male. This has great ecological signifi-

Gravidity in snakes is often very obvious—viewing the snake from overhead will make the swollen section rather obvious. This attractive Mexican Rosy Boa, *Lichanura trivirgata trivirgata*, for example, is obviously gravid. Photo by K. H. Switak.

cance. Beyond that, the long-term survival of sperm from one egg-laying or birth until the next makes possible the maintenance of normal reproduction. As a result, female snakes of some species are able to lay fertile eggs repeatedly for years, even without the chance to mate again. This delayed sexual reproduction through sperm storage is called amphigonia retardata.

GESTATION PERIOD OF SELECTED SNAKE SPECIES.

Species	Egg-laying or live-bearing	Period in days
Boa Constrictor (Boa constrictor)	l	119-294
Slender-Boas (Epicrates sp)	l	160-220
Emerald Tree-Boa (Corallus caninus)	l	184
Asian Rock-Python (Python molurus)	l	79-120
Reticulated Python (Python reticulatus)	l	81
Common Garter Snake (Thamnophis sirtalis)	l	87-116
Four-lined Rat Snake (Elaphe quatuorlineata)	e	54-63
Desert Horned-Viper (Cerastes cerastes)	e	78
Asian Cobra (Naja naja)	e	49-103
Caissaca Pit Viper (Bothrops moojeni)	l	175-276
Western Diamondback Rattlesnake (Crotalus atrox)	l	167-253
Cottonmouth (Agkistrodaon piscivorus)	l	166-390

AMPHIGONIA RETARDATA IN A FEW SNAKE SPECIES

Boa Constrictor (Boa constrictor)	22 months after litter birth of young without intervening copulation.
Striped Fish Snake (Xenochrophis vittata)	laying of fertile eggs every 4-5 weeks over $1^{1}/_{2}$ years.
Red-bellied Water Snake (Nerodia erythrogaster)	live youngster 1 year after last litter.
Indigo Snake (Drymarchon corais)	live sperm confirmed 52 months after the last possible copulation.
Banded Cat-eyed Snake (Leptodeira annulata)	developing eggs were laid for 5 years after the last possible copulation.
Mangrove Tree Snake (Boiga dendrophila)	14 months after the last eggs were laid another fertile clutch was laid.
Long-nosed Tree Snake (Ahaetulla nasuta)	young were born after 28 months of solitary keeping.
Rhombic Night-Adder (Causus rhombeatus)	7 clutches within half a year with decreasing fertilization rates (1st, 2nd clutches 100%, 3rd clutch 65%; 4th clutch 56%; 5th to 7th clutch 0%).
Cottonmouth (Agkistrodon piscivorus)	3 young after $3^{1}/_{2}$ years of solitary keeping.
Plain-scaled Pitviper (Agkistrodon halys)	young born 3 years after last copulation.

In egg-laying snakes we must distinguish between the actual period of pregnancy [the prematuration time of the embryo in the maternal reproductive tract] and the incubation period [the time from egg-laying to the hatching of the young]. In the livebearing snakes there is no difference between the prematuration period and the incubation period; the period of pregnancy is considerably extended and is identical with the developmental period of the embryo. In addition, the total period of embryonic development in the mother as well as outside of her is dependent on many internal and external influences.

Thus it is not surprising that data on the internal or external developmental period can differ substantially even within a species. Moreover, the data presented often are based on preconditions of observation that are not tenable. It is generally assumed:
1) that one ejaculation occurred in mating;
2) that the fertilization of the eggs occurred immediately after that ejaculation;
3) that the fertilized egg cells developed continuously; and
4) that the ready-to-lay eggs and the developed young were deposited as soon as possible.

In snakes it often happens that a hemipenis is inserted without releasing sperm. Data on the last observed mating are not particularly valid: successful mating may already have taken place days or weeks earlier. Was the last observed mating really the last? Also insufficiently considered is the possibility of delayed and irregular development.

Furthermore, in egg-laying species substantial delays in egg-laying (egg retention) can occur when, for example, no suitable laying site is offered. Consequently, a gestation period of at least nine months has been reported in the Steppes Rat Snake (*Elaphe dione*), though the more typical incubation period actually is only 13 days. In closely related *Elaphe* species, the normal incubation period ranges from 60 to 70 days.

Even more confusing is the determination of the true period of pregnancy, the time from the fertilization of the ovum (amphigonia) to the release of the eggs or young, since there is a possibility of delayed fertilization (amphigonia retardata). Amphigonia retardata is based on the storage of viable sperm as described previously.

Data on amphigonia retarda in snakes show that the preservation of viable sperm in the female for up to five years has been demonstrated. It is certain that all of the sperm do not remain viable during this time, however, decreasing numbers being available each year.

Parthenogenesis, as is found in several lizard species but rarely in snakes, is reproduction involving only females, in which offspring arise from unfertilized eggs. Parthenogenesis has been proved so far only in the Braminy Flowerpot Snake (*Ramphotyphlops braminus)* and suspected in the Brown Filesnake (*Acrochordus javanicus*). In the autopsy of a Brown Filesnake that was kept separately for eight and a half years, a fully developed, dead fetus was found. This could possibly have been a case of amphigonia retardata, which would, however, be a record. Amphigonia retardata has been described for at least 29 snake species from six families—this reproductive strategy apparently is not more common in any particular taxonomic lineage than in any other.

Because of the possibility of amphigonia retardata, the snake breeder is advised to incubate all clutches. Both with female snakes kept for a fairly long time without mates and even more with newly purchased females—particularly wild-caught animals, there definitely is a chance to produce young.

The recognition of pregnancy can be of decisive importance for the propagation of snakes in the terrarium, such as when suitable laying conditions were not provided in time for egg-laying or the terrarium was not escape-proof with livebearing species and the often tiny newborns scattered long before the birth was noticed. The lack of a laying site with sufficient moisture can cause the female to lay the eggs randomly in the terrarium, sometimes even in the water vessel, so that they are hopelessly damaged within a short time.

Surprisingly, most snakes don't mind being observed while laying their eggs, as this albino Bullsnake, *Pituophis sayi*, is doing, but it is still advised that the keeper provide as much privacy as possible during this time. Photo by R. T. Zappalorti.

Above: A gravid Cuban Slender-Boa, *Epicrates angulifer*, one month before egglaying. Photo by I. Vergner. **Below:** This radiograph shows eggs in the process of shell formation in a Burmese Python, *Python molurus bivittatus*. Photo by L. Sassenburg.

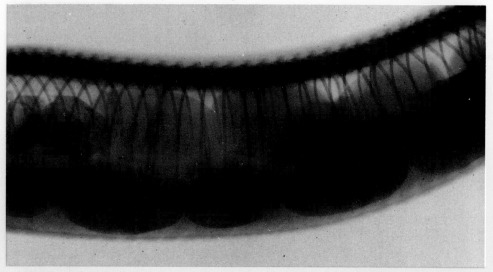

FIRST EVIDENCE OF PREGNANCY AFTER COPULATION THROUGH PALPATION

Species	Palpation after copulation (days)	Size of yolk balls	Total gestation period (days).
Amur rat snake (*Elaphe schrencki*)	9 14	lentil-to-pea-sized cherry-sized	28 ... 31
Garter Snake (*Thamnophis* spec.)	6 14 25	lentil-to pea-sized cherry-sized	62 ... 71

The observant snake keeper can recognize the first signs of successful mating by changes in the behavior of the snakes. The advances of courting males, which often are still in breeding condition, are repulsed by clearly defensive reactions or flight on the part of the female. In many cases food intake is reduced and finally ceases completely. Of course exceptions also exist. Both younger and older females not in breeding condition try through further food intake to improve their chances of survival and survival of their offspring. Well-fed females occasionally stop feeding after the last copulation. I once observed how a breeding female Common Kingsnake (*Lampropeltis getula*) for many years ate nothing at all between the end of hibernation and egg-laying.

Despite refusing food, the increase in body mass of the female is an important indication of an advanced state of pregnancy. Starting at about the second third of pregnancy, examination of the female through palpation (feeling of the abdomen) can detect eggs. For this examination the snake is lifted so that the last third of the body hangs freely. In pregnant snakes an increase in girth up to the cloaca is visible and lumps can be seen and felt. The eggs also can be detected by resting the thumb on the back and placing the fingertips against the belly and letting the snake crawl between them. For the experienced hobbyist, a diagnosis is possible in this way in the first third of pregnancy.

Palpation through the cloaca is possible only in larger snakes under local anesthesia and therefore must be left to the veterinarian.

Special devices permit the diagnosis of pregnancy with x-rays or ultrasound. At late stages of development, these devices can be used to detect the eggs or the partially calcified skeletons of the fetuses of livebearing species.

The Brown Filesnake, *Acrochordus javanicus*, is truly rare in one respect—it may be one of the few snakes that can reproduce parthenogenically, meaning only the females are involved in reproduction, the young developing from unfertilized eggs. Photo by K. T. Nemuras.

Development of Growing Snakes

After fertilization, a series of cell divisions takes place in which the new cells become smaller and smaller and at first do not increase in volume. These cells are still undifferentiated with respect to their future functions, but soon three germ layers (ectoderm, entoderm, and mesoderm) develop from which the individual organs arise in the course of further development. The majority of the snake egg consists of the large supply of yolk that serves as food for the embryo. The embryo or embryonic disk thus develops only in a specific region of the egg, at the animal pole. The yolk supply is surrounded by a thin-walled membrane [the yolk sac, formed by the embryo] that is attached to the embryo by the umbilical cord. In addition to the yolk sac, three other membranes develop: the amnion, surrounding the embryo floating in a fluid; the chorion, surrounding the yolk sac and amnion and connected to the egg shell and its membranes; and the allantois, a membranous pouch that forms as an evagination of the hindgut and pushes between the amnion and chorion. The allantois initially has the task of collecting the waste products of embryonic metabolism.

With advancing development the allantois in part fuses with the chorion to form the chorio-allantois, which becomes strongly vascularized and exchanges oxygen and carbon dioxide with the atmosphere.

Whether an embryo develops into a male or female snake is already determined by the chromosomes in the unfertilized ovum (the mother's genes determine the sex of the offspring). Further sexual differentiation proceeds through the immigration of primary germ cells from the inner germ layer (entoblast). Only then does the differing development of the reproductive organs and other morphological sex characters take place.

The formation of the fibrous egg shell occurs from the outside through special glands of the ovary just before the egg is laid. In the livebearing snakes, egg shell formation is greatly reduced, and a limited metabolic exchange between mother and young still is possible. Finally, in various species placentalike structures can form from the egg membranes, and the ovary (in which all of the eggs lie one after the other like a string of pearls) develops a close connection with the embryonic membranes (chorion—allantois—placenta) or the yolk sac (yolk sac—placenta). In this manner an effective gas exchange and in some cases the intake of nutrients are made possible. Such placentalike structures have been found in the nocturnal Australian elapids of the genus *Denisonia* and in *Pseudechis porphyriacus* from western Australia. Placental structures also are thought to be present in sea snakes and some North American garter and water snakes (*Thamnophis* and *Nerodia*). Transitional forms also exist, extending from egg-laying through egg-livebearing to livebearing snakes. A clear separation of these types of reproduction often is difficult.

Now let us turn to the often contradictory concepts of oviparous (egg-laying), ovoviviparous (egg-livebearing), and viviparous (livebearing) reproduction and their definitions. The hobbyist basically knows what is meant by these terms; however, the explanation of the concepts, such as is required in herpetological publications and would also be desirable for popular terrarium articles, often is unclear.

In fact, according to some authorities, in the terrarium hobby we should not distinguish between oviparous and ovoviviparous reproduction, because they are part of the same biological process and there are only gradual differences between them (i.e., the two ends of a continuous spectrum). Moreover, the differences between the various forms of livebearing should be set forth, although even in the terrarium hobby this

Development of the snake in the egg.

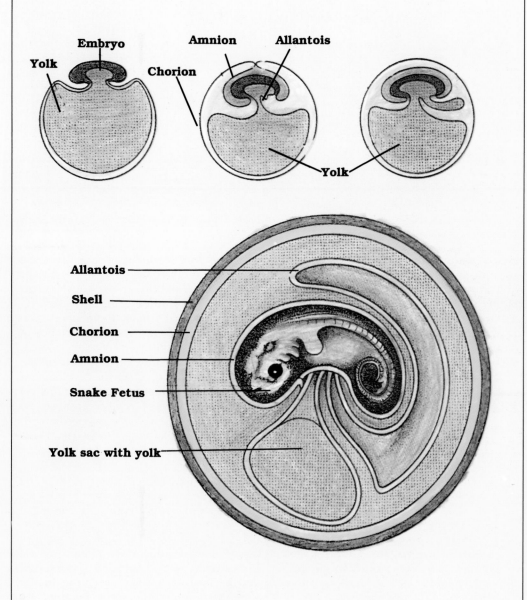

Uterus of a Florida Water Snake, *Nerodia fasciata pictiventris*, with fetuses. Two small unfertilized eggs can also be seen on the bottom. Photo by D. Schmidt.

cannot always be determined experimentally for the individual species.

The following overview should help to clarify these concepts.

1) Ovulipary: Laying of unfertilized eggs that are dependent on external fertilization (as in most frogs).

2) Ovipary: Laying of fertilized eggs or ready-to-hatch fetuses that have received no maternal nourishment.

2.1) True ovipary: Laying of fertilized eggs with more or less advanced embryonic development. Numerous snake species belong to this group.

2.2) Viviovipary: Giving birth to "ready-to-hatch" fetuses or young that have already hatched in the mother's body but were not nourished by the mother. This group includes the majority of snake species that usually are designated as ovoviviparous, like the boas, numerous vipers, and many pitvipers.

3) Vivipary: Birth of fetuses that were nourished inside the mother.

3.1) Aplacental vivipary: Birth of fetuses that have hatched inside the mother and that during a particular period have received supplemental nourishment in addition to the nourishment derived from the yolk, but without a placenta. Various *Thamnophis* and *Nerodia* species practice this type of reproduction.

3.2) Placental vivipary: Birth of fetuses that underwent their entire development inside the mother, with which they were connected by a placental organ. Probably the most familiar snake with placental development is the Common Garter Snake (*Thamnophis sirtalis*).

Now we may ask ourselves, what is the sense of bearing live young? Egg-laying certainly represents the primitive mode of reproduction. Viviovipary and vivipary cannot be explained as adaptations to low environmental temperatures alone, because there are too many examples of egg-laying and livebearing species occurring in the same area under the same temperature conditions. Even within numerous snake genera, such as *Daboia*, *Agkistrodon*,

Embryonic development in the Dice Snake, *Natrix tessellata*, with the incubation temperature at 77°F/25°C.

On the day of laying

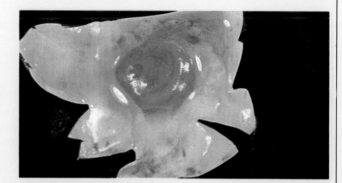

After two weeks

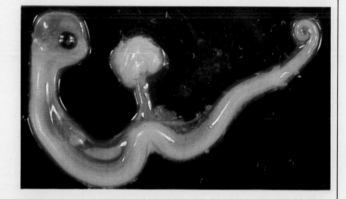

Just before hatching

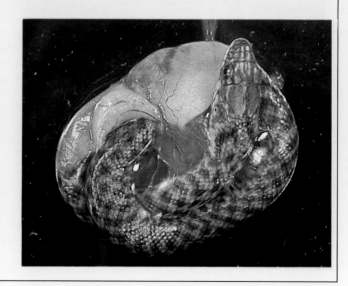

Trimeresurus, and *Elaphe*, both types of reproduction have evolved. (But beware: these genera may not be "real" genera in the modern sense, representing several lineages of only somewhat related species. This seems to be true in *Elaphe* and *Agkistrodon* and may be true in the other examples as well.) There are even transitional stages, as is found in the Okinawan Himehabu (*Trimeresurus okinavensis*); it both gives birth to living young and lays eggs with a four-day incubation period. Within its genus it thus stands between the egg-laying Okinawan Habu (*Trimeresurus flavoviridis*) and such species as the Common Green-Pitviper (*Trimeresurus stejnegeri*), which always are viviparous. All of this is evidence of the evolutionary changes that have taken place within the genus. (But again beware, as several authorities split *Trimeresurus* into three or more genera.)

Although sweeping questions about "livebearing" and its advantages still need to be answered, the following examples should prove illuminating. Snakes like the aquatic and semi-aquatic North American *Nerodia* and *Thamnophis* species need not be concerned about laying moisture-sensitive eggs in their wet living space, an advantage of livebearing. With snakes that can defend themselves effectively, like the large boas and many poisonous snakes, the young are better protected in the mother's body than in a nest clutch. Other giant snakes such as the pythons and poisonous snakes such as the cobras, which lay eggs, have instead developed specialized brood care. Livebearing is of course also an advantage under extreme conditions at higher altitudes and latitudes, where suitable climate for egg development is rare.

Let us now return to the development of the fetus. Although most organs appear at very early stages of development—the heart and eyes are soon visible even with the naked eye in very tiny embryos—the body scales do not develop until late, the head scales even later. This explains why deformities in the scales can be caused relatively easily by external influences. The egg tooth also appears late and does not protrude from the gums until shortly before the youngster hatches. This tooth, positioned on the premaxillary bone and pointing forward, is used to cut open the egg shell. The tooth is lost a few days after hatching—for example, after two to seven days in the Viperine Water Snake (*Natrix maura*) and after four to eight days in the Burmese Python (*Python molurus bivittatus*). The fact that even the young of livebearing snakes have an egg tooth shows that egg-laying is the primitive mode of reproduction. The Northern Adder (*Vipera berus*) is curious in this respect because the egg tooth points to the rear and is therefore useless for penetrating the egg membranes. At birth, a young Common Viper must use its snout to push its way through the egg membranes.

The yolk sac, the content of which (mostly fats and proteins, lipoproteins) provides nourishment for the developing embryo, is gradually used up. At hatching the remains are left behind in the egg shell. To a large extent, the yolk is absorbed by the fetus before birth. Consequently, in the newborn American Copperhead (*Agkistrodon contortrix*) the yolk mass can still make up 14 to 29% of the total weight of the young snake and is not used up completely until 14 days after hatching.

A rarity that has been observed in various snake species is the hatching of two snakes from the same egg. Often these twins remain stuck in the egg or die in an early stage of development. Theoretically the formation of twins is possible in two ways: in early stages of cell division in the embryo, as a result of internal or external factors, a separation into two independent embryos takes place with both fetuses sharing all or several egg membranes (single-egg twins); or two ova from a follicle are enclosed in a common egg shell, two yolk sacs, amnions, and allantoises being present (two-egg twins). One-egg twins were first described in 1981 with the Northern Viper (*Vipera berus*); both young snakes were only half as large as their siblings and exhibited identical markings.

The thin, opaque membrane that encases many newborn snakes usually gets broken out of only a few moments after birth. Every now and then a young snake will have trouble breaking free of this membrane and will die in the struggle. Shown are Northern Copperheads, *Agkistrodon contortrix mokasen*. Photo by R. T. Zappalorti.

Brooding and Birth

Though the duration of pregnancy is dependent on various factors and can be influenced externally in snakes, the birth of living young and the laying of eggs at the conclusion of pregnancy are regulated by hormones. External influences play a role here as well, as in the effect of stress, which can lead to miscarriage or egg-binding.

EGG-LAYING

In all egg-laying species we can speak of brood care when the eggs are laid in a place where the best possible conditions for their incubation appear to exist. This has to do with protecting the clutch from possible predators, providing favorable temperature and humidity for embryonic development, and probably also meeting the requirements for the survival of the young after they hatch (brood care). The search for a favorable laying site sometimes leads to mass layings by many females in the wild. For example, up to 3,000 eggs of the Eurasian Ringed Snake (*Natrix natrix*) have been found in one site, and at least a dozen other snake species exhibit similar behavior. As experiments in the terrarium with female Rough Greensnakes (*Opheodrys aestivus*) showed, the ready-to-lay females, when offered several equivalent potential laying sites, preferred those in which eggs had already been laid. This searching out of favorable laying sites is to be considered the first stage of brood care. Advanced brood-care behavior with nest building, incubation of the clutch, and guarding of the clutch or the young is known only in a few species of snakes. Brood-care behavior should be put to use in the propagation of snakes in the terrarium by offering laying facilities that are known to be preferred, thus helping to prevent the eggs from being laid in the wrong place.

Adding a substrate suitable for egg-laying and later incubation, especially with hiding places under roots or flat rocks, is the most natural method in the terrarium. The problem here is that this is difficult to realize. For medium colubrids, a fairly loose, slightly moist mixture of, for example, peat moss, garden soil, and sand would have to be at least 15 cm (6 in) deep in the terrarium. Simpler, on the other hand, is a plastic or metal box of the proper depth filled with a preferred substrate and inserted in the substrate of the terrarium.

I have had success with a method often called the "pickle-jar method" by hobbyists. Depending on the size of the species of snake, for this method we need a ceramic pot with a diameter of 15 to 25 cm (6-10 in). An upper diameter of about 20 cm (8 in) is adequate for a 1.5-meter (5-ft) female rat snake (*Elaphe*). This pot is filled more than half full with moist but not dripping wet peat moss and is filled to the rim with loose, slightly moist moss.

Under relatively dry conditions and with only a shallow substrate in the terrarium—a method of keeping that can be recommended even for moisture-loving snakes—the female snake in advanced stages of pregnancy will at first search in vain for a suitable site to lay her eggs and under certain circumstances will roam for days in the terrarium and tunnel into corners and nooks.

Now the time has arrived to introduce the prepared ceramic pot into the terrarium. Often the searching female will disappear into the pot in only a few minutes. By turning its body it forms a depression in the peat moss. The moss layer protects it from curious eyes and gives it a feeling of security. Now all disturbances must be avoided. As a rule, egg-laying will be completed by the following day and the snake will already have moved away from the clutch. The female may have to be removed from the laying container, depending on its temperament either without problems or only after a fierce defensive reaction. The eggs then are carefully harvested from the peat moss, with which they have more or less been covered in the meantime. It is possible that the snake deliberately pushes peat moss over the eggs. The eggs should be cleaned of bits of clinging peat moss and then transferred to the prepared, prewarmed incuba-

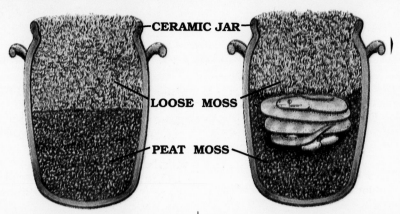

tor. Eggs that are stuck together are not separated. Most keepers recommend that snake eggs not be turned like chicken eggs—keep the upper side up, the lower side down as much as possible, and certainly never jar or shake the eggs. A dot or small cross from a wax pencil may serve to mark the upper side. (There have been suggestions that the ink from some felt-tip markers penetrating the egg shell may cause developmental abnormalities.)

Incubating in the ceramic pot is not recommended because it would be impossible to maintain the proper moisture level of the brooding substrate or to monitor the condition of the eggs during incubation. If the pot is heated from below, the eggs can quickly dry out.

Whether searching for a hiding place in the terrarium under roots or in cavities in rocks in which to lay the clutch, pressing the eggs into the soft substrate, or seeking out a laying container can be considered as nest-building behavior is a matter of opinion. Rat snakes (*Elaphe*) were observed forming depressions in the substrate by means of turning and pressing movements. Female Desert Horned-Vipers (*Cerastes cerastes*) have been observed in the terrarium "burying" the clutch after scraping away the sandy substrate with the head and neck. It is possible that the natural habits of the Desert Horned-Viper in sandy deserts with a lack of other hiding places are of significance here.

True nest-building among snakes has been documented only for the largest species of elapid, the King Cobra (*Ophiophagus hannah*). Although cobra nests of this kind have been known for a long time in the wild, their construction was first observed in captivity. In 1956 in the Bronx Zoo, a female King Cobra was observed grasping plant pieces with coils of the front part of her body and heaping them up to build a mound, forming an egg chamber in the middle by means of turning movements, and covering the nest with plant pieces after laying the clutch. Finally the female remained coiled on the nest mound and guarded the clutch.

Because as far as possible all the eggs of a clutch should be hatched and ideal incubation conditions usually are lacking in the terrarium, the clutch is removed as soon as possible after it is laid. This of course means that observations of brood-care behavior will be sacrificed. From observations in the wild and also in the terrarium, it is known that females of some species coil around the clutch and "guard" it. This raises the question of whether the female stays on the clutch for hours or days only because it is exhausted from egg-laying. Defensive reactions should not be overestimated because of the stressed physiological and psychological conditions. The author was able to drive rat snakes (*Elaphe*) and kingsnakes (*Lampropeltis*) from the clutch without difficulty and was even able to lure them away with a mouse. The Mud Snake (*Farancia abacura*), repeatedly cited in the literature as a clutch guardian, ig-

As soon as a snake's eggs are laid, you should remove them and place them in an incubator. A few snakes may display a sharp aggression towards this, but most seem indifferent. Shown is the egglaying of a Gray-banded Kingsnake, *Lampropeltis alterna*. Photo by L. Trutnau.

nored its clutch in the author's terrarium and showed absolutely no aggression. Reports of brood-care behavior often are contradictory even within a species. Based on the present level of knowledge it must be assumed that individual differences, dependent on the terrarium conditions and possibly also territorial differences or differences between subspecies, could exist.

PYTHON BROODING

The most pronounced form of brood care is the incubation of the clutch by a number of larger pythons. By means of thrusting body movements, these snakes heap up and coil around the eggs. Although a few species display true brooding behavior and produce heat from muscular twitching, others coil around and guard the clutch without raising the temperature and without the twitching movements of the body typical of the true brooders. Such non-heat-producing species include the African Rock-Python (*Python sebae*), Ball Python (*Python regius*), Reticulated Python (*Python reticulatus*), Children's Python (*Liasis childreni*), and the Diamond Python (*Python spilotus*).

True incubation has been demonstrated in both subspecies of the Asian Rock-Python (*Python molurus*) as well as the Blood Python (*Python curtus*), Scrub Python (*Python amethistinus*), and Green Tree-Python (*Chondropython viridis*). Incubation with temperature elevation by the Asian Rock-Python has been known since 1832, but was disputed and incorrectly interpreted. Erroneous measuring conditions yielded different incubation temperatures. More accurate observations showed that temperature differences of up to 7.3°C (about 13°F) above the temperature of the environment (air, substrate) apparently depended in their fluctuations on the body mass of the incubating female. The differences were correlated with conspicuous twitching of the body musculature—the frequency of contractions increased as environmental temperatures fell, and simultaneously the oxygen consumption of the animals rose. The oxygen consumption of incubating pythons corresponded to that of warmblooded animals. In non-heat-producing pythons, the

Certain pythons are among the only snakes that regularly display an instinct for brood care. In short, this means the mother will incubate her own eggs by wrapping herself around the clutch and twitching her muscles to create warmth. Photo of a Reticulated Python, *Python reticulatus*, by K. Dedekind.

Three stages of the birth of a Western Cottonmouth, *Agkistrodon piscivorous leucostoma*. Top—Neonate being expelled from the cloaca. Middle—Moments after birth, struggling in the membrane. Bottom—Breaking through with the aid of the pointed snout. All photos by L. Trutnau.

oxygen consumption curve, as in all poikilothermic creatures, is temperature-dependent.

Studies of Diamond Pythons (*Python spilotes*) showed a median temperature increase of 7°C (about 12°F) above room temperature. The body of the incubating female shuddered up to 50 times per series, each of these shuddering movements being made up of a series of twitching muscle contractions. The frequency of body movements, the body temperature, and the simultaneously measured oxygen consumption of the snake showed a clear daily rhythm with a peak between 6:00 and 10:00 PM and a dip between 3:00 and 6:00 AM. At air temperatures of 24°C (75°F) and below, the twitches stopped and the body temperature fell. Possibly the enormous energy expenditure of the animal for the incubation of a clutch at relatively low temperatures is one reason why these pythons reproduce only every other year in the terrarium.

Interestingly, it has been observed that female pythons left their clutches at rising terrarium temperatures and returned at sinking temperatures. It remains to be explained by what means unfertilized or ready-to-hatch eggs are recognized as such and are then abandoned.

BIRTH

The course of birth in livebearing snakes has been observed frequently. This process can extend over several hours: Gaboon Viper (*Bitis gabonica*)—25 young in 4 hours, 40 minutes; Saw-scaled Carpet-Viper (*Echis carinatus*)—8 young in 8 hours, 20 minutes. For rattlesnakes (*Crotalus, Sistrurus*) it has been documented in the wild that birth was completed considerably faster than in the terrarium.

At birth, dead but normally developed, deformed dead youngsters, undeveloped eggs, and living young in the normal egg membranes all are delivered. The undeveloped, probably unfertilized eggs as a rule are amber yellow and have a rough, glassy structure; they often are called "wax eggs." Under certain circumstances, some young are so feeble at birth that they are unable to

Some brood-care species do not perform the muscle-twitching that creates warmth for their eggs, but instead simply cover the eggs with their bodies. Species shown is an African Rock-Python, *Python anchietae*. Photo by Paul Freed.

make their way out of the membranes on their own and are unable to breathe.

In boa births it occasionally has been observed that the mother ate both infertile eggs and egg membranes, and a Green Anaconda (*Eunectes murinus*), perhaps "by mistake," also swallowed a newborn youngster. This feeding behavior could have something to do with loss of fluids, acute nutrient and mineral deficiencies, and perhaps also with preventing birthing remains at the birthing site from attracting predators.

With livebearing snakes, an absorbent substrate is recommended in the terrarium to absorb liquids released during birth and is easy to remove along with the egg membranes and yolk remains. For births with large boas, a wire grating can be installed in the terrarium so that youngsters that do not free themselves from the egg membranes quickly enough do not run the risk of being crushed by the mother.

NUMBERS

Of particular interest to the hobbyist is the number of offspring obtainable per clutch or birth. Statistical data for 100 species of snakes yielded an average clutch size of seven eggs. For all snake species the estimated average number of offspring per clutch or birth ranged from 8 to 15. Such data are of little use to the hobbyist. Species-specific and individual differences are great and as a rule are influenced by the age and size of the particular female.

Clear correlations between the body length of the mother snake and the number of eggs have been observed. A comparison between body length and egg number shows that differences occur between species and also between individuals of the same species.

For egg-laying snake species, in general the females of larger species lay larger clutches than do the smaller species.

Very productive species are known among the livebearing snakes. The Puff Adder (*Bitis arietans*), native to the arid regions of Africa, has repeatedly set the record for propagation rate in snakes. In December, 1971, a Puff Adder in the Nairobi Snake Park gave birth to 134 young; in 1976 a record birth of 156 young was reported from the Dvur Králové Zoo. Currently the record stands at 157

Part of a litter of Boa Constrictors, *Boa constrictor*, with 33 young snakes and three infertile eggs. Photo by I. Vergner.

live young from a female only 1.1 meters (3.6 ft) long.

Many factors other than size play a role in the average number of offspring. The average litter size of the Western Rattlesnake (*Crotalus viridis*), for example, increases from northeast to southwest from 2.6 to 11.4. The American Copperhead (*Agkistrodon contortrix*), on the other hand, it is almost the reverse: its litter sizes get smaller toward the southwest. The water snakes of the genus *Natriciteres* from tropical Africa have an average of 3.2 offspring in the plains and 6.3 offspring in the mountains. In most species, however, changes in clutch or litter size are completely random. The frequency of breeding even plays a role, the species that breed less often having a larger number of offspring per reproductive event. Second clutches usually are smaller than the first.

RELATIONS BETWEEN THE LENGTH OF THE MOTHER SNAKE AND THE NUMBER OF OFFSPRING.

Species	Length of mother snake (cm)	Average number of eggs per clutch/litter (young)
Tiger Keelback	70-79	8,3
(*Rhabdophis*	80-89	10,9
tigrinus)	90-99	14,2
	-100	16,7
Asian Rock Python	305	15
(*Python molurus*)	550	33-50
	630	57
	700-790	103
Habu	110-119	4,4
(*Trimeresurus*	160-169	11,4
flavoviridis)		

Generally speaking, viviparous snakes have larger litters than oviparous snakes have eggs. It is not unusual for a livebearer to have 20 or 25 young, whereas most egglaying snakes lay around five to fifteen eggs. Photo of a Northern Copperhead, *Agkistrodon contortrix mokasen*, being born, by R. T. Zappalorti.

BODY LENGTH OF THE MOTHER SNAKE AND THE NUMBER OF EGGS OR YOUNG (*=LIVEBEARER) OF SEVERAL SNAKE SPECIES

Species	Length of mother snake (cm)	Number of off-spring per clutch or litter
House Snake (Boaedon fuliginosus)	86	8
Flying Snake (Chrysopelea ornata)	128	8
	132	14
	115	8
American Racer (Coluber constrictor)	114	9
Horseshoe Snake (Coluber hippocrepis)	140	6
Corn Snake (Elaphe g. guttata)	102	16
	114	12
Aesculapian Rat Snake (Elaphe l. longis-sima)	140	6
Black Rat Snake (Elaphe o. obsoleta)	185	11
Gray Rat Snake (Elaphe obsoleta spiloides)	146	8
Yellow Rat Snake (Elaphe obsoleta quadrivittata)	141	18
Four-lined Rat Snake (Elaphe quatuorlineata)	173	3
Speckled King Snake (Lampropeltis getula holbrooki)	145	13
	145	9
Eastern Milk Snake (Lampropeltis t. triangulum)	92	8

Species	Length of mother snake (cm)	Number of off-spring per clutch or litter
Viper Water Snake (Natrix maura)	74	7
	76	8
	74	10
Ringed Snake (Natrix natrix helvetica)	96	11
	92	26
	95	19
Emerald Tree Boa (Corallus caninus)	168	7*
Madagascan Tree Boa (Sanzinia madagas-cariensis)	140	7*
Western Ribbon Snake (Thamnophis proximus)	83	12*
Eastern Garter Snake (Thamnophis s. sirtalis)	87	27*

RECORD CLUTCH AND LITTER SIZES FOR SEVERAL SNAKE SPECIES

Common Garter Snake (Thamnophis sirtalis)	73 young
Green Anaconda (Eunectes murinus)	90 young
Mud Snake (Farancia abacura)	104 eggs
Asian Rock Python (Python molurus)	107 eggs
Common Puff Adder (Bitis arietans)	157 young

Eggs and Incubation

The shape and surface structure of snake eggs are quite variable, but all have more or less soft shells. The Desert Horned-Viper (*Cerastes cerastes*) is an example of a species with "chicken-egg"-shaped eggs that are smooth and only slightly porous, but which exhibit dark blotches. Snake eggs usually conform in shape to the tube-shaped ovary and are cylindrical, equally rounded at each end, or they exhibit an elliptical longitudinal section. Their surface structure is variable: smooth and shiny like ivory, with the finest pores (example: Rough Greensnake, *Opheodrys aestivus*); smooth, dull, and pure white (many rat snakes, like *Elaphe obsoleta*); finely marked with an irregular pattern (Leopard Rat Snake, *Elaphe situla*); with punctate elevations (Aesculapian Rat Snake, *Elaphe longissima*); with ring-shaped dimples (Dice Snake, *Natrix tessellata*); or with the finest downlike hairs with a strongly punctate belt around the middle of the egg (Sonoran Whipsnake, *Masticophis bilineatus*). The listing of different examples could be continued, but it must be kept in mind that these structures need not be species-specific. The female Dice Snake mentioned in the example had laid completely smooth-shelled eggs the previous year, from which healthy young snakes also hatched. Variable coloration of the egg shell also can occur immediately after laying, but it is more common toward the end of incubation.

Unfertilized eggs display clear changes in shape and structure. As a rule they are considerably smaller than the remaining eggs of the clutch, are cylindrical or taper to a point (but can be spherical), usually have a smooth surface, the shell does not harden much or at all after laying, and they often are yellowish to amber in color. The outer chorion sometimes is translucent.

Ideally, eggs should be incubated separately rather than in a clump. If you are fortunate enough to be around when your snake lays, do your best to remove the eggs one at a time and immediately set them up in the incubator. Species shown is an albino Sonoran Gopher Snake, *Pituophis catenifer affinis*. Photo by Jim Merli.

Typical forms of snake eggs and measuring points for their length (L) and breadth (B).

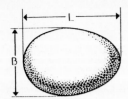 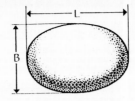 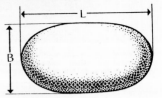

EXAMPLES OF BODY LENGTHS OF FEMALE SNAKES AND THE SIZE AND WEIGHT OF THEIR EGGS

Species	Length of the mother snake (in cm)	Egg Size Length (in cm)	Diameter (in cm)	Average egg weight (in grams)
Brown House Snake (Boaedon fuliginosus)	86	3,8-4,2	2,3-1,4	11,8
Flying Snake (Chrysopelea ornata)	128	3,4-3,6	1,3-1,4	4,9
American Racer (Coluber constrictor)	114	3,1-3,5	1,8-1,9	7,4
Corn Snake (Elaphe guttata)	114	3,7-3,9	1,9-2,0	8,3
Aesculapian Rat Snake (Elaphe longissima)	140	3,4-4,0	2,0-2,1	11,2
Gray Rat Snake (Elaphe obsoleta spiloides)	146	4,6-5,2	2,3-2,4	16,8
Yellow Rat Snake (Elaphe obsoleta quadrivittata)	141	3,5-3,9	2,2-2,3	13,2
Four-lined Rat Snake (Elaphe quatuorlineata)	173	6,6-6,8	2,4-2,5	30,6
Milk Snake (Lampropeltis triangulum)	92	2,7-2,9	1,3-1,4	4,2
Common Kingsnake (Lampropeltis getula)	145	3,6-4,2	2,3-2,4	8,5
Viperine Water Snake (Natrix maura)	74	3,4-3,7	1,8-1,9	8,0
Ringed Snake (Natrix natrix helvetica)	96	2,8-3,0	1,6-1,8	5,3

Eggs of an Aesculapian Rat Snake, *Elaphe longissima*. Note the obvious granular texture. Photo by D. Schmidt.

Whether the snake breeder wants to take a risk and measure and weigh all eggs after laying will depend on the rarity of the offspring. Clutches that are not discovered immediately after laying often are stuck together, and the eggs can no longer be separated from one another without damaging the egg shells. Handling individual eggs for the purposes of measuring and weighing is less risky shortly after laying than in later stages of incubation. A mark placed on the top side of each egg with a soft pencil can serve as a reference point so that the position of the eggs—and thereby that of the embryo

INCREASE IN WEIGHTS AND SIZES OF SNAKE EGGS

Species	Average egg weight				Average egg size	
	At laying (in grams)	After weeks	Final weight (in grams)	In-crease %	At laying (in mm)	Before hatching (in mm)
Flying Snake *(Chrysopelea ornata)*	4,9	9	6,6	35	35x14	36x17
American Racer *(Coluber constrictor)*	7,4	8	10,7	45	34x19	35x25
Corn Snake *(Elaphe g. guttata)*	5,0	7	7,6	52	28x17	30x24
	8,3	7	15,8	90 (!)	38x19	40x26
Aesculapian Rat Snake *(Elaphe longissima)*	11,2	8	16,6	48	37x21	38x29
Yellow Rat Snake *(Elaphe obsoleta quadrivittata)*	13,2	7	19,1	45	37x22	39x28
Common Kingsnake *(Lampropeltis getula)*	8,5	8	14,1	66	39x24	42x30
Milk Snake *(Lampropeltis triangulum)*	4,2	8	6,4	52	29x13	30x19
Viperine Water Snake *(Natrix maura)*	8,0	8	11,9	49	36x19	38x25
Ringed Snake *(Natrix natrix)*	5,2	7	7,8	50	29x17	31x24

in relation to the yolk sac—is not changed. For size data, two parameters that can be measured the most precisely with calipers are sufficient: the greatest length and the greatest width (diameter). The entire clutch can be weighed simultaneously on a scale (postal scale, laboratory scale) and the median value calculated.

The length of freshly hatched eggs varies within a species far more than does the diameter, because the reproductive tract of the female snake does not allow large variations in egg diameter. Only normal, fertilized eggs are measured and weighed. The egg size and egg weight are positively correlated with the body size of the mother snake and are negatively correlated with the clutch size.

The dimensions and mass of the individual egg are subject to changes. Should a clutch be laid in too dry a site, dehydration soon occurs; the eggs collapse, but need not be given up for lost immediately. If dehydra-tion is not too advanced, the embryos can survive. After transferring the eggs to a moist substrate, they absorb water and become taut again. This water intake (imbibition) continues during incubation and, together with the growing embryo, at first leads to an increase in size and weight of the eggs. For this reason only measurements of freshly laid eggs say something about the performance of the mother snake.

The egg weights of different clutches clearly differ more from one another than do the length and diameter, as the data for eggs of the Asian Rock-Python (*Python molurus*) show: mass 140 to 305 grams (5-10.7 oz), length 82 to 106 mm (3.2-4 in), diameter 50 to 66 mm (2-2.6 in). In some cases the eggs increase substantially in size. For example, the average weight of ten eggs of a King Cobra (*Ophiophagus hannah*) increased by about 66% during the more than ten weeks of incubation, the diameter by 26%, and the

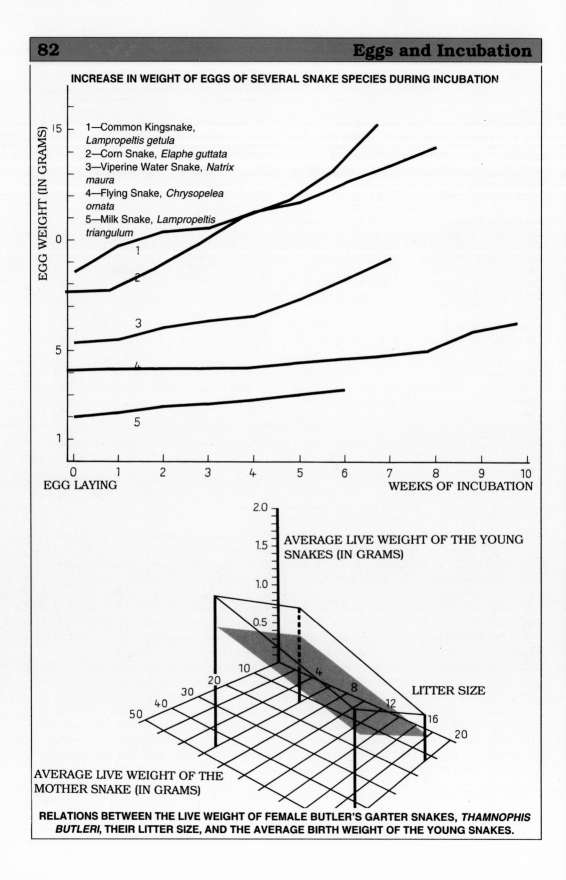

INCREASE IN WEIGHT OF EGGS OF SEVERAL SNAKE SPECIES DURING INCUBATION

EGG WEIGHT (IN GRAMS)

1—Common Kingsnake, *Lampropeltis getula*
2—Corn Snake, *Elaphe guttata*
3—Viperine Water Snake, *Natrix maura*
4—Flying Snake, *Chrysopelea ornata*
5—Milk Snake, *Lampropeltis triangulum*

EGG LAYING   WEEKS OF INCUBATION

AVERAGE LIVE WEIGHT OF THE YOUNG SNAKES (IN GRAMS)

LITTER SIZE

AVERAGE LIVE WEIGHT OF THE MOTHER SNAKE (IN GRAMS)

RELATIONS BETWEEN THE LIVE WEIGHT OF FEMALE BUTLER'S GARTER SNAKES, *THAMNOPHIS BUTLERI*, THEIR LITTER SIZE, AND THE AVERAGE BIRTH WEIGHT OF THE YOUNG SNAKES.

length by 8%. Interruptions in development during incubation caused by periods of low temperatures or fluctuations in ambient moisture mean that the size of the eggs does not increase continuously up to hatching. Just before hatching the dimensions decrease again as a result of elimination of water. The eggs of many species develop longitudinal creases that can assume alarming proportions, so occasionally the successful conclusion of incubation can scarcely be expected. Eggs of the Asian Rock-Python (*Python molurus*) can weigh as much as 20% less just before hatching than immediately after laying. Eggs of the African Common Egg-eating Snake (*Dasypeltis scabra*) increased in length by 5.1% after 60 days of incubation, but just before hatching weighed 8.1% less than at the start of incubation.

Few studies have been done so far to determine whether differences exist between egg sizes in wild and captive clutches. It would be expected that the greater availability of food in the terrarium could lead to larger and heavier eggs and perhaps even to larger numbers of eggs. For *Xenochrophis vittata*, a water snake from Southeast Asia, data in the literature exist on this subject—in the wild:

egg length 19 to 28 mm (0.8-1.1 in), average weight 1.57 grams (0.045 oz); in the terrarium: 20 to 33 mm (0.8-1.3 in) and 1.77 grams (0.06 oz). In the same way that the size of the eggs is dependent on the size of the mother snake and the number of eggs in the clutch, similar relations can be inferred in livebearing snakes. For Butler's Garter Snake (*Thamnophis butleri*), herpetologists calculated relations between the length, body weight, or the ratio of mass to body length to the same values of the mother snake; there was a positive correlation. On the other hand, there was a negative correlation to litter size. As a measure of the reproductive performance of the mother snake, the so-called relative litter weight was calculated from the ratio of the total weight of the litter to the weight of the mother. The relative number did not vary with increasing size of the mother snake.

Let us now turn to the incubation of snake eggs. Although the term incubation period is not always used consistently in the herpetological literature, in the terrarium hobby it has proved practical to understand by incubation only the maturation of the eggs of oviparous species from the time they are laid

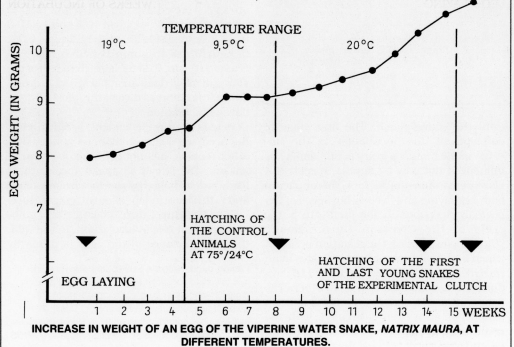

INCREASE IN WEIGHT OF AN EGG OF THE VIPERINE WATER SNAKE, *NATRIX MAURA*, AT DIFFERENT TEMPERATURES.

**CONTROL OF THE TEMPERATURE OF
INCUBATORS FOR SNAKE EGGS**

Type of temperature control	Heat source	Comments
external heat source	heating plate	danger of overheating in absence of thermostat
	lighting box of the terrarium	danger of overheating, day-night rhythm achieved
	heated empty terrarium	day-night rhythm, advantage with the operation of several incubators
built-in heat source	aquarium heater, heating cable	affordable, but danger of overheating
	heater with thermostat	expensive, above all with the simultaneous operation of several incubators; constant temperature ensured
	heater with thermostat and timer	expensive, but timer can be used for several incubators. Advantage of the day-night rhythm

ing of the gestation period by four and a half days.

A virtually uniform control of incubation temperature, as in the clutch of a true incubating python or under conditions of the tropical rainforest, scarcely exists in the wild. Nighttime cooling influences the length of incubation, but not the hatching result. Although it is easier to achieve constant incubation temperatures under terrarium conditions, they are not necessary. In fact, when embryonic development is not accelerated too much because of uniformly high temperatures of 30°C (86°F) and above, better hatching results with stronger and healthier young snakes can be expected. Nighttime cooling of 5 to 10°C (10-18°F), over even just a few days, does not have a negative effect on the quality of the young. Too much cooling, especially sudden cooling, however, can lead to deformities, difficulties in hatching, and death of the embryos.

Under laboratory conditions eggs of the Common Kingsnake (*Lampropeltis getula*) were subjected to different incubation temperatures: **A**: 30.1°C (29.2 to 31.2°C); **B**: 32.8°C (32.0 to 33.8°C); and **C**: 34.8°C (34.2 to 35.2°C). The young snakes of experimental group A were on average 281.3 mm (280 to 282 mm) long and weighed 10.6 grams (10.3 to 11.1 grams) (11.25, 11.2-11.28 in—0.37, 0.36-0.39 oz). In group B (263.0 mm, 9.6 grams) (10.5 in, 0.34 oz) more than half of the young displayed tail anomalies, and in group C all of the embryos died at the latest after 21 days of incubation.

A temperature-dependent, arbitrarily influenced sex determination, as is known in other reptiles, has not yet been observed in snakes. The sex of all snake species most likely is determined by specific chromosomes and is therefore independent of temperature.

Besides temperature, moisture also plays an important role in incubation. In the wild, the water balance of the eggs is primarily

Facing page: Note the blue-coated wire running into this clutch of snake eggs. It is attached to a digital thermometer for precise monitoring of the ambient temperature in the incubator. This is a highly crucial consideration when dealing with reptile eggs of any kind. Photo by Isabelle Francais, courtesy of Eugene L. Bessette.

until the young hatch. The first stage of development, the "incubation" of the embryos in the mother's ovary (= pregnancy), is influenced not only by species-specific but also by environmental factors. This applies to both egg-laying and livebearing species. Repeatedly described in the literature is the cycle of the Common Garter Snake (*Thamnophis sirtalis*), the gestation period of which in the wild amounted to 87 days in an extremely warm summer, but up to 116 days during longer periods of cold weather. The temperature dependency of the gestation period has even been calculated, with the result that an elevation of the average temperature by 1°C (2-3°F) results in a shorten-

SKETCHES ILLUSTRATING THE PRINCIPLES OF DIFFERENT TYPES OF INCUBATORS

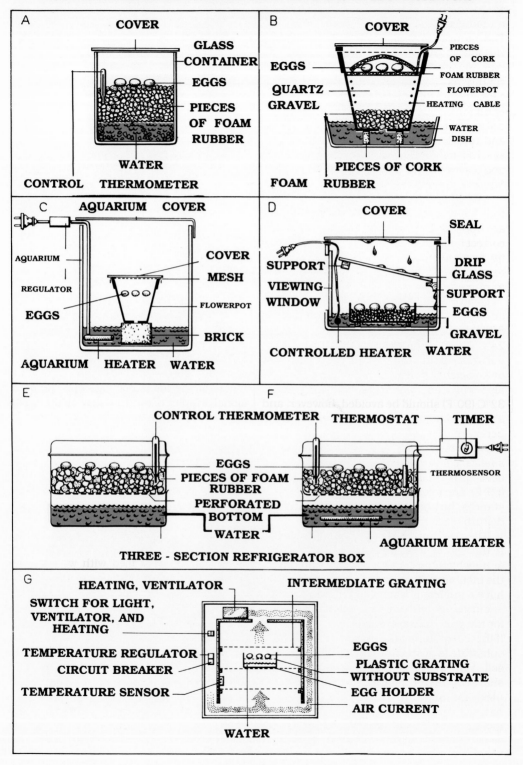

A — COVER, GLASS CONTAINER, EGGS, PIECES OF FOAM RUBBER, WATER, CONTROL THERMOMETER

B — COVER, PIECES OF CORK, FOAM RUBBER, FLOWERPOT, HEATING CABLE, WATER DISH, EGGS, QUARTZ GRAVEL, PIECES OF CORK, FOAM RUBBER

C — AQUARIUM COVER, COVER, MESH, FLOWERPOT, BRICK, AQUARIUM, REGULATOR, EGGS, AQUARIUM HEATER, WATER

D — COVER, SEAL, DRIP GLASS, SUPPORT, EGGS, GRAVEL, WATER, SUPPORT, VIEWING WINDOW, CONTROLLED HEATER

E — CONTROL THERMOMETER, EGGS, PIECES OF FOAM RUBBER, PERFORATED BOTTOM, WATER

F — THERMOSTAT, TIMER, THERMOSENSOR, AQUARIUM HEATER

THREE - SECTION REFRIGERATOR BOX

G — HEATING, VENTILATOR, INTERMEDIATE GRATING, SWITCH FOR LIGHT, VENTILATOR, AND HEATING, TEMPERATURE REGULATOR, CIRCUIT BREAKER, TEMPERATURE SENSOR, EGGS, PLASTIC GRATING WITHOUT SUBSTRATE, EGG HOLDER, AIR CURRENT, WATER determined by the moisture-holding capacity of the substrate surrounding the eggs. The humidity fluctuates greatly in most climates. The natural brooding substrate can be of various origins and properties. It must, however, no matter what the particular local conditions, have a favorable water-holding capacity and be sufficiently permeable to air. Sand for the Desert Horned-Viper (*Cerastes cerastes*); probably humus-rich soil, moss, and rotten wood for most colubrid species; sawdust for the Ringed Snake (*Natrix natrix*); and leaves for the King Cobra (*Ophiophagus hannah*) are suitable substrates.

Every successful snake breeder believes that his method and the incubator he uses are optimal. In principle, however, only the correct temperature range, favorable humidity, and sufficient ventilation of the clutch are important. This can be achieved technically in numerous ways.

Good development of the fetus is achieved at daytime temperatures of 27 to 30°C (81-86°F) and nighttime temperatures of 20 to 24°C (68-75°F), on average. This of course does not rule out that constant temperatures or somewhat higher or lower temperatures also will lead to success. Warming above 32°C (90°F) should be avoided, however, and should never be maintained over an extended period of time, because the development of the fetuses will be accelerated and the young snakes could be too weak to hatch or to develop normally. Brief periods below 15°C (59°F) are tolerated under certain circumstances, but here too there is the danger of disturbances in development.

The moisture necessary for supplying water to the eggs is obtained from the substrate in or on which the eggs lie and the humidity in the incubator. Therefore, the substrate must have a sufficient water-holding capacity, be low in germs, and be unsuitable as a medium for the growth of microorganisms and fungi. If these requirements are fulfilled, the type of substrate is of secondary importance. Sand, soil, peat moss (perhaps mixed with wood shavings), moss, vermiculite, plastic granules, and foam rubber in sheets or pieces have all been used successfully. Optimal moisture can be achieved and controlled very easily with foam rubber cut into small pieces

Some snake eggs have a rough, granular texture, whereas others, like these of the Gray-banded Kingsnake, *Lampropeltis alterna*, are smooth. Notice also the the substrate they are being incubated in—ordinary soil. Photo by L. Trutnau.

about 1 centimeter (a bit under half an inch) on a side. The pieces of foam rubber are washed thoroughly and squeezed out slightly before use. No disinfectant should be used. The relative humidity in the incubator should approach 100%; this is achieved when the inside of the incubator fogs up. The occasional dripping of condensation on the eggs is not harmful. It can be prevented, however, by a pane of glass placed diagonally over the eggs.

Several types of incubators commonly are used by hobbyists and scientists. I have had success for years with an incubator in which the temperature is controlled by putting the incubator in an unoccupied terrarium. This incubator was made from a transparent three-part refrigerator storage box, the bottom section of which was filled with water. Holes were drilled in the bottom of the central section, which was then filled with pieces of foam rubber. The top section was equipped only with a hole for a thermometer. A single filling of water lasted the entire incubation period. Opening the cover every three to five days for inspections provided adequate ventilation for the clutch. The incubator was placed in a fairly dark location.

A separate incubator should be used for each clutch. The young snakes of different clutches do not all hatch at the same time, and snakes that have already hatched burrow through the substrate and mix up the eggs. Hatched young should be taken from the incubator as soon as possible. If an egg is turned over, the ready-to-hatch youngster still tries to cut open the top of the egg shell. Now, however, the yolk sac is on top and prevents penetration. The result: The young snake cannot hatch and dies in the egg.

If young snakes of different clutches of the same species hatch simultaneously in an incubator, the parentage of the young snakes will be unknown. This should be avoided as a matter of principle. Furthermore, youngsters of different subspecies often are difficult or impossible to distinguish.

Freshly laid eggs are sticky and shiny and become harder only after several hours or days. There is no rush to transfer them from the laying container to the incubator, but they must not be allowed to dry out. Slightly collapsed eggs will become taut again in the incubator. In many cases several eggs will be stuck together. They should be left together to avoid damaging the shells. An infertile egg

or one in which the embryo subsequently dies and becomes moldy usually does not have a detrimental effect on healthy eggs fused together in a pile. Moldiness of the eggs can be minimized by dusting the eggs with charcoal dust and removing the superficial deposit of mold with a soft brush.

Infertile eggs often can be recognized when laid or become unsightly and moldy after a period of incubation and when touched are hard and not as elastic as normally developing eggs. When they are cut open it will be discovered that fetuses in the most diverse stages of development can be contained in these rotten eggs. Such fetuses can be preserved in approximately 70% alcohol as illustrative material or for scientific purposes.

Numerous data exist on the incubation period of snake eggs. These are easily measured values but should be supplemented by average and range values of the incubation temperature, and if possible also by values of the average relative humidity. These values give practical reference points for further breeding attempts with the species in ques-

This incubator has an interesting substrate—small blocks of moistened foam rubber. Such a medium would be good not only for retaining the moisture, but also for keeping the eggs firmly in place.

Note the relative size of these python eggs compared to the coin on the left. Photo by Roberta Kayne.

tion, so, for example, prematurely discarding or opening the eggs is avoided.

Observations in the wild of the incubation period are useful to the hobbyist only so far as they are indications of maximum incubation times. Less favorable incubating conditions in the wild usually require considerably longer periods, as is shown by the example of the South African Boomslang (*Dispholidus typus*), which has been bred repeatedly in captivity. The incubation of the eggs of this snake took about 210 days in the wild; under constant terrarium conditions at 28°C (82°F) and virtually 100% relative humidity it was shortened to 84 to 94 days. Among the pythons, the Australasian species exhibit relatively short incubation periods under natural incubation, without special brooding. In python species there seems to be a relation between the body length of the mother snake and the incubation period. The brood-tending species apparently require somewhat shorter times for the young to hatch under natural brooding than under artificial incubation. For example, the Reticulated Python (*Python reticulatus*) took 55 to 94 days in nature versus 92 to 105 days in captivity.

Data on the incubation period should always include the time of hatching of the first and last youngster of a clutch. Unfortunately, often only an average value or the day that hatching began are recorded.

The diversity of the large family Colubridae suggests quite variable incubation periods. Within a genus, even with species that come from similar climates, differences occur. Rat snakes (*Elaphe*) of the temperate zone exhibit incubation periods of 36 to 109 days (even among the subspecies of the American Rat Snake, *Elaphe obsoleta*, the range is 53 to 109 days). Equally variable is the 23 to 118 days range in the genus *Lampropeltis*. Differences caused by nonuniform temperatures or retention of the eggs also are known: Rough Green Snake (*Opheodrys aestivus*) 4 to 34 days instead of 21 to 26 days in the incubator; Steppes Rat Snake (*Elaphe dione*) 12 days instead of 60 to 70 days.

Hatching

The actual hatching of the young snakes of a clutch in most cases takes place over one to four days. By way of exception, individual snakes also can appear considerably before or after the hatching date of the majority of their siblings. The impending hatching usually is indicated a few days beforehand by the eggs losing water and developing indentations and longitudinal creases. Occasionally brown to blackish spots appear. Finally the first openings cut in the top of the egg with the egg tooth become visible—usually there are several parallel longitudinal cuts, but V-shaped and star-shaped cuts also appear. A peculiarity was observed in the Ornate Flying Snake (*Chrysopelea ornata*), in which all of the young snakes from all eggs of three clutches hatched through cuts at the poles of the egg.

First the tip of the snout is pushed through the opening cut in the egg shell. The first breaths taken by the young snake cause small bubbles to form in the liquid seeping from the egg around the opening. Finally the head and neck appear. The young snake still is prepared at all times to withdraw back into the protective egg shell immediately when disturbed. If it does so, the danger of suffocation cannot be ruled out. It can spend up to two days in this position. The young of some species already are quite aggressive at this stage and bite at the hand they think is threatening them. The venomous snake breeder is reminded that the youngsters have an effective toxin and that a bite in a sensitive place could have serious or even fatal results.

When the egg is left completely, in most cases the remnants of the yolk sac still in the egg also are torn out. Occasionally parts of the umbilical cord or the yolk sac remain attached to the freshly hatched snake; they are not lost until the snake starts to crawl around or they dry up within a short time and fall off.

Detail of the egg tooth of a newborn snake. This tooth will fall off shortly after the animal cuts through the shell.

Yolk still remains in the body cavity of hatchlings and is used as food for the first days of life. The hobbyist should *never* attempt to remove yolk sac remnants from hatchlings—nature must take its course.

Sometimes not all of the fully developed fetuses are able to hatch. The reasons for this are not always clear. If these snakes have not died some time before the hatching of the clutch, hatching assistance can be useful. Hatching assistance is controversial, because occasionally some fetuses are not yet fully developed and still have a large yolk sac. The careless opening of the eggs can damage the yolk sac and lead to the death of the snake. However, I have had good experiences with cutting open eggs that showed no signs of opening on their own two to three days after the first eggs of the clutch have opened independently. With fine scissors, an incision can be made along a longitudinal crease without danger of injuring the snake. If a small amount of clear fluid leaks out in the process, this is a sign that in all probability the fetus is still alive. If a fetus has died recently, a cloudy to milky fluid will be apparent; firm contents with the consistency of soft cheese indicate that the fetus has been dead for some time. Individual eggs can be very taut even though the rest of the clutch is ready to hatch. By carefully puncturing the shell with pointed scissors, the emerging fluid can be inspected. Lowering the pressure inside the egg by this procedure often causes the young

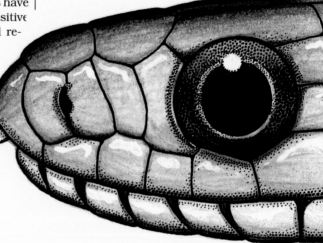

Top: A Ball Python, *Python regius*, opens its shell after the 70th day of incubation. Photo by I. Vergner.
Bottom: Hatching Black-lipped Cobras, *Naja melanoleuca*. Photo by L. Trutnau.

snake to cut through the shell on its own. It can be observed occasionally that youngsters have made four or six parallel cuts in the egg shell and still apparently have difficulty in hatching. In such a case it is beneficial to connect the longitudinal slits with one or two transverse cuts, thereby producing a larger escape hole. This type of hatching assistance should cause no problems.

The body length of the young snakes depends on the species and the size of the eggs—and therefore also on the length of the mother and the clutch size. Differences between different individuals of a clutch usually are smaller than those between different clutches. Occasionally, however, there are one or two runts in a clutch. Youngsters of this kind, if it is not a question of a special breeding, should be culled and killed painlessly. They usually have problems in feeding and in subsequent growth. In the interest of healthy propagation over as many generations as possible, young snakes with deformities should of course also be destroyed.

Sometimes the hobbyist will be surprised by the appearance of his newly hatched young snakes (neonates)—they might not resemble their parents at all in color and markings. There are numerous examples of this. For this reason subspecies may not be identifiable in juvenile coloration, as is the case for several subspecies of the American Rat Snake (*Elaphe obsoleta*) and the Four-lined Rat Snake (*Elaphe quatuorlineata*). In the latter, young snakes of the subspecies *E. q. quatuorlineata* and *E. q. sauromates* cannot be distinguished on the basis of markings. While the western (nominate) subspecies develops with increasing age the stripes responsible for its common name, the eastern subspecies *E. q. sauromates* retains the dorsal blotches found in juveniles of both subspecies. It is even more confusing when variable juvenile markings occur in the youngsters within a clutch. For example, both uniformly green and brown youngsters of the South American Long-nosed Green Snake (*Philodryas baroni*) have been hatched from one clutch with no intermediates; taxonomic separation of the color varieties therefore is not justified. The same applies to the striped or banded young of the California Kingsnake (*Lampropeltis getula californiae*) from the same clutch. It is hard to believe that the yellow, orange, brownish, or red young-

This photo clearly shows the difference between a healthy snake egg (white, clean) and a bad one (discolored and covered with fungus). Photo by W. P. Mara.

A pair of Burmese Python, *Python molurus bivittatus*, eggs. Note their size, which is quite large compared to those of most other snake species. Photo by Jim Merli.

sters of the Green Tree-Python (*Chondropython viridis*) or the yellow-brown youngsters of the Emerald Tree-Boa (*Corallus caninus*) will take on the green ground color of their parents after only a few molts. Green Tree-Pythons change color after about three years, Emerald Tree Boas after about only 190 days.

The gorgeous red to orange belly coloration of the young Florida Water Snake (*Nerodia fasciata pictiventris*) unfortunately becomes paler with increasing age, usually becoming a dingy yellow; in some individuals the belly can become almost uniformly dark grayish brown. The vividly banded youngsters of the Cottonmouth (*Agkistrodon piscivorus*) turn mottled brown in most areas, with some old individuals almost solid black.

Snake eggs should not be handled once they have been set in their incubator. If, for whatever reason, you do have to pick them up, remember to set them back down again in the exact same position. Photo of the eggs of a Cape Cobra, *Aspidelaps lubricus*, by Jim Merli.

EXAMPLES OF DIFFERENT COLORATION AND MARKINGS OF YOUNG SNAKES IN COMPARISON TO ADULTS

Flying Snake *(Chrysopelea ornata ornatissima)*	juvenile: adult:	light crossbarring no crossbarring
Eastern Yellowbelly Racer *(Coluber constrictor flaviventris)*	juvenile: adult:	longitudinal rows of black-brown spots, decreasing in intensity toward the tail, uniform dark-brown from about the tail back plainly colored
Caspian Racer *(Coluber jugularis caspius)*	juvenile: adult:	dark-brown barred markings on a light background blue-gray ground color, dark scales with a light center
Aesculapian Rat Snake *(Elaphe longissima)*	juvenile: adult:	longitudinal rows smaller, brown spots, in the hind third so dense that a longitudinal striation is almost produced; on each side of the head a large, yellow spot. plainly colored
Black Rat Snake *(Elaphe o. obsoleta)*	juvenile: adult:	light-gray ground color rows of dark-brown to black spots uniform black dorsal side
Gray Rat Snake *(Elaphe obsoleta spiloides)*	juvenile: adult:	like *E.o. obsoleta* speckling is retained; becomes somewhat darker overall
Yellow Rat Snake *(Elaphe obsoleta quadrivittata)*	juvenile: adult:	like *E. o. obsoleta* yellowish to brownish with 4 brown to black longitudinal stripes
Everglades Rat Snake *(Elaphe obsoleta rossalleni)*	juvenile: adult:	like *E. o. obsoleta*, somewhat lighter iris yellow brown to orange, weakly suggested brown longitudinal stripes
Speckled Kingsnake *(Lampropeltis getula holbrooki)*	juvenile: adult:	suggested whitish crossbarring crossbarring no longer discernible
Eastern Milk Snake *(Lampropeltis t. triangulum)*	juvenile: adult:	gray ground color with three rows of reddish spots with black borders brown spots with black borders

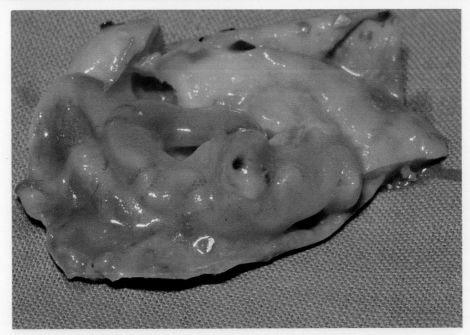

Detail of a snake embryo, five weeks into development, in this case a Scarlet Snake, *Cemophora coccinea*. Photo by W. P. Mara.

After a snake cuts through its shell, it may still remain in the egg for awhile. Do not attempt to remove the animal; it will come out eventually. Species shown is an Eastern Milk Snake, *Lampropeltis triangulum triangulum*. Photo by William B. Allen, Jr.

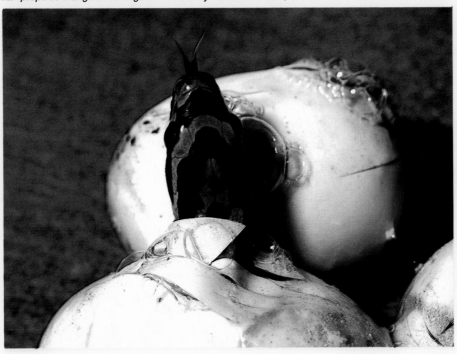

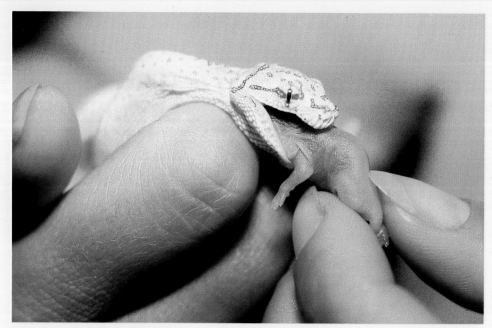

Young snakes often are eager feeders, taking food right from the fingers. This Green Tree Python, *Chondropython viridis*, had to be coaxed into biting a pinkie, but it eventually swallowed it on its own. Photo by I. Vergner.

Young venomous snakes, like the pretty Eyelash Viper, *Bothrops schlegeli*, shown here, should be offered food via forceps. Even at this age their bites can be harmful and possibly deadly. Photo by Jim Merli.

Rearing the Young

"With the handling of the eggs and the hatching of the young, the breeder's work is not done yet. I almost want to say that the biggest problems do not start until now." With these words of the grand old man of the terrarium hobby, Klingelhöffer, we turn to the problems facing the lucky hobbyist who, after weeks of effort to ensure the successful development of a clutch or the birth of an expected litter, now has a whole bunch of tiny young snakes on his hands. Are suitable terraria available? Will it be possible to procure adequate amounts of suitable food? Is enough time available to care for these young snakes?

Should doubts arise in answering these questions, it is better to give some of the offspring to other hobbyists as soon as possible. The careful rearing of young snakes is the basis of the successful propagation of our charges over a further generation. Optimal growth, early maturity, and a long life span will be the rewards for our efforts.

As a matter of principle, young snakes are reared separately from the parents. This is due not only to the danger of being crushed to death or even of being eaten by large conspecifics, but above all to different requirements in housing and diet. Often the mistake is made of immediately housing young snakes in relatively large terraria, which may even be thickly planted, thus offering innumerable uncontrollable hiding places. Young snakes are real escape artists. Millimeter-wide cracks are big enough, and if the little snakes are not found again by accident they will remain hopelessly lost. Breeders of boas and pythons have fewer problems in this respect with the youngsters. For most colubrid species, special small rearing terraria should be built. Small cages, placed in groups against one another or on top of one another and needing floor space no larger than 20 X 30 cm (8 X 12 in) for three to six youngsters of most species, have proved effective.

For some kingsnakes (*Lampropeltis*) and other ophiophagus (snake-eating) species, individual housing is highly recommended.

Not only is there the danger that even a sibling of the same size will suddenly be swallowed after months of harmony, but the voracious snake itself often will perish by choking on the oversized portion. Separate keeping also is advisable for the rearing of venomous snakes, since bites with fatal consequences can occur during feeding. (Actually, this is rare, as most venomous snakes possess at least partial immunity to the venom of their own species.)

The furnishing of the rearing terraria should be as simple as possible and readily accessible. Elaborately formed rear walls of bark offer innumerable hiding places that make it impossible to keep track of all the youngsters. Decorative elements made of cement, plastic, or similar materials must not have any cracks or uncontrollable nooks. Pieces of bark are sufficient for the young snakes to satisfy their need for hiding places providing close body contact.

The daytime and nighttime temperatures should be somewhat higher for young snakes than for their parents. Fresh, clean drinking and bathing water always must be available in a shallow-rimmed container. In larger, steep-walled water vessels, even water snakes drown in a few hours. Moss, somewhat damper in one spot, as a rule is sufficient as a substrate; for species that like to burrow, loose earth, peat moss, or sand is put in the terrarium. Young snakes of many species like to rest on elevated surfaces or fairly thin branches.

Sudden temperature changes and drafts absolutely must be avoided. Young snakes are more susceptible to colds than are their parents.

Rearing can be considered as half successful when the youngsters have taken their first food independently. Our lack of knowledge about the natural prey animals of the young of individual species and the likely impossibility of obtaining these foods probably are the biggest problems. Exotic frogs and salamanders theoretically could be bred as food animals, but the productive breeding of lizards for feeding purposes is hardly feasible.

What is left is substitute foods. This concept should in no way be denigrated. It usually is a matter of natural food that normally is not taken in the wild at a particular age or by a particular species, but is still of high quality. In this manner many young snakes that otherwise feed primarily on the lizard species that occur in abundance in their biotope can be imprinted on nestling (pinkie) mice from an early age. When young Corn Snakes (*Elaphe guttata*) barely 25 cm (10 in) long are observed having trouble eating a baby mouse only a few hours old, it becomes clear that young snakes of this size could hardly have access to sufficient quantities of nestling mice of suitable size in the wild. To what extent young snakes of the most diverse species would accept insects, even if they do not belong to insect-eating genera such as *Eirenis* and *Opheodrys*, is unknown. Young snakes that refuse food should be offered freshly molted crickets, tiny grasshoppers, wax moth larvae, and similar terrestrial food insects to see if they will accept them.

Absolute freedom from disturbance and a small terrarium promote feeding. It seems that repeated encounters with the offered prey have a stimulating effect, so finally the animal will be snapped up. Young nocturnal snakes can be put individually in a box or cloth bag together with a pinkie mouse; in the dark and quiet they often feed. Some young snakes seem to be afraid of struggling mice (and well they might—a mouse can kill a small snake) and prefer dead prey. Others are stimulated to take food by smelling the blood sticking to freshly killed mice. When young snakes refuse food, their biting reflex often can be used to advantage by allowing the snake to bite a dead young mouse held in front of it. It probably will let go again several times, but finally the swallowing reflex will be triggered and the prey will be gulped down. If the young snake is not aggressive, repeatedly striking the prey against the tip of the snout ultimately will cause it to bite. Forceps can be used to feed dead prey. If no young mice are available, offer parts of killed older mice, if possible with bits of bone and fur.

Many snakes that reject pinkie mice and have to be force-fed eventually grow large enough to hunt, grab, and swallow live, hairy young mice, so-called jumpers or fuzzies. The vigorous movements of mice of this age group trigger the hunting reflex. Youngsters of many species of boas and pythons immediately take young hairy mice without problems.

There is a growing trend today to attempt to wean as many snakes as possible onto frozen, thawed mice and chicks. Frozen mice are readily available commercially, can be injected with supplements as needed, are convenient to store in the freezer until needed, and are not expensive if only a few snakes are to be fed. Mouse colonies are smelly and take up room that could be better occupied by snakes, while chicks usually cannot be raised in homes and cities because of health and zoning laws. Additionally, living mice—anything bigger than a pinkie—can cause serious wounds to small snakes and occasionally kill snakes if left together unattended. In several areas there are restrictive laws about feeding living animals to other animals, and feeding mammals to snakes always angers some people. If possible, try to wean your snakes onto frozen mice, but always be sure the prey is fully thawed before feeding.

Often some of the young snakes of a clutch or litter refuse food, and whether they could catch prey in the wild either is open to question. In any case, separate keeping is effective for these snakes—not only because otherwise the control of food intake is difficult or more voracious siblings would repeatedly snatch the proffered pinkie mouse away from them, but because they may be more sensitive to being repeatedly disturbed by more robust cagemates. With voracious young snakes, mutual biting and strangleholds often occur. Bitten and injured animals become timid and refuse to take food. Consequently, it is not rare that in the eagerness to catch food, conspecifics are grabbed and swallowed or simple accidents happen when two snakes grab the same mouse and the larger snake swallows the second snake along with the mouse. Observation and careful control of feeding are thus always necessary.

Water snakes as a rule present fewer problems with their first feeding. Thus with

Three stages of force-feeding.

Top—The annoyed snake
opens its mouth

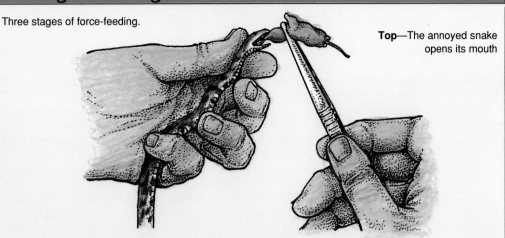

Top—The annoyed snake opens its mouth

Middle—The food item is pushed deep into the gullet

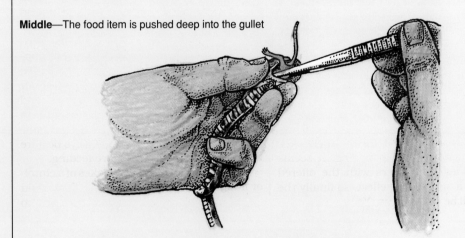

Bottom—Now the food is gradually massaged down into the stomach

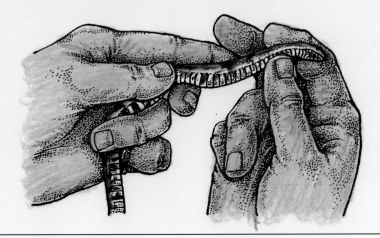

the livebearing water snakes and garter snakes, *Nerodia* and *Thamnophis*, feeding usually starts by the second day of life. Tiny aquarium fishes such as guppies, mollies, platies, or small barbs or tetras should be available. If you know a tropical fish breeder you ought to be able to get underdeveloped specimens or fishes with undesirable colors or forms for almost nothing. Pet shops usually have very cheap small fishes (especially wild-type guppies) at very low prices. Avoid bait minnows and wild-caught fishes; the former often carry too many diseases, while the latter may have special regulations controlling their collection. Many amphibian-eating species can be fed with fishes, but if nothing else works, we must turn to frogs and salamanders as well as their larvae bred in the terrarium. Fortunately, most fish and amphibian eaters also accept dead fish, including strips of fresh or frozen and thawed fish. Young garter snakes (*Thamnophis*) will take as their first meal tiny pieces of fish without bones or scales, fed from a dish. In so doing they orient themselves with their sense of smell and find the food dish very quickly. This is a somewhat surprising finding, because fish eaters in nature must try to find fish or amphibian larvae swimming in the water with their eyes.

Good complementary foods for many of these species are earthworms from the garden (whole or pieces of suitable size) as well as small slugs, though the exclusive feeding of earthworms cannot be recommended for most water snakes (but some garter snakes, brown snakes [*Storeria*], and other small burrowers feed largely on earthworms).

In addition to fish, many individuals also readily accept lean meat or poultry, particularly heart. Many species of water snakes accept heart cut into strips and if necessary placed between pieces of fish. Larger specimens also take pinkie mice, but there are great individual and species differences in food choices. Pronounced amphibian eaters can be fooled by disguising pinkie mice with "fish aroma." For example, a hobbyist found the following method of feeding young African Herald Snakes (*Crotaphopeltis hotamboeia*) to be effective. Several frogs were pureed in a food processor and the resulting paste was thinned with water and frozen in ice-cube trays. Before feeding, a cube was thawed and the liquid was used to cover pinkie mice. The young snakes accepted the unfamiliar prey, finally without even having to disguise the scent.

Occasionally, however, none of these tricks work and a young snake stubbornly refuses to eat any food. Then we feel compelled to try force-feeding. This should not be started too early. Any force-feeding means stress for the animal and always should be viewed as a last resort. The larger the species and therefore the young snake, the later force-feeding must be started. With medium-sized rat snakes (*Elaphe*), force-feeding should be delayed for at least four weeks. The power of resistance that newly hatched snakes can exhibit is shown by the example of one of my little Corn Snakes (*Elaphe guttata*). The snake escaped from its terrarium on the fifth day of life, before the first molt and before the first feeding, and could not be found, even though it could not have left the room. After 11 weeks, the snake was found one morning crawling across the floor. It defended itself fiercely against capture. After being put back in the terrarium, it drank very greedily, and immediately after drinking the water it ate a pinkie mouse.

The suggestion to hibernate youngsters that refuse to feed seems to be a harsh solution to the problem, but it sometimes works. This was practiced repeatedly with American Rat Snakes (*Elaphe obsoleta*), and all the youngsters survived hibernation well and ate voluntarily in the spring.

The most suitable foods to be used for force-feeding are natural foods or at least the prey animals accepted voluntarily by the little snake's siblings, such as pinkie mice or fish. In many species, force-feeding is relatively easy. The youngster opens its mouth when held gently with the thumb and index finger behind the head. In many cases touching the mouth with the food held in rounded forceps will work. The food is placed in the mouth, the snake bites, and, if we are lucky, chewing and swallowing movements begin after a few tries. If the snake refuses to swallow, the piece of food is pushed lightly into the gullet and the snake is gently put down; sometimes the swallowing reflex then sets in.

If the food is spit out again and again, it should be massaged down to the stomach region, but no farther than about the middle of the body. To do this we hold the young snake with the thumb and index finger behind the head and try to stretch the front part of the snake slightly with the remaining fingers of the same hand. Pinkie mice, killed beforehand with slight pressure of the forceps on the head and moistened with water to increase their slipperiness, are best placed in the snake's mouth belly-up and pushed as far into the gullet as possible with the forceps. Then with the thumb and index finger of the other hand, the mouse is detected from the outside and massaged in the direction of the stomach. In so doing, the thumb can be effectively placed on the underside of the snake with the index finger pressing against it from on top, or both fingers can massage the sides of the body. If the mouse is not too large and the young snake does not become too agitated, it will not attempt to regurgitate the mouse. If the snake tries to regurgitate the food, it is put in the water bowl; this will force it to swim, which could stop regurgitation. Fish-eating snakes are easier to force-feed. With young pythons and boas or if the hobbyist is unpracticed in force-feeding, it can be useful to have an assistant hold the animal.

Force-feeding becomes somewhat more complicated if the snake refuses to open its mouth. With tiny baby snakes, using a small, pointed brush to tickle the corner of the mouth can cause the mouth to open. Otherwise the mouth must be opened carefully with a small, flat piece of wood (a beveled match, toothpick, or the like) pushed laterally into the mouth opening. Then the food is brought in front of the mouth, the piece of wood is slowly pulled out, and the insertion of the piece of food can begin.

Small fishes such as guppies also are well-suited for the force-feeding of those snake species that normally do not eat fish. For example, it is very easy to push a small fish into the gullet of a tiny Corn Snake (*Elaphe guttata*). As a last resort when suitable food is not available, particularly with very delicate snakes, strips of lean meat can be used for force-feeding. The meat is cut into very thin, long strips and is enriched with a multivitamin and mineral supplement.

The force-feeding of venomous snakes requires special care. Accidents can happen in the feeding of young venomous snakes. Bites on the fingers, especially the cuticle, are the most common. When holding young venomous snakes the keeper must be aware of the fangs, which sometimes extend beyond the lower jaw.

Some young snakes present problems in force-feeding even to experienced keepers. For example, in rearing North American Mud Snakes (*Farancia abacura*), I never succeeded in opening the mouths of the baby snakes wide enough to stuff them with little fishes. As an alternative food, a pap of boneless fish was prepared and, supplemented with traces of vitamins and minerals, used to fill a syringe. In portions of 1 milliliter—later 2 to 3 milliliters—this pap was pressed deep into the gullet through a plastic tube of the sort used by veterinarians for treating the teats in cows. With larger young snakes the food pap can be conveyed directly to the stomach through a thin plastic or rubber tube. Feeding with food pap is very effective when a fairly large number of young snakes must be force-fed. Many keepers of egg-eating snakes (*Dasypeltis*) rear young snakes by this method using chicken egg yolk as the basic ingredient when the necessary tiny eggs of cage birds are not available.

When young snakes refuse food for psychological reasons, a few force-feedings often will be enough to "break the spell" and encourage them to feed independently. If the snakes are not ready to accept alternative food, it may be necessary to force-feed them for months. Despite the best efforts, force-fed youngsters will lag in development behind their conspecifics that feed independently. Moreover, boneless fish is no substitute for whole fishes. On the other hand, through force-feeding some very difficult snakes can be kept alive and reared until they begin feeding on their own.

The frequency of feeding depends on the speed of digestion, which can be determined by the amount of droppings after a single feeding. As a rule of thumb, it can be assumed that one feeding a week is adequate. In any case, snakes that feed well regulate this rhythm independently; it is interrupted by a pause in feeding only for the molt that occurs about once a month. Fish-eaters digest faster than mouse-eaters and must be fed every two to three days.

Generally, an abundant food supply combined with high temperatures leads to more rapid growth in captivity than in the wild. But this also leads to the danger of nutritional deficiencies.

Direct exposure to sunlight or doses of artificial ultraviolet light as a rule is unnecessary. A suitable vitamin preparation supplies adequate amounts of vitamin D3, and enough calcium is present in the bones of food animals. Insect-eating snakes or animals that are fed exclusively with earthworms, on the other hand, are more susceptible to rickets. Here it is advisable to dust the food animals with a calcium preparation or to add water-soluble calcium lactate to the drinking water.

A balanced diet including occasional pauses in feeding ensures more vigorous and resistant animals than does "forcing" specimens. The latter often are obese and have problems in breeding despite or because of their early sexual maturity.

Above: A diet that includes the occasional vitamin/mineral supplement will do wonders for your snakes' health. Vitamins can be obtained in both powder and liquid form. Photo of a California Kingsnake, *Lampropeltis getula californiae*, by Isabelle Francais.

Left: Newborn snakes will eat more frequently than adults, plus they will have a slightly greater need for vitamin/mineral supplmentation. Photo of a litter of Boa Constrictors, *Boa constrictor*, by William B. Allen, Jr.

Growth and Life Expectancy in the Terrarium

Growth in snakes is reflected in increasing total length and body mass. Data on length in snakes, unless noted otherwise, normally apply to the total length. The ratio of the head-body length (tip of the snout to the cloaca) to the tail length (cloaca to the tip of the tail) varies in individual snake species, and even between males and females of a species. The range of variation is shown by the proportionally tiny tail of the Puff Adder (*Bitis arietans*) compared with the long tail of a Long-nosed Tree Snake (*Ahaetulla prasina*). It would therefore be more appropriate, instead of giving the total length (TL) of the snake, to give the head-body length (HBL) and the tail length (TL) separately.

The precise measurement of length in live snakes, however, is problematic in any case. Various tricks, like letting them crawl through a glass tube, have been used with varying success. Probably the easiest and relatively most precise measurement technique consists of laying a tape measure along the back of a snake held by a second person, who tries to stretch the snake carefully, at least by stages. It makes no sense to give the length of a large snake in millimeters. A truly precise measurement is possible only with freshly dead or at least anesthetized animals. Preserved animals usually shrink a little. The measurement of snake skins leads to inadvertent overestimates of up to 25 percent. The same is true of the length of the shed skin, though the straightforward measurement of complete sheds dried without stretching can provide valuable indications of the rate of growth of a snake.

Conscientious and regular measurement will reveal that hatching lengths within a clutch can vary by more than 50% and hatching weights by as much as 100% between the smallest and lightest and the longest and heaviest youngsters. The further development of snakes of a clutch is determined by the environment and in many cases also depends on the sex.

The question of whether snakes continue to grow their whole lives is controversial. It is likely that after the rapid increases in length during juvenile development the annual increases decline with advancing age and come to a standstill when too much calcium has been deposited at the places of attachment of the bones and joints. The growth rates of large boas and pythons decrease rapidly. For example, a python grew by 7.6 cm (3 in) a month and 92 cm (37 in) a year up to an age of two years, and in the following 12 years grew only an additional 107 cm (43 in). Growth records in the specialist literature stand at about 140 cm (56 in) a year for the African Rock-Python (*Python sebae*) and 105 cm (42 in) a year for the somewhat smaller Asian Rock-Python (*Python molurus*).

Despite numerous fantastic reports of the record lengths of giant snakes, only six species attain lengths of more than 5 meters (16.5 ft). The absolute record length of 11.44 meters (37.75 ft) has been held for many years by a Green Anaconda (*Eunectes murinus*) measured in 1944 on the Orinoco (though this record is questioned by many). A Reticulated Python (*Python reticulatus*) caught in 1979 in Thailand that was 12.2 meters (40.3 ft) long and had a live weight of 220 kilograms (484 pounds) has reputedly outstripped the Anaconda. Record lengths of the remaining giant snake species are as follows: African Rock-Python (*Python sebae*) 7.63 meters (25.2 ft); Scrub Python (*Python amethistinus*) 6.71 meters (22.1 ft); Asian Rock-Python (*Python molurus*) 6.1 meters (20 ft); and Boa Constrictor (*Boa constrictor*) 5.64 meters (18.6 ft).

Additional interesting lengths of snakes, taken from the *Guinness Book of World Records*, include lengths of 5.71 meters (18.8 ft) for a King Cobra (*Ophiophagus hannah*) from the London Zoo and 2.18 meters (7.2 ft) for an Aesculapian Rat Snake (*Elaphe longissima*) from Austria, as well as a maximum of 12 cm (5 in) for the smallest snake species of all, a blindsnake species (*Leptotyphlops bilineata*) from Martinique, Barbados, and St. Lucia. The smallest poisonous snake, *Homoroselaps dorsalis*, a species from South Africa, is said to grow to at most 15 cm (6 in) in length.

It is easier and considerably more precise to follow the development of a snake by measuring its body weight. Weighing should of course be done only on an empty stomach. The pregnancy of females should also be taken into account. Regular, quick weighings permit a dependable control of the condition of the animal and its stage of pregnancy. Controlled weighings before and after hibernation allow important inferences to be drawn.

Careful long-term observations of the increase in weight of most snakes are rare; however, there are numerous data on the development of individuals. For example, there are data on the Four-lined Rat Snake (*Elaphe quatuorlineata*), which in the first year of life increased its hatching mass sevenfold and in four years thirty-fold, and for the Boa Constrictor (*Boa constrictor*), which increased its body weight by up to twenty-fold within a year between the sixth and eighteenth months of life. Some record weights for snakes are almost 227 kilograms (500 pounds) for a Green Anaconda (*Eunectes murinus*) with a maximum circumference of 111 cm (3.7 ft); a live weight of 15 kilograms (33 pounds) for a 2.36-meter (7.8 ft) Eastern Diamondback Rattlesnake (*Crotalus adamanteus*); and 12.75 kilograms (28 pounds) for a 4.39-meter (14.4 ft) King Cobra (*Ophiophagus hannah*).

As a general rule, as snakes grow longer, the slower is their rate of growth, but the increase in weight is maintained. It can be observed occasionally that growth rates slow down at the onset of sexual maturity. As a rule of thumb, snakes attain sexual maturity when they have reached 50 to 75% of the ultimate length typical of their species. Large species of boas and pythons are an exception: they are already sexually mature at 25 to 30% of their ultimate length. Virtually nothing is known about the termination of sexual maturity in old age (senescence).

Molting (ecdysis, shedding, sloughing) is closely related to the increase in length and body weight in snakes. The outer horny layer (stratum corneum), consisting of dead keratinized cells, has only limited elasticity; it becomes too tight and therefore is subject to a hormonally regulated, periodic sloughing. These relationships explain why young, fast-growing snakes molt more often—six to eleven times a year—than older animals, which sometimes shed their skins only once or twice a year. Besides the food supply, temperature and moisture also influence the endocrine regulation of molting.

The first molt of freshly hatched snakes usually takes place 8 to 20 days after hatching. Some livebearing species, like garter snakes (*Thamnophis*) and water snakes (*Nerodia*), molt within the first hours of life, and a few species molt while they are still within the chorion. Obviously there is a great deal of variation in the time of first molt, and hobbyists should expect anywhere from two or three days to a week or more in commonly bred egg-layers. The start of the molting process can be recognized by the gradual clouding of the eyes, often distinctly bluish in tone; additionally, the whole body turns grayish and the colors become pale and dull. The eyes clear up two to three days before the molt, when the milky fluid that had been present between the old and new layers of skin has been resorbed by the body. The scales of the upper and lower lips look slightly swollen. By rubbing its head against objects, the snake now tries to loosen the skin on the margins of the lips and work it back over the head. By forcing their way between obstacles, healthy animals slough the skin in one piece, now turned inside out. Although the old skins (exuviae) are a true-to-nature copy of all scales of snakes, the color and pattern are reproduced only poorly or not at all. Large boas and pythons slough in large shreds, not in one piece. Otherwise, an incomplete or tattered molt indicates unfavorable moisture levels, a dietary deficiency (usually a vitamin deficiency), a generally weak nutritional state, or mite infestation (acariasis).

Snakes that either molt incompletely or do not molt at all must be given a forced bath for at least 15 minutes in water with a temperature of between 30 and 35°C (86-95°F). (But take care! Very weak animals can die while

AGE RECORDS OF SELECTED SNAKE SPECIES

(The snakes marked with an * were still alive at the time the data were collected)

Species	Age (years—months)	Species	Age (years—months)
Boa Constrictor (Boa c. constrictor)	40-3	Common Garter Snake (Thamnophis s. sirtalis)	10-0
Green Anaconda (Eunectes murinus)	31-9	Black-lipped Cobra (Naja melanoleuca)	29-1
Indian Python (Python molurus molurus)	31-1	Asian Cobra (Naja naja ssp.)	22-2
Ball Python (Python regius)	28-1	King Cobra (Ophiophagus hannah)	17-2
Rainbow Slender Boa (Epicrates cenchria maurus)	27-4	Banded Krait (Bungarus fasciatus)	14
Brown Sand-Boa (Eryx johni)	12-5	Eastern Green Mamba (Dendroaspis angusticeps)	13-5
African Rock Python (Python sebae)	26-6*	Long-nosed Viper (Vipera ammodytes)	22
Garden Tree-Boa (Corallus enydris cooki)	14-3	Desert Horned-Viper (Cerastes cerastes)	17-1
Scrub Python (Amethistinus sp.)	10-2	Common Puff-Adder (Bitis a. arietans)	12-10*
Indigo Snake (Drymarchon corais couperi)	25-11	Saw-scaled Carpet-Viper (Echis carinatus)	12-4
Leopard Rat Snake (Elaphe situla)	25	Levantine Viper (Daboia lebetina)	10-5*
Corn Snake (Elaphe g. guttata)	21-9	Canebrake Rattlesnake (Crotalus horridus atricaudatus)	28-1
Eastern Milk Snake (Lampropeltis t. triangulum)	21-5	Western Diamondback Rattlesnake (Crotalus atrox)	24-4
Northern Pine Snake (Pituophis m. melanoleucus)	20-9	Broad-banded Copperhead (Agkistrodon contortrix laticinctus)	21-6
Eastern King Snake (Lampropeltis g. getula)	20-7	Cottonmouth (Agkistrodon piscivorus)	18-11
Yellow Rat Snake (Elaphe obsoleta quadrivittata)	17-11	Massasauga (Sistrurus catenatus)	14-0
Asian Chicken Snake (Ptyas mucosus)	10-7	Eyelash Palm-Pitviper (Bothrops schlegeli)	13-8
		Bamboo Pitviper (Trimeresurus elegans)	10-3

The molt, or shed, is a natural part of a snake's life. In captivity, it is the keeper's job to see that this cycle runs smoothly, i.e., all skin comes off completely (particularly around the eyes). Photo of a South American Rattlesnake, *Crotalus durissus terrificus*, by L. Trutnau.

being bathed!) The old skin will become so soft that it can be stripped off in one piece by hand or in shreds with forceps. The skin covering the eyes and the tip of the tail also must be removed to prevent subsequent blindness or necrosis of the tip of the tail. The skin of the forked tongue (shed in its own cycle), the hemipenes, and even the anal spurs in giant snakes also are molted.

Many snakes like to bathe before molting. It is not clear, however, whether bathing serves only to soften the old skin or to compensate for increased water loss through the skin before molting. It has been shown that healthy snakes can molt without problems and in one piece even under very dry keeping conditions.

A long life for snakes in the terrarium is certainly a reflection of excellent care and keeping conditions. Good reproductive rates and a high life expectancy probably are mutually exclusive, because very productive individuals are subject to too many risk factors. All the same, snakes can live considerably longer in the terrarium than their conspecifics in the wild.

Changes in weather and innumerable enemies, including man, limit the length of a snake's life. Snakes probably almost never die from old age in the wild.

Until recently, the record age for snakes probably was held by a 1.8-meter Boa Constrictor (*Boa constrictor*) named Popeye. Resident in the Philadelphia Zoo, he had to be destroyed for medical reasons on March, 15, 1977, after a life span of 40 years, 3 months, and 14 days. On October 7, 1992, a Ball Python (*Python regius*) in the same zoo died after being in captivity for over 47 years (*Bull. Chicago Herp. Soc.*, 28(4): 77-78) setting a new record. Also a male, he died of liver disease. Many large boas and pythons have a high average life expectancy, often in the 10 to 30 years range.

An Indigo Snake (*Drymarchon corais couperi*) of the Florida subspecies with a length of 2.3 meters (7.6 ft) apparently holds the record for colubrids, almost 26 years. Rat snakes, kingsnakes, and bullsnakes often reach 20 years or more, but garter snakes and water snakes are relatively short-lived. A Black-lipped Cobra (*Naja melanoleuca*) has apparently reached the greatest age of any poisonous snake in captivity, over 29 years, but several rattlesnakes (*Crotalus*) have reached more than 20 years of age.

Disturbances in Reproduction

Besides the most diverse systemic and specific diseases that affect the organ systems of snakes and can be detrimental to the well-being of the animals and the incidence of reproduction, diseases of the reproductive organs are the direct cause of far-reaching disturbances in reproduction. Calcium deposits in the testes, in the oviducts, and apparently also in the ovaries can be the result of systemic irregularities in calcium metabolism. As a rule, such changes are not recognized in the living animal. A balanced vitamin supply, in particular with sufficient vitamin D3, has a prophylactic effect.

Inflammations of the male and female reproductive organs are rare and usually are the consequence of a systemic infectious illness. For example, in amebiasis, which is so dangerous to snakes, necrotic inflammations have been observed in the testes. Salmonella bacteria have been found in the ovaries, where they caused a degeneration of the follicles. Acute inflammations, the formation of abscesses, and other pathological changes to the testes can occur with severe infections of aeromonas, pseudomonas, and tuberculosis bacteria, as well as other pathogens. Delayed egg-laying (egg retention) and the subsequent disintegration of the eggs usually leads to progressive inflammations and necrosis of the oviducts.

Physical overexertion, constipation, and injury to or heavy soiling of the hemipenes during mating may be responsible for making it impossible to withdraw one or both hemipenes again. The consequences usually are skin injuries and secondary bacterial infections that lead to inflammation and necrosis. If the mucous membrane of the hemipenis still is intact, a case of this kind can be remedied by carefully pushing the hemipenis back in with the aid of a lubricant such as glycerin. With repeated occurrences, an experienced veterinarian may have to partially sew up the cloacal opening. Antibiotic ointments promote the healing process. With inflammation or necrosis there is no choice but to amputate the hemipenis. Subsequent successful mating is still possible if only one hemipenis was affected.

Tumors of the ovary and testes are relatively rare in snakes; tumors occur mainly in the digestive tract.

A recently completed molt is detrimental to the breeding behavior of male snakes. The absence of mating despite active courtship behavior also can be traced to the incomplete molting of the skin of the hemipenes. On closer inspection of the openings of the hemipenes in the cloaca, remnants of skin that may have started to decompose and cause inflammation may be visible. After the application of an oily liquid in the blind pouches of the hemipenis and a thorough bath at a temperature of 30 to 35°C (86-95°F), with some luck it may be possible to massage out these remnants while simultaneously pulling on them with forceps.

Difficulties in mating with male snakes also are caused by vertebral deformities in the rear third of the body, possibly caused by rachitis; by healed tail injuries and cropped tails; by disturbances in coordination of the tail movements; as well as by nonfunctional hemipenis musculature.

Occasionally the absence of copulation has a completely different cause. In one instance an apparently painful mandibular disease of a male Amur Rat Snake (*Elaphe schrencki*) prevented it from performing the nape biting that normally accompanies copulation; this disrupted the entire mating behavior.

A disturbance during copulation can lead to the "hanging up" of the hemipenis in the female's cloaca. When the often larger and stronger female snake tries to take flight or even rotates around its longitudinal axis while trying to escape, the erect hemipenis may be dislocated. This causes the hemipenis to swell up and prevents it from being released from the cloaca. Under certain circumstances, surgical treatment under local anesthesia and medicinal treatment are required to remedy the situation.

Obstacles to copulation in females take the form of prolapse of the cloaca and greatly swollen postanal glands. In the majority of cases veterinarians have been able to reinsert the prolapses of the cloaca under local anesthesia of the mucous membranes. The postanal glands can be surgically removed.

Female snakes in heat can be injured if they are impatient and injure themselves, particularly their rostrum, while fleeing from the male. Especially common are collisions with the glass of the terrarium. Even if infection and renewed injury are prevented, injuries of this kind heal relatively slowly over a period of several months.

Irregularities during pregnancy are common causes of reproductive disturbances in female snakes. Long-term studies of these problems have involved various species of garter snakes (Thamnophis). Cases of overfertilization (superfetation) were observed; here females mated again despite already being pregnant. A female of the Common Garter Snake (Thamnophis sirtalis) was mated twice at an interval of three weeks and gave birth 71 and 52 days after copulation to young at different stages of development. Another female of this species also copulated twice within three weeks and gave birth after 79 and 55 days to litters at an above-average state of development, as well as a quantity of yolk and decomposed fetuses after 12 months. Interrupted embryonic development has been documented in other female garter snakes. The successful treatment of pneumonia and the refusal to feed for several months caused the suspension of embryonic development for a fairly long time. After a total of 234 days this female gave birth to 41 young, of which 25 were alive and healthy. Another female garter snake, after refusing to feed and undergoing hibernation, gave birth to 14 live and two dead young 253 days after copulation. The possibility of delayed fertilization (amphigonia retardata) is considered part of the problem of recognizing apparently prolonged gestation.

Disturbances during the period of time before laying eggs or giving birth to young are egg-binding (dystocia) and miscarriage (abortion). Delayed egg-laying (retention) caused by unfavorable keeping practices can still lead to a successful hatch, but frequently ends in egg-binding. Causes of egg-binding that can also lead to miscarriage—that is,

premature birth in an environment also detrimental to development—include the lack of suitable sites for laying eggs; unsuitable moisture levels; too high or too low temperatures; unfavorable psychological influences, such as transport stress and frequent disturbances by cagemates or people; and pathological organic changes of the reproductive duct. Young snakes or individuals with a large number of eggs not infrequently fail to lay all the eggs of a clutch. If this is not noticed in time and countermeasures are not attempted, the fetuses will die and decompose. Bacterial infections also occur, and a rapidly progressing inflammation with necrosis finally leads to death.

The cause of death also can be acute calcium deficiency at the time of egg-laying. The greatly increased calcium requirement during pregnancy, combined with an undersupply, leads to weakness of the oviduct musculature and to egg-binding.

Obvious symptoms usually are not present in the case of psychological disturbances. Renewed food intake and the absence of searching for a suitable egg-laying site often are overlooked. Symptoms of acute egg-binding include persistent thrusting and stretching of the tail, occasionally a mucous discharge from the cloaca, and finally lethargy and apathy. Decisive points to consider in the diagnosis are the presence of eggs in the body, the general condition of the female, and information on the previous history (mating, new purchase, lack of appetite, keeping conditions, among others).

If egg-binding is suspected, the first therapeutic measures should be directed toward a rapid improvement in the general physical condition of the animal. These measures include the injection of a multivitamin preparation and calcium borogluconate or calcium gluconate (1 g Ca^{++} per kilogram body weight). In acute egg-binding the first action attempted should be the removal of the eggs by massaging after the introduction of a sterile water-soluble lubricant or an oily vitamin preparation into the cloaca. Mineral oil should not be used as a lubricant, because it could have a detrimental effect on gas and water exchange of the eggs during subsequent incubation. Simultaneously increasing the body tem-

EGG-BINDING IN SNAKES				
Development of the fertile egg	Physiological time of laying	Unphysiological development of the egg in the mother's body (water uptake)	Death of the fetus (necrosis)	Mummification; resorption of the dead fetus
	▽	▽	▽	▽
	△ △	△	△	△
Course of egg-binding	rejection acute egg-binding	chronic egg-binding	infection, inflammation of the oviduct (salpingitis), poisoning through the uterus	chronic inflammation of the oviduct (salpingitis), fatal in the long run
Therapy	oxytocin, surgical intervention (salpingotomy)	surgical intervention (salpingotomy)	surgical removal of the oviduct (salpingectomy)	
Behavior of the female	unrest, burrowing, labor pains, involuntary egg laying	crawling to a cooler location; no labor pains	apathy	throes of death, death

perature to 30 to 36°C (86-97°F) is especially effective for relieving muscle cramps.

Particularly in psychologically caused egg-binding, the application of oxytocin, a hormone that among other things induces birth, can be successful. After preliminary injections of calcium gluconate distributed over several points on the body, labor can be induced and promoted through the intramuscular injection of 2 to 3 I.U. of oxytocin per kilogram of body weight, which then leads to the laying of the eggs. If none of these measures works, the soft-shelled eggs can be punctured through the disinfected skin with a syringe—if necessary after temperature elevation and oxytocin administration—and the contents sucked out. The remaining egg remnants are easier to remove.

A cesarean section performed by a veterinarian is a last resort in cases of egg-binding that have not responded to other therapy. After radiographs are taken to determine the number and position of the eggs, under general anesthesia an incision is made along the median line of the belly and the thin wall of the oviduct is split (salpingotomy); the eggs are then massaged out individually. It is essential that both oviducts are cleared out. Often the eggs are already decomposing and are fused to the oviduct; then the removal of the oviduct (salpingectomy) usually is necessary, which naturally results in the permanent sterility of the snake. After the operation the oviducts and the opening in the skin must be sewed up. Follow-up treatment with antibiotics is recommended. The sutures can be removed after about two weeks if the animal is not too weak. This kind of operation is quite simple for the experienced veterinarian.

Disturbances in the development of the embryos in the laid egg occur primarily at the start of the period of maturation. Examples include: symptoms of deficiency in the mother, such as vitamin deficiency; environmental toxins; technical defects causing rapid temperature changes, overheating, or excessive dryness or wetness; and genetic factors.

We have already discussed hatching assistance in the form of "windowing" of the eggs. Youngsters that do not move after the eggs are opened still can be saved under certain circumstances. Physical defects, clear underdevelopment, a bluish coloration in the belly area, and a milky fluid in the egg all indicate, however, that efforts to activate such youngsters would be a waste of time. Fully developed young that show no signs of life first have the mucous removed from the mouth and nostrils and then are submerged for at least ten minutes alternately for half a

mals exhibit normal behavior in every respect, except that they are no longer able to father young.

Occasionally anomalies can turn up during embryonic development that—if they do not have a lethal effect—can lead to deformities. By deformities are meant congenital changes in form or shape affecting either the body as a whole or individual body parts.

Here's an interesting example of a developmental anomaly—this Burmese Python, *Python molurus bivittatus*, hatched without eyes. Photo by D. Schmidt.

minute at a time in two water baths with temperatures of 35 and 15°C (95° and 59°F). In this way it may be possible to stimulate a scarcely detectable heartbeat and finally deep breathing.

The decision to sterilize snakes may seem absurd at first glance. The reasons for it become clear, however, when you are aware of the problems facing, for example, a keeper of Puff Adders (*Bitis arietans*) who regularly obtains litters of 30 or 40 young venomous snakes that he is unable to distribute in his circle of acquaintances. In such cases the sterilization of the male through the surgical removal of a 2-cm (almost 1-in) section of the sperm duct (vasectomy) under general anesthesia is recommended. Vasectomized ani-

Whether such changes are genetically determined or can be traced back to disruptive factors during embryonic development cannot be determined externally. The extent of developmentally dependent anomalies is determined by the timing of the disturbance in the course of development. Because they often are played up sensationally, deformities frequently are described in the specialist literature. Newspaper photographs and reports of two-headed "monster snakes" appear regularly.

Duplications, particularly of the head, are the most commonly reported type of deformity. Double heads usually are based on bifurcations of the vertebral column. Both heads then as a rule have a brain and both feed; one head may be dominant over the other. Snakes with two heads often have survived for many years in captivity.

More common than described in the literature are curvatures of the vertebral column, either upward (kyphosis), downward (lordosis), or to the side (scoliosis). If such deformities occur in the vertebrae of a number of siblings, temperature disturbances in the course of embryonic development usually are the cause.

A cystlike protrusion of the eyes (exophthalmos) was observed by the author in a freshly hatched Radiated Rat Snake (*Elaphe radiata*). Puncturing the outer chamber of the eye released a watery, clear fluid; the eyes appeared completely normal. After several days, however, the original condition returned and the eye pressed against the upper jaw, preventing the mouth from closing.

The life expectancy of deformed snakes depends on the extent of the changes. Slight curvature of the vertebral column does not necessarily cause any problems in locomotion, food intake, or reproduction. The absence of eyes in a Burmese Python (*Python molurus bivittatus*) did not impede food intake.

Many two-headed snakes do not live past the infancy stage, but a few grow normally and do fine. This trait is not genetic, however, meaning you cannot breed two-headed snakes and expect to get more. Photo of a Texas Rat Snake, *Elaphe obsoleta lindheimeri*, by W. P. Mara.

Egglaying should always run smoothly, with the eggs sliding gently out of the mother in an easy fashion. If you suspect egg-binding in any of your snakes, you should react at once. Egg-binding can be deadly. Photo of a Bullsnake, *Pituophis sayi*, by William B. Allen, Jr.

DEFORMITIES IN SNAKES

Deformity	Specific example
Double head (bicephaly)	several hundred cases described
Albinism in various forms	28 North American Snake species, Ringed Snake *(Natrix natrix)*, Four-lined Rat Snake *(Elaphe quatuorlineata)*, Asian Rock-Python *(Python molurus)*, Ball Python *(Python regius)*, plus others
Clefts in lips and gums	Western Rattlesnake *(Crotalus viridis)*
Shortened body	Northern Water Snake *(Nerodia sipedon)*
Shortened jaw (brachygnathus)	Common Garter Snake *(Thamnophis sirtalis)*
Scale anomalies - Missing body scales - Anomalies of the lip scales - Divided preocular scales - Paired pits in the parietal scales - Deformity of the umbilical slit	 Pine Snake *(Pituophis melanoleucus)* Asian Rock-Python *(Python molurus)* Southern Water Snake *(Nerodia fasciata)* Ringed Snake *(Natrix natrix)* Common Garter Snake *(Thamnophis sirtalis)*
Eye anomalies - small eyes *(microphthalmus)* - pop eyes *(exophthalmus)* - lack of eyes *(anophthalmus)*	 Four-lined Rat Snake *(Elaphe quatuorlineata)* Rhinoceros Viper *(Bitis nasicornis)* Gaboon Viper *(Bitis gabonica)*
Curvature of the spine *(kyphosis/scoliosis)*	Water Moccasin *(Agkistrodon piscivorus)*
Hydrocephaly	Common Garter Snake *(Thamnophis sirtalis)*
Fusion of the ventral plates	Viperine Water Snake *(Natrix maura)*
Openings in the chest and abdominal wall *(thoracogastroschisis)*	Madagascar Tree-Boa *(Sanzinia madagascariensis)*
Absence of kidneys	Pine Snake *(Pituophis melanoleucus)*

Genetics

The crowning achievement of the terrarium hobby is the production of offspring (reproduction) and the increase of the number of individuals in reproduction (propagation). Well-known herpetologists and zookeepers often use the concepts of breeding and rearing to describe mating, pregnancy, maturation of eggs, and hatching or birth under human care in the terrarium. The producer of agricultural domesticated animals as well as the aquarist who works with cultivated strains understand by the term breeding the systematic, planned mating of individuals, directed toward a specific breeding goal, which in particular serves to elevate their traits and performance. The elevation of traits has been a goal for a several years in the breeding of snakes.

In the propagation of terrarium animals we usually strive to maintain their species-typical traits, but we cannot rule out a certain influence by man and the artificial manmade environment. The culling of runts and deformed animals corresponds roughly to natural selection, but this selection is even stricter because only the most vital animals are allowed to reproduce.

Inheritance results in close similarity between the parents and their offspring. Moreover, the genetic material acts together with the environment to determine development and change. Under terrarium conditions, maintaining the typical traits of a species is made more difficult, if not impossible, in breeding over many generations without introducing "new blood."

The carrier of the material of inheritance is a complex organic molecule, deoxyribonucleic acid (DNA), localized in the form of genes on the chromosomes. Each somatic (body or non-sex) cell contains a double complement of chromosomes (diploid, 2N). The sex cells always contain only one complement of chromosomes (haploid, N); the fusion of sperm and egg restores the diploid complement and thereby makes possible the combination of paternal and maternal genetic information. Snakes often have numerous dot-like microchromosomes in addition to large straight or V-shaped macrochromosomes. In their entirety, the chromosomes make up the species-typical karyotype (chromosome picture) according to their form and number. Extreme numbers in snakes include 32 in the Spotted Blindsnake (*Typhlops punctatus*) and 50 in the Ring-naped Mussurana (*Clelia occipitolutea*).

In addition to the paired chromosomes present in identical form and size in both sexes, snakes also have two sex chromosomes that can be distinguished morphologically. They are similar (isogametic) in the male and of dissimilar form (heterogametic) in the female. Through the combination of the sperm, all of which exhibit the same sex chromosome, with the eggs—here two types of sex chromosomes are present in equal proportions—a sex ratio of 50:50 is achieved in the offspring. This equality of sexes can shift because of specific influences, such as differing mortality of one sex during embryonic development, but in principle it is not influenced by external factors. (In turtles, for instance, sex of the offspring is at least partially determined by temperature in the nest at crucial developmental periods.)

The entire stock of genes of a snake is called the genotype, which is expressed in the externally visible phenotype: the traits, characters, and performance resulting from the interaction of the genotype with the environment. A closed genetic system with a specific store of genes is designated as a species (sp., plural spp.). A species is made up of populations—not of unrelated individual organisms—that as a result of reproductive isolation from other species preserve its traits. Nevertheless, these traits are subject to change in the course of evolution. A subspecies (ssp.) is a group of populations differing in certain morphological characters, sometimes only in coloration and markings; living in geographic isolation from one another; and exhibiting unrestricted fertility with one another. This raises the danger of mixing when subspecies of the same snake

Hybridizing snakes of differing genera produces some interesting specimens. This, for example, is believed to be the product of a cross between a Gray-banded Kingsnake, *Lampropeltis alterna*, and a Corn Snake, *Elaphe guttata guttata*. Photo by W. P. Mara.

species are kept together, which must be avoided in the interest of the preservation of original and typical traits of the animals. The only exception worth discussing is the propagation of a specific subspecies in the terrarium when, for example, only a few specimens of the same sex are available and the acquisition of a mate of the same subspecies is impossible. Through a one-time cross with a similar subspecies, the foundation material can be obtained that can be used over several subsequent generations always to mate only with individuals of the foundation population, thereby eventually suppressing the genes of the foreign subspecies (displacement crossing).

Little selective breeding has been attempted so far in the propagation of snakes, but it should be conceivable in the future to breed for new traits in the species that can be propagated regularly without much difficulty.

The first step would be the selection of snakes from an available group. Unlike natural selection, this artificial selection could be carried out for desired characters. These characters also could be random, heritable changes (mutations). A prerequisite for artificial selection is the variability of traits.

Another path of true selective breeding in snakes would be the combination crossing of subspecies, through which new genetic combinations would be produced. This combination crossing followed by culling of unwanted varieties would be particularly promising if only one or two qualitative traits, determined by only one or a few genes and subject to few environmental influences, were involved. Such qualitative traits include coloration and color distribution.

Because of the countless possible combinations of genes in the mating of two individuals, all snakes are genetically different.

Top: Amelanism is the condition in which a snake loses much of its dark pigmentation, producing an "amelanistic," or "albinistic," specimen. Shown is an amelanistic Corn Snake, *Elaphe guttata guttata*.
Bottom: Striped varieties of the California Kingsnake, *Lampropeltis getula californiae*, have been selectively bred to produce unbroken dorsal striping. On most specimens, however, this stripe is broken in at least a few places. Both photos by L. Trutnau.

M = Melanophores present	E = Erythrophores Present
m= Melanophores Absent	e = Erythrophores Absent

a) Mating of recessive amelanistic snakes

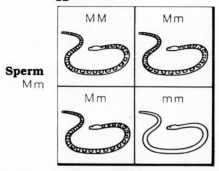

Egg cells Mm

	MM	Mm
Sperm Mm	Mm	mm

Result: 3 normal-colored Snakes (75%)
1 amelanistic Snake (25%)

b) Mating of recessive amelanistic-anerythristic snakes

Egg cells

	ME	Me	mE	me
ME	MMEE	MMEe	MmEE	MmEe
Sperm **Me**	MMEe	MMee	MnEe	Mmee
mE	MmEE	MmEe	mmEE	mmEe
me	MmEe	Mmee	mmEe	mmee

Result: 9 normal-colored Snakes (56%)   **3 amelanistic Snakes (19%)**

3 anerythristic Snakes (19%)   **1 "albino" Snake (6%)**

KNOWN HYBRIDS BETWEEN SPECIES OF SNAKES

Name	Scientific name	Name	Scientific name
Blacktail Rattlesnake X Western Rattlesnake	(Crotalus molossus X viridis)	Ringed Snake X Dice Snake	(Natrix natrix X tessellata)
Western Rattlesnake X Red Diamond Rattlesnake	(Crotalus viridis X ruber)	Dice Snake X Viperine Water Snake	(Natrix tessellata X maura)
Western Rattlesnake X Mojave Rattlesnake	(Crotalus viridis X scutulatus)	Asp Viper X Long-nosed Viper	(Vipera aspis X ammodytes)
Mojave Rattlesnake X Cascabel Rattlesnake	(Crotalus scutulatus X durissus)	Common Puff-Adder ~ Gaboon Viper	(Bitis arietans ~ gabonica)
Corn Snake X American Rat Snake	(Elaphe guttata X obsoleta)	Fischer's Slender-Boa ~ Rainbow Slender Boa	(Epicrates striatus ~ cenchria)
Central Asian Sand-Boa X Tartar Sand-Boa	(Eryx miliaris X tataricus)	Silent Sandsnake ~ Red-Striped Sand Snake	(Psammophis sibilans ~ subtaeniatus)
Yellow Anacona X Green Anaconda	(Eunectes notaeus X murinus)	Plains Garter Snake ~ Common Garter Snake	(Thamnophis radix ~ sirtalis)
Ringed Snake X Viperine Water Snake	(Natrix natrix X maura)	Long-nosed viper ~ Northern Adder	(Vipera ammodytes ~ berus)
		Asp Viper ~ Northern Adder	(Vipera aspis ~ berus)

Only maternal twins possess the same genetic makeup. In the mating of pure (homozygous) animals, Mendel's laws of inheritance would apply. In our further explanations, however, we will avoid theoretical discussions and instead will concentrate on the actual breeding of snakes.

First let us turn to the old breeder's concept of inbreeding, by which is understood the mating of animals that are more closely related to each other than is the average of the animals of a population. This very often is the case with snakes in the terrarium. Sometimes virtually all captive individuals of a species in a country are descended from a single pair or even one imported pregnant female.

Although close inbreeding, the mating of related animals of the first degree (mother to son, father to daughter, brother to sister, etc.), usually results in genetically healthy mates in the first generations without detrimental results, there is always the possibility that the foundation animals carried hidden (recessive) genetic defects. In the mating of distantly related or unrelated animals the chances of such factors coinciding in the fusion of the male and female gametes is quite remote. To be sure, the recessive "defective" genes also are handed down, but they are masked by the corresponding dominant gene from the mate. In the mating of closely related animals, these negative factors can turn up in a double dose (homozygous) and be expressed in the phenotype. The result can be deformities, very feeble offspring, or even stillbirths. An example is described in the literature in which six albinos appeared after the third inbred generation in one litter of 12 young Common Garter Snakes (*Thamnophis sirtalis*). The snakes were red-eyed, flesh-colored, and had only three rows of gray spots instead of the usual broad black bands. The majority of the albinos exhibited a variety of other genetic defects. The longest life span of the albinos was less than one year.

The simplest and surest way to avoid inbreeding defects and to produce strong, viable offspring is the breeding of unrelated animals. If there are no prospects of obtaining such animals, two separate breeding lines should be established in the second generation. Then after a few generations of close to extremely close inbreeding within these lines, an individual from the first line should be bred into the second line, and vice versa. This is called line breeding.

Little is known about the inheritance of qualitative traits such as coloration in snakes or in reptiles in general. It can be assumed, however, that the inheritance of color characters often is recessive and is determined by a single gene.

The first proof for this claim came in the 1940's, when a normal-colored male San Diego Gopher Snake (*Pituophis catenifer annectens*) was mated with an albino female and, in accordance with Mendel's laws of inheritance, the expected normal-colored off-spring were produced. (Normal color is dominant, so all offspring would be phenotypically normal, but they also would all carry the albino gene from the mother, making them genotypically heterozygous for albino). When a male of this generation was mated with the mother, the colors split up according to Mendel's second law: normal to albino in a ratio of 3 to 1. Later the same results were obtained with other species in the selective breeding of the Corn Snake (*Elaphe guttata*), California Kingsnake (*Lampropeltis getula californiae*), and the American Rat Snake (*Elaphe obsoleta*). Today professional snake breeders, especially in the United States, raise albinos in numerous snake species.

The form of albinism is determined by four types of pigment cells (chromatophores) in the skin (melanophores with black, erythrophores with red, xanthophores with yellow pigment, and iridophores that contain tiny iridescent crystals). In the Corn Snake (*Elaphe guttata*), for example, we find, besides complete albinos (lacking all pigment), amelanistic albinos lacking only the black pigment and anerythristic black-and-white specimens lacking the red pigment. The increased deposition of dark pigments in the skin (melanism) probably also is inherited recessively. Melanistic specimens (melanos) are common in the the the European *Vipera aspis* and *Vipera berus* and are a regularly available variety in the Common Garter Snake (*Thamnophis sirtalis*).

The inheritance of markings in snakes also has been studied. In the Viperine Water Snake (*Natrix maura*), for example, the striped pattern proved to be dominant over the spotted pattern. Subspecies crosses of the plain nominate form of the Ringed Snake (*Natrix n. natrix*) with spotted *Natrix natrix persa* yielded—to be sure in animals of different provenance—contradictory results. In one case the spots, in the other the lack of markings, was dominant.

Breeding attempts with Asian Cobras (*Naja naja*) showed that the variability of the spectacled markings probably is not geographically determined. Even within a clutch, variations ranging from the absence of spectacled markings through monocular to binocular

Whenever a species is offered to hobbyists in an albino variety for the first time, it commands a very high price. Subsequent breedings, however, usually cause those prices to gradually drop. Photo of an albino Diamondback Water Snake, *Nerodia rhombifer*, by R. D. Bartlett.

markings occurred. Differences in coloration of young snakes from a single clutch or litter—recall color variation in babies of the Green Tree-Python (*Chondropython viridis*) and the Emerald Tree-Boa (*Corallus caninus*), or the striped and banded young of the California Kingsnake (*Lampropeltis getula californiae*)—belong to this sphere of problems. Only the breeding of such species over many generations will allow conclusions to be drawn about the inheritance of such variation.

Only recently has the state of knowledge of reproduction of snakes in the terrarium reached the point that biotechnical techniques, such as have long been customary in the breeding of domesticated animals, are being used on occasion. Through the systematic administration of sex hormones, the events of reproduction, including ovulation, mating, egg-laying, and birth, can be stimulated and synchronized.

Artificial insemination opens up new opportunities above all in the propagation of snakes that show no interest in mating. With this method behavioral barriers to mating preventing natural crossing also could be overcome. Preliminary results of the long-term preservation of snake sperm by freezing and many years of storage in liquid nitrogen at -196°C (-320°F) show that in this area as well there are unforeseen prospects for the systematic breeding of snakes.

Hybridization

Now a few comments on hybridization in snakes. The modern definition of the species refers to the reproductive isolation of the population, not necessarily of the single individual. In the sense of a strict definition, only the products of crosses between animals of different species (interspecific hybrid) or higher taxonomic categories (intergeneric, interfamilial) would be called hybrids. Today, however, the term hybrid also is used (though incorrectly) to describe the product of a mating between individuals of different subspecies. This often occurs in nature where the ranges of neighboring subspecies touch. In scientific circles animals of such mixed populations are called "intergrades." Examples are "hybrids" between the Eastern Kingsnake (*Lampropeltis getula getula*) and the Florida Kingsnake (*L. g. floridana*), which occur as different varieties: the Blotched Kingsnake in the Florida Panhandle and the Outer Banks Kingsnake on the islands off North Carolina.

Hybrids between different species and genera have rarely been described in the wild. Under terrarium conditions crosses are less rare. This is because in the terrarium animals that in their natural ranges never would have encountered one other can come together; ecological differences that normally serve to isolate species are not present; and because of the absence of mates of the same species even differences in reproductive behavior could be overcome.

Verifiable hybridization becomes possible in the terrarium because the parents are known. Natural hybrids usually are questionable. Characteristic traits of both foundation populations as well as shared traits must be taken into account. As a symbol for these hypothetical hybrids, in which the mother and father cannot be classified in one or the other foundation form, the names are given in alphabetical order.

While there usually are few problems with respect to viability and reproduction in the crossing of subspecies of snakes, the situation is different with hybrids between species. Even after successful fertilization, embryos die prematurely and the youngsters are stunted or sterile.

Hybrids between animals of different families of reptiles generally are not known. Alleged crosses between the Common Viper (*Vipera berus*) and the Ringed Snake (*Natrix natrix*) have not been substantiated; the proof for this kind of hybridization apparently was falsified. Two older reports of intergeneric hybrids of reptiles are known: Timber Rattlesnake (*Crotalus h. horridus*) X Massasauga (*Sistrurus c. catenatus*) and Graham's Water Snake (*Regina grahami*) X Red-sided Garter Snake (*Thamnophis sirtalis parietalis*). Both were found in the wild and are considered to be hypothetical hybrids on the basis of the external characters of their assumed parents. Recently snake breeders have produced hybrids said to be between species of the genera *Elaphe, Lampropeltis,* and *Pituophis,* though scientific documentation of these claims apparently has not been published; the offspring, however, do seem to have characters of the purported parents. It should be noted that all these reported intergeneric hybrids belong to groups that are very closely related and sometimes considered by taxonomists to be artificial genera. *Sistrurus* has been considered a synonym of *Crotalus, Regina* species are of uncertain relationship to the genera *Thamnophis* and *Nerodia,* and the North American species assigned to *Elaphe, Lampropeltis,* and *Pituophis* are closely related and perhaps all belong to one genus. Just looking at generic names on a list of hybrids may be misleading.

Among the known snake hybrids, those involving rat snakes (*Elaphe*) might be of particular interest to the hobbyist. They include (among an ever-growing list because of increased captive-breeding) a cross between the Corn Snake (*Elaphe g. guttata*) and the Everglades Rat Snake (*Elaphe obsoleta rossalleni*) known both as a wild hybrid and documented as a terrarium cross, and crosses between the Texas Rat Snake (*Elaphe obsoleta lindheimeri*) and the Great Plains Rat Snake (*Elaphe guttata emoryi*) as well as between the Corn Snake and the Yellow Rat Snake (*Elaphe obsoleta quadrivittata*). In the latter hybridization, a hybrid female hatched and proved to be fertile when backcrossed with the father. A remarkable cross between the geographically widely separated Amur Rat Snake (*Elaphe schrencki*) and the American Yellow Rat Snake (*Elaphe obsoleta quadrivittata*) unfortunately could not be verified because the remaining egg was opened prematurely and the embryo died. Hybrid rat snakes, usually involving subspecies of *Elaphe obsoleta* crossed with *Elaphe gutta,* lave unfortunately become rather common on dealer price lists. Many seem to be fertile, resulting in a further mix of genes with continued cross-breeding. The same situation exists with *Lampropeltis* crosses.

Crosses among subspecies are more common and would seem—unfortunately—to occur far more often in the terrarium of the hobbyist than is reported in the herpetological literature. Consequently, the interbreeding of the subspecies of the Boa Constrictor, *Boa constrictor constrictor, imperator,* and *occidentalis*, is all the more lamentable because pure subspecies have already become very rare in the terrarium. About the same thing is true of crosses of subspecies of the Rainbow Boa (*Epicrates cenchria*). Also known are crosses between the subspecies of the Asian Rock-Python (*Python molurus*); they presented problems in some cases, because the hybrid offspring were not viable or proved to be sterile when backcrossed.

Crosses between subspecies of colubrids are relatively common, especially in the Ringed Snake (*Natrix natrix*), the American Rat Snake (*Elaphe obsoleta*), the Common Kingsnake (*Lampropeltis getula*), and the Pine and Gopher Snakes (*Pituophis melanoleucus* and *catenifer*).

Specific crossing attempts can provide information about phylogenetic relationships, particularly if the viability and fertility of the hybrids are analyzed. Taxonomic changes have been made based on the ability to hybridize and reproduce in the wild. For instance, *Storeria tropica* and all its subspecies were reclassified as subspecies of the Brown Snake (*Storeria dekayi*) because of naturally occurring intermediates, while intergradation of subspecies of the various garter snakes (*Thamnophis*) has proved very useful in trying to understand that confusing genus. Hybrids formed under captive conditions generally are not given much taxonomic value.

Propagation of Specific Snakes

Of the more than 2,500 snakes species classified in over 400 genera, there is no doubt that scarcely more than 10% have been bred so far in captivity. The majority of the breedings, particularly of rare species, were achieved in zoos and public terraria. Often they were simply a lucky and unique accidental occurrence. Many reports on the propagation of snakes are based on egg-laying or the birth of young snakes by pregnant wild-caught females. Frequently even then the rearing of the offspring proved unsuccessful. Consequently, statistical data such as appear in the *International Zoo Yearbook* and other zoo reports provide misleading information on actual breeding results. Requiring that both parent snakes are captive-bred for actual captive breeding to be recognized would contribute to the consistency of data.

To some extent breeding reports tend to come from the homelands of the animals. Temporally shifted seasons, tropical or subtropical conditions, and rainy and dry seasons often present the hobbyist in the cool and not especially reptile-friendly northern and central Europe and United States with hard-to-solve problems in the care of such species.

Despite all obstacles to breeding, the quite extensive palette of snake species bred in the terrarium makes it impossible to include all species in a book of this kind. Data on reproduction are for the most part taken from the literature,

COMPILATION OF BREEDING DATES IN PYTHONS

Species	Reproductive event	Quarter I.	II.	III.	IV.	Incubation temperature (C°)	Incubation period days
White-lipped Python (*Liasis albertisi*)	Mating		●	● ●		32...33 (28...30)	(72...74)
	Egglaying			●	●		
	hatched				●		
Scrub Python (*Python amethystinus*)	Mating					24...29	(77)
	Egglaying			●			
	hatched			●	●		
Children's Python (*Liasis childreni*)	Mating		●			25...32	(41... 66)
	Egglaying	● ●	● ● ●		● ● ●		
	hatched	●	●	● ●	●		
Australian Water Python (*Liasis mackloti fuscus*)	Mating					24...29	(61...64)
	Egglaying				●		
	hatched				●		
New Guinea Water Python	Mating	●				31...32 (26...33)	57...89
	Egglaying		● ●	● ●			
	hatched			●	●		
Black-headed Woma (*Aspidites melanocephalus*)	Mating					24...27	
	Egglaying			●			
	hatched				●		
Diamond Python (*Python spilotus*)	Mating	● ● ●				24...32	37...102
	Egglaying	●	● ● ●	●	● ●		
	hatched	●	● ● ●	● ● ●	●		
Reticulated Python (*Python reticulatus*)	Mating	●		●	● ● ●	29...32	(54...105)
	Egglaying	● ● ●			●		
	hatched		● ● ● ●				
Asian Rock-Python (*Python molurus*)	Mating	● ●			● ●	29...32	56...85
	Egglaying	● ●	●				
	hatched		● ●	● ●			
African Rock-Python (*Python sebae*)	Mating	● ●			●	30...32 (...33)	75...109
	Egglaying	●	● ● ●	●	● ●		
	hatched	● ●	●	●	●		
Ball Python (*Python regius*)	Mating	● ●		●	● ●	29...32 (...33)	59...81 (58...105)
	Egglaying	● ●	● ● ●	●			
	hatched		●	● ● ●	●		
Angolan Dwarf Python (*Python anchietae*)	Mating					28...30	72...75 (60...)
	Egglaying				●		
	hatched	●					
Green Tree-Python (*Chondropython viridis*)	Mating	●	● ●	●		28...31	50 (...65)
	Egglaying	● ●	●	● ●	● ●		
	hatched		●		● ●		

although all authors cannot be named individually. In addition, species were chosen that have become rare in the wild today or, like the venomous snakes, do not belong in the hands of every hobbyist.

If you compare the breeding conditions and results published in the literature with one another, you will notice large deviations again and again. Success was possible, however, because of the adaptability of many species. This shows that no universal recipe for the preprogrammed reproduction of a species in the terrarium exists. Often related species or species that live under the same environmental conditions exhibit very similar reproductive behavior and can be kept and propagated under the same terrarium conditions.

The hobbyist has to learn from his own mistakes, particularly since these mistakes usually have tragic results for his animals. But this does not rule out the need to experiment. Without intuition and patience, the assimilation of the experiences of others, and reflection on your own failures, success will be a long time coming. Then successful breeding will be all the more satisfying.

Birth of a Cuban Boa, *Epicrates angulifer*. Photo by K. H. Switak.

Species

BOAS AND PYTHONS

The superfamily of the giant snakes and their allies (Henophidia) is made up of five families, some 40 genera, and about 150 species. The family of the giant snakes (boas and pythons, Boidae), which alone contains about 25 genera and 90 species, plays an important role in the terrarium hobby. The remaining families, the pipesnakes (Aniliidae) with largely unknown biology, the filesnakes (Acrochordidae), and the shield-tailed snakes (Uropeltidae), as well as the sunbeam snakes (Xenopeltidae) represented by one or two species, probably are all livebearers but are rarely kept in the terrarium. Observations of the reproduction of these snakes would contribute fundamentally to our knowledge of the natural history of the families.

GIANT SNAKES (BOIDAE)

Pythons and boas have highly variable requirements in captivity. This should not be surprising, because they come from the most diverse climatic and ecological regions and some are barely 50 cm (20 in) long, while others grow to over 10 meters (33 ft) in length. Many species of the genera *Python*, *Eunectes*, and *Liasis*, because they grow to such large size and are so aggressive, can be kept in the terrarium only under special conditions. Although not all species of giant snakes appear to be facing imminent extinction, the captive breeding of as many species as possible could make it unnecessary to import specimens for the terrarium hobby. The mass slaughter of giant snakes for the production of luxury leather goods still commonplace in many countries is an abomination. Using them for food can only be eliminated by intensive education of the native populations and by raising the standard of living.

NEOTROPICAL PYTHONS (LOXOCEMINAE) AND ROUND ISLAND SPLITJAW BOAS (BOLYERIINAE)

The Loxoceminae contains only one species, the approximately 1.2 meters (4 ft) Central American *Loxocemus bicolor*, the Neotropical or Mexican Python. It primarily burrows in the ground and lays eggs. Because it is rarely seen in collections, hardly any keeping experiences exist.

Unlike other giant snakes, the Round Island boas or splitjaws (so-called because the upper jaw is divided) do not possess vestiges of the pelvis. The two species, *Bolyeria multocarinata* and *Casarea dussumieri*, live on Round Island near Mauritius; both have terrestrial habits. Though the Burrowing Splitjaw (*Bolyeria multocarinata*) apparently became extinct by the late 1960's, in the late 1970's it was estimated that about 100 sexually mature individuals of the Slender Splitjaw (*Casarea dussumieri*) still existed. Three to ten eggs are laid by this species, providing additional reason to include it in its own subfamily rather than the true boas (which all give live birth). A hatched youngster weighed only 4 grams (0.14 oz). Feeding proved to be problematic; presumably insects are part of the natural diet. The species changes in color from bright brown to a deep blue black.

PYTHONS (PYTHONINAE)

The pythons are native to Africa, Asia, and Australasia. Differences that separate them from the boas (Boinae) include the presence of teeth on the premaxillary bone and their egg-laying habits.

Ross, in an international study of the propagation of these snakes in the terrarium, collected the following information on measures that stimulate pythons to breed:
1) separating of the sexes for several weeks before mating;
2) having an excess of males for mutual sexual stimulation in ritual fights and to reduce the risk of having sexually inactive animals;
3) keeping the snakes at fairly cool temperatures for two to four weeks before mating at nighttime temperatures of just above 20°C (68°F); this applies both to snakes kept at constant high temperatures of 29 to 32°C (84-90°F) and those already exposed to daily nighttime cooling.

With artificial maturation of the clutch in

the incubator, which is generally recommended to reduce the risk of failed clutches, optimal brooding temperatures of 29 to 32°C (84-90°F) as well as a relative humidity of 90 to 100% have proved effective. The brooding of the eggs by the mother is considered advisable only when:

1) the breeder has too little experience with the artificial incubation of snake eggs;
2) the eggs cannot be removed and the size and form of the clutch do not allow the use of an incubator;
3) the clutch is laid unexpectedly and no incubator is available.

WHITE-LIPPED PYTHON (*LIASIS ALBERTISI*)

Until a few years ago, the White-lipped or d'Alberts' Python was considered to be a subspecies of the Water Python (*Liasis mackloti*). It is a characteristic species of the herp fauna of New Guinea and is chiefly found in monsoon forests, gallery forests along rivers, and palm swamps near the coast. It grows to a length of up to 3 meters (10 ft).

Keeping: Like other *Liasis* species, it needs a roomy terrarium heated to 28 to 30°C (82-86°F) during the day, with climbing and bathing facilities. The acclimation of wild-caught specimens presents considerable problems; acclimated specimens, on the other hand, prove to be quite hardy, but they often continue to be very aggressive.

Propagation: Liasis albertisi has seldom been bred so far in the terrarium. In one attempt the eggs rotted because the female apparently was not ready to breed. In another case, after 72 to 74 days only four youngsters hatched from 17 eggs incubated artificially at 28 to 30°C (82-86°F) on water-holding plastic granules. The rearing of the 40-45-cm (16-18-in) young snakes, which caught and swallowed almost hairless mice after the first molt, was without problems. Other hobbyists had to force-feed the youngsters with young mice at first.

SCRUB PYTHON (*PYTHON AMETHISTINUS*)

The Scrub or Amethystine Python can—though only in exceptional cases—grow to over 8 meters (26.4 ft) in length. Numerous Southeast Asian islands, plus New Guinea and northern Australia, are its homeland. Most imports seem to be from Indonesia.

Propagation: Scrubs lay 7 to 15 eggs, which the female coils around and incubates. An approximately 2-meter (6.6-ft) female laid two unfertilized and ten fertilized eggs, 11.2 X 5.2 cm (4.5 X 2 in), from which the first of seven youngsters with an average length of 65 cm (26 in) and a live weight of 50 grams (1.75 oz) hatched at 28°C (82°F) after 77 days. The initially brown youngsters did not assume the typical tapestrylike markings until they had undergone several molts.

CHILDREN'S PYTHON (*LIASIS CHILDRENI*)

The barely 1.5-meter (5-ft) Children's Python from Australia and neighboring islands is primarily terrestrial and usually stays in a hiding place during the day.

Keeping: Because of the small size of this snake, a medium-sized terrarium with plenty of hiding places is adequate. The air temperatures of 25 to 30°C (77-86°F) can safely fall by nearly 10°C (18°F) at night.

Propagation: Ritual fights have been observed between sexually active males. Pregnant females lie coiled in a tight spiral, as also is observed in other species, with the head as the upper terminus, the body often twisted around its longitudinal axis. In ten clutches described in the literature, the number of eggs ranged from 5 to 14. A few infertile eggs as well as several dead fetuses in different stages of development apparently are normal for captive breeding. The incubation period was 41 to 54 days at 30°C (86°F); at 28°C (82°F) it increased to 61 to 66 days.

OTHER SPECIES

The Australian Water Python (*Liasis mackloti fuscus*) by no means lives exclusively in water, as its name might imply. Like other *Liasis* species, however, it likes high humidity in the terrarium and spraying with lukewarm water. In an Australian terrarium, the animals mated in mid-August; one female laid 11 eggs, which she incubated herself after a gestation period of 53 days. After 61 to 64 days the 40-centimeter (16-in), 45-

White-lipped Python, *Liasis albertisi*. Photo by L. Trutnau.

gram (1.6-oz) youngsters hatched; they molted for the first time within five days and soon after that took nestling mice.

The New Guinea Water Python (*Liasis mackloti mackloti*) is a forest-dweller. Separating the sexes at temperatures of 26 to 33°C (79-91°F) and 100% humidity stimulates the readiness to breed and leads to the laying of 9 to 17 eggs about 6.0-6.7 X 3.5-3.8 cm (2.5-2.8 X 1.4-1.5 in) weighing 44.2 grams (1.5 oz). Under artificial incubation the youngsters hatched after 57 to 65 days (incubation temperature 28 to 30.5°C, 82-87°F), producing identical twins as a rare event. In another case they did not hatch for 87 to 89 days (incubation temperature 29°C, 84°F). The young New Guinea Water Pythons were between 40 and 50 cm (16-20 in) long and weighed about 30 grams (1 oz). The coloration of the parents was attained at an age of about six months; at nine months one youngster weighed 186 grams (6.5 oz) and had grown to a length of 89 cm (36 in).

The rare Black-headed Woma (*Aspidites melanocephalus*), a crepuscular terrestrial snake from northern Australia, probably has been bred so far only once in Australia, where two youngsters hatched from ten fertile eggs.

DIAMOND PYTHON (*PYTHON SPILOTUS*)

The slender, 3-4-meter (9.9-13.2 ft) Diamond Python is considered to be quite delicate and is rarely very persistent in the terrarium. It lives in Australia, New Guinea, and the Tokelau Islands, chiefly in dry forest and shrubby steppes. The Diamond Python and the Carpet Python (*P. s. variegatus*) usually are considered to be subspecies or ecological forms of a single species or group of very closely related species. This form once was called *M. argus*.

Keeping: In general, Diamond Pythons voluntarily feed on small mammals and birds in the terrarium.

Propagation: In a successful breeding of the subspecies *P. s. variegatus*, the 1,150-gram (40 oz) male and 2,325-gram (81.4 oz) female mated in late August/early September at terrarium temperatures of about 31°C (88°F). Additional matings took place the following January and February at 28°C, 82°F (22°C, 72°F, at night). In June, 13 eggs were laid and incubated at 32°C (90°F). After 55 and 56 days, seven very aggressive youngsters hatched which were 31 to 46.5 cm (12.5-18.6 in) long and weighed 10 to 26 grams (0.35-0.9 oz). Interestingly, the coloration and markings of young Diamond Pythons are very variable. Several were very dark and displayed fine markings, one youngster was very light in color with large rhomboid markings, and others resembled their parents. The first molt took place after barely three weeks; two young immediately ate young fuzzy mice and the others had to be force-fed repeatedly before they fed independently.

From another clutch of 32 eggs, ten healthy young pythons hatched after 77 to 79 days (incubation temperature 29°C, 84°F), even though the eggs had collapsed completely and seemed to be spoiled. Barely 11 months later the same female laid a new clutch that weighed a total of 1,850 grams (64.75 oz) and from which 37 young hatched after 70 to 73 days at an incubation temperature of 30°C (86°F). The incubation temperature, which had been raised by 1°C (2°F), shortened the incubation period by a week.

After another 11 months a third clutch (1,820 grams [63.7 oz], 36 eggs) was laid,

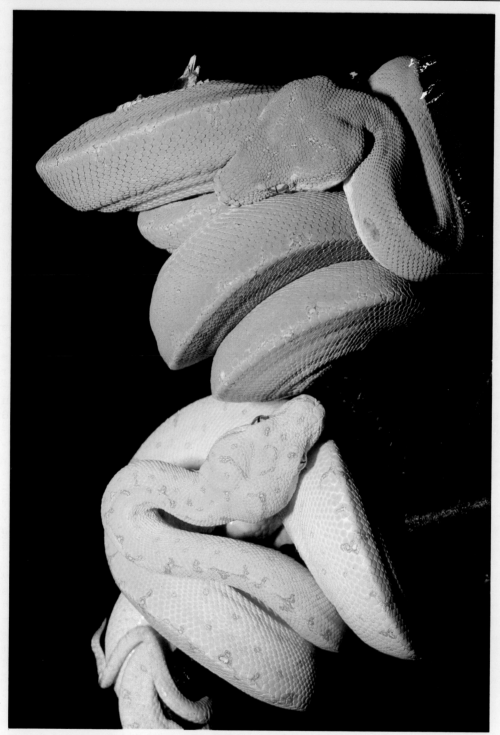

Green Tree Python, *Chondropython viridis*. Photo by I. Vergner.

from which only 12 youngsters hatched after the eggs had been cooled to 20°C (68°F) several times because of power failures. The young Diamond Pythons were 43 to 55 cm (17-22 in) long and weighed 28 to 35 grams (1-1.2 oz). They had to be force-fed at first and later preferred the most active prey animals. After barely a year they had reached a length of 83 to 105 cm (33-42 in) and a weight of 68 to 264 grams (2.4-7.9 oz).

RETICULATED PYTHON (*PYTHON RETICULATUS*)

Southeast Asia, Indonesia, and the Philippines are the homelands of this giant snake, which usually grows to a length of 5 to 6 meters (16.5-19.8 ft). It is an inhabitant of the warm rainforest but is also found in settled regions.

Keeping: This python, which usually spends the day resting, is easy to keep in a roomy terrarium with sturdy climbing branches. It is not fussy with respect to diet, eating everything from chicks to mice to chickens, rabbits, and young pigs; any prey that can be overpowered is devoured.

Propagation: In the Reticulated Python copulations often lasted for hours and usually were observed from October to December. After three to four months, 18 to 49 eggs weighing about 250 grams (8.8 oz) were laid; they had to be incubated artificially if the female abandoned the clutch prematurely. The clutch often included a few unfertilized eggs, and some eggs contained dead fetuses in different stages of development. Twitching movements of the body, as have been described in some other incubating female pythons, have not been observed in the Reticulated Python. Whether incubating female pythons feed depends on their physical condition. One snake took only dead rats and another ate nothing and lost 15 kilograms (33 pounds). The natural and artificial incubation periods of the Reticulated Python apparently vary depending on the most diverse conditions during incubation. Combined data for natural and artificial incubation periods ranged from 54 to 105 days. Individual young take up to 36 hours to leave the opened egg.

Rearing: Newly hatched Reticulated Pythons weigh 105 to 170 grams (3.7-6 oz) and usually are 60 to 80 cm (24-32 in) long. After about two weeks the youngsters molt for the first time, and soon after that they catch their first medium-sized mice. With a good food supply their growth could scarcely be slowed down. A length of 1.3 meters (4.3 ft) after three months is reported. One youngster ate 46 rats, 27 mice, and 10 hamsters in its second year of life and was 2 meters (6.6 ft) long and weighed 1,500 grams (52.5 oz). After an additional 60 rats and 65 mice in the third year of life, it reached 2.6 meters (8.6 ft) and 4,500 grams (157.5 oz). In the rearing of another brood, 26-month-old Reticulated Pythons were 222-240 cm (89-96 in) long and weighed 6,450 to 8,850 grams (226-310 oz).

ASIAN ROCK-PYTHON (*PYTHON MOLURUS*)

The paler nominate form (Indian Python, *P. m. molurus*) of the Asian Rock-Python is native to India and Sri Lanka and is very rare. The darker subspecies (Burmese Python, *P. m. bivittatus*) of Burma, Southeast Asia, southern China, and Indonesia is kept more frequently in the terrarium and is considered to be the most hardy and "sociable" python. At a length of 6 to 8 meters (19.8-26.4 ft), it grows significantly larger than the nominate form. Moist sites, especially in proximity to bodies of water, are preferred.

Propagation: Although daytime temperatures between 28 and 32°C (82-90°F) and nighttime temperatures 5 to 8°C (9-15°F) cooler generally are recommended, animals from the northern part of their range given an eight- to ten-week overwintering at temperatures of about 18 to 20°C (65-68°F) without terrarium lighting were stimulated to start mating activities. Other breeders succeeded in propagating Burmese Pythons without changing the light and temperature cycles. After matings in December and January, the females of both subspecies laid their eggs primarily from March to May, with clutch sizes of 13 to 35. However, extreme clutch sizes of 100 to 107 also are known.

During incubation the terrarium temperature should be kept as constant as possible at about 30°C (86°F). At this temperature the incubation of the eggs of the Indian subspecies took 61 to 85 days, those of the Burmese

Burmese Python, *Python molurus bivittatus*. Photo by Mella Panzella.

subspecies 58 and 69 days. Twenty-two eggs of a female Indian Python weighed on average almost 250 grams (8.8 oz) and measured on average 10.1 X 6.9 cm (4 X 2.8 in). In five clutches of the Burmese Python consisting of an average of 29 eggs, the eggs weighed only 180 to 200 grams (6.3-7 oz) and were 9.4 X 6.0 cm (3.8 X 2.4 in). Much of this difference probably is due to the larger number of eggs in the Burmese. From the 22 large Indian eggs, 16 youngsters weighing 142 grams (5 oz) hatched; 46 young Burmese Pythons weighed 120 to 135 grams (4.2-4.7 oz) and averaged 58 cm (23 in) in length. Breeding and raising Asian Rock-Pythons in the terrarium certainly is not an uncommon event, as is shown by a female that laid three clutches at two-year intervals.

AFRICAN ROCK-PYTHON (*PYTHON SEBAE*)

The African Rock-Python lives in the open African savannah and reaches a length of 6 meters (19.8 ft). In the terrarium it usually accepts willingly any warm-blooded prey of appropriate size. The daytime terrarium temperature should be between 25 and 32°C (77-90°F) and can be allowed to sink at night to 18 to 22°C (65-72°F). In South Africa it hibernates for two to three months.

Propagation: In the captive breedings described by several authors, African Rock-Pythons laid from 17 to 56 eggs in January, April to July, or November. Artificial incubation lasted 75 to 89 days, depending on temperature (25 to 33°C, 77-91°F). The 60- to 70-cm (24-28-in) hatchlings grew rapidly and were up to 2.5 meters (8.3 ft) long at five years of age.

BALL PYTHON (*PYTHON REGIUS*)

The colorful Ball Python of western and central Africa is a nocturnal snake that usually specializes in a particular species of nocturnal prey. For this reason wild-caught specimens often present problems in feeding. Their terrarium can be relatively small but must offer ample climbing facilities. The temperature should be about 26 to 32°C (79-90°F) and should fall as little as possible at night.

Propagation: How a well-thought-out scheme for keeping the Ball Python can stimulate its reproduction is shown by the following examples.

At first two males and one female were kept separately at an ambient temperature of 27 to 31°C (81-88°F), a relative humidity of 80 to 90%, and a 14-hour day length. From May to August the animals were given a 40-50-minute sun bath every five days and from August to October a daily five-minute irradiation with ultraviolet radiation, as well as vitamin supplements in the food. In August the nighttime temperature was lowered to 22°C (72°F) for 20 days and after that a male was put with the female. On the following night the first matings were observed. After a gestation period of 120 to 140 days, the female laid a clutch of eight soft-shelled white eggs. The body temperature of the incubating female, which was checked with an electronic thermometer, was 31 to 32°C (88-90°F), and that of the male only 27 to 29°C (81-84°F). On the 68th day the first young Royal Python cut through its shell; all eight young pythons hatched and weighed an average of 46 grams (1.6 oz) and averaged 42.5 cm (17 in) in length.

Another hobbyist succeeded in propagating his Royal Pythons after he had first simulated the native rainy season from June to August by spraying the terrarium three times a day; he followed this with an absolutely dry season from December to March. The snakes mated from December to February. The female laid ten fertile eggs in early June that weighed 85 to 90 grams (3-3.2 oz) and were 4.5 to 5 cm (2 in) long. Artificial incubation at 29 to 33°C (84-91°F) on moist peat moss took 58 to 59 days. Eight youngsters hatched; they were 33 to 38 cm (13.2-15.2 in) long and weighed between 28 and 65 grams (1-2.3 oz). All were reared.

Other authors reported clutches of six to nine eggs, and quite notable egg sizes of 7.2 to 8.7 X 5.2 to 6.1 cm (2.9-3.5 X 2-2.4 in) and incubation periods of 90 to 97, even 105 days, were recorded. The length of the youngsters was reported as 23 to 43 cm (9.2-17.2 in). There were no problems with food intake in any of the breedings.

OTHER SPECIES

The Blood Python (*P. curtus*) from Southeast Asia and the Angolan Python (*P. anchietae*) usually are difficult to acclimate in the terrarium and are short-lived. Since the first description of the Angolan Python over 100 years ago, relatively few specimens have reached the museums of the world and it remains a very uncommon snake in captivity. From the clutch of a collected pregnant female, young snakes hatched after 69 to 74 days. Five other Angolan Pythons left their eggs after 60 to 65 days.

The Blood Python, on the other hand, has been bred repeatedly in the terrarium. For example, after an observed mating in late January at an ambient temperature of only 26°C (79°F), a clutch of 16 fertile and three infertile eggs was found on March 1 in the female's shelter box; a portion of the clutch obviously had become too warm there. The eggs rested on damp moss and were incubated artificially at 29 to 30°C (84-86°F)—27°C (81°F) at night—and 90% average relative humidity. After 69 to 72 days, three young Blood Pythons hatched. They weighed 44.3, 64.5, and 68.9 grams (1.55, 2.26, 2.41 oz) and were 35 to 45 cm (14-18 in) long. They had to be force-fed with nestling rats at first. With natural incubation, young Blood Pythons usually hatched after 70 to 75 days and were 33 to 45 cm (13.2-18 in) long and weighed 37 to 69 grams (1.3-2.4 oz).

GREEN TREE-PYTHON
(*CHONDROPYTHON VIRIDIS*)

The Green Tree-Python grows up to 1.8 meters (72 in) long. It is native to New Guinea, neighboring small islands, and northern Australia, where it lurks in wait for prey in a characteristic resting posture in branches of tropical rainforest trees.

Keeping: A warm, moist, well-planted, roomy terrarium with ambient temperatures of about 25 to 32°C (77-90°F), which should fall only slightly at night, offers good conditions for propagating this snake. Its color usually is bright green, but it also can be yellow-green or, rarely, blue. Dead mice, small rats, and birds are taken from forceps.

Propagation: Mating was stimulated by shortening the day length from 12 to 14 hours to 8 hours in January and February while simultaneously lowering the temperature by 5 to 6°C (9-11°F) and separating the sexes.

After pairs were kept separately from April to August, matings took place from late August to November. The gestation period is approximately 105 to 112 days. Clutches of 15 to 23 eggs were laid from late November to February or, after winter matings, from March to July directly on a moderately moist substrate of peat moss or in a plastic tub with moist sphagnum moss in the climbing tree.

Eggs of the Green Tree-Python reached an average size of 3.9 X 2.5 cm (1.6 X 1 in) and weighed about 15 grams (0.53 oz). The eggs were laid in batches of two or three. With naturally incubated eggs the young snakes, about 30 cm (12 in) long and weighing about 9 grams (0.32 oz), hatched after 50 to 62 days. Artificial incubation at 28 to 29°C (82-84°F) took 60 to 65 days. After cutting open the egg shell, the youngsters stayed in the eggs about 12 more hours and left them at night. Remnants of the yolk sac sometimes did not fall off for a week.

Rearing: The coloration of young Tree-Pythons is surprising. Even from the same clutch the handsomely colored snakes can be bright yellow, brownish white, reddish brown, or, more rarely, even red. Only in the course of several molts do they change color and assume the green color of their parents. Frequently young Tree-Pythons refuse food after the first molt. They then must be force-fed with pinkie mice or pieces of mice until they feed on their own. This can take months.

Forced-feeding often is quite difficult. It was reported that some youngsters lost consciousness because of fairly strong pressure on the neck area, and in one case a youngster could only be saved through artificial mouth-to-mouth respiration through a tube. Although drinking water was always available, the young Tree-Pythons preferred to drink water drops after the spraying of the terrarium furnishings. The growth of the young pythons was highly correlated with the amount of food eaten. The largest and most voracious young snakes were twice as heavy at three months of age and twice as long after six months as at hatching.

Green Tree Python, *Chondropython viridis*. Photo by I. Vergner.

BOAS (BOINAE)

In contrast to the oviparous Old World pythons, the boas are ovoviviparous and are principally snakes of the New World, although the genera *Acrantophis* (Madagascar ground-boas), *Sanzinia* (Madagascar tree-boas), and *Candoia* (Pacific island-boas) occur far from the Americas. The systematic classification of the boas is not settled; burrowing representatives sometimes are placed in their own subfamily, Erycinae.

BOA CONSTRICTOR (*BOA CONSTRICTOR*)

Keeping: Native to both dry and wet forested regions of Central and South America, the Boa Constrictor usually grows to a length of only 3 meters (9.9 ft) and therefore feels at home in a not particularly roomy giant-snake terrarium with localized bottom heating, a climbing tree, and a large water basin. Temperatures of 25 to 32°C (77-90°F), which can sink to 20 to 22°C (68-72°F) at night, are adequate. Healthy animals are good food exploiters, but obese animals are scarcely capable of reproducing. For that reason, Boa Constrictors as well as other snakes should not be overfed. Instead, they need a varied diet. Younger boas, for example, take house and field mice, white mice, young laboratory rats, hamsters, sparrows, chicks, and nestling pigeons; older boas take adult rats, guinea pigs, rabbits, and pigeons that have fallen from their nests. (Feeding feral domestic pigeons raises the danger of transmission of salmonella.)

Propagation: Boa Constrictors have been bred many times in the terrarium. The nominate form, the form most often kept in captivity, is the one usually bred. Breedings of *B. c. occidentalis* and *B. c. ortonii* as well as the most diverse subspecies hybrids have been reported more rarely. As a result, the "terrarium boa" has almost attained the position of a house pet, but unfortunately pure-blooded subspecies are now rare.

Boa Constrictors do not seem to need specific stimuli to promote their readiness to breed. They mate throughout the year with peaks in August to September and February to May. Possibly certain manifestations of domestication in snakes bred over many generations play a role here. After the male often wanders restlessly for days, copulations lasting several hours finally take place. Because in most cases all of the copulations are not observed, it is not known which mating led to pregnancy. Consequently, the gestation periods of Boa Constrictors reported in the literature exhibit considerable variation, from 17 to 42 weeks. Finally the day arrives when the young boas, usually still inside the transparent chorions (egg membranes), are born. A bubble with a young snake appears every three minutes or even faster. A few youngsters may stick their heads out of the chorions and actively test their new environment with their tongues immediately after leaving the mother. Most of the young free themselves soon after that. There is no sign of an egg tooth. The entire process of birth can last two to three hours. The mother snake loses about 4 kilograms (8.8 pounds) of weight, about half her body mass. The usual litter size is 20 to 30, but the range is 12 to more than 60 young. The number of unfertilized eggs and fetuses that have died in different stages of development is variable.

Good females are very productive. In nine years one Boa Constrictor gave birth to almost 350 live young. This of course demands a good constitution and excellent care.

Though the majority of newborn boas begin their existence in the terrarium with no human assistance at all, a little "obstetrics" can be useful. Sometimes it is necessary to tear the chorion. At first the newborns are still connected to the yolk sac by an umbilical cord about 15 cm (6 in) long; if the umbilical cord does not soon tear on its own, it can be cut with scissors. A piece about 10 cm (4 in) long still attached to the snake soon shrivels up and falls off after a few days. A lukewarm bath after birth cleans the young snakes of mucus deposited during birth. Young Boa Constrictors are 35 to 55 cm (14-22 in) long and weigh 45 to 95 grams (1.6-3.3 oz); typically they are barely 50 cm (20 in) long and weigh about 60 grams (2.1 oz).

Rearing: Each youngster has unique mark-

Boa Constrictor, *Boa constrictor*. Photo by R. D. Bartlett.

ings that it retains its whole life. As a rule, rearing presents few problems. Newborn snakes have been observed making the first attempts to catch young mice only eight hours after birth, without, however, eating them. The first molt is completed one to three weeks after birth; at that time the excretion of firm, yellowish droppings also is observed. Soon after that the first half-grown—by the most robust youngsters even fully grown—mice are eaten. Nestling sparrows are a special "delicacy," and usually even youngsters that refuse to eat mice cannot resist them. In the meantime, under certain circumstances even on the day of birth the mother has started to feed again. Well-fed young snakes grow fast. One-year-old individuals reached lengths of about 80 cm (32 in) and weighed almost 300 grams (10.5 oz). Reproductive maturity can be attained, assuming adequate development, at an age of three years. A Boa Constictor only 135 cm (54 in) long gave birth to six live young as well as two unfertilized eggs but certainly was not yet sufficiently developed to have been bred.

RAINBOW SLENDER-BOA (*EPICRATES CENCHRIA*)

Of the slender boas of the genus *Epicrates*, the Rainbow Slender-Boa is the most frequently bred species. Unfortunately, this species has the same problems of subspecific hybridization as the Boa Constrictor (*Boa constrictor*). The ten subspecies, distributed in the forests and rocky regions from Costa Rica to Argentina, usually are hard to tell apart, which contributes to the problem of hybridization.

Keeping: Rainbow Slender-Boas are about as adaptable as Boa Constrictors and can be kept under the same conditions. Because they seldom grow longer than 2 meters (6.6 ft), they are more suitable for the normal beginner's terrarium than their larger relatives.

Propagation: Separating the sexes for a short period of time can stimulate the readiness to breed, but keeping them together the whole year also leads to success. In one instance a hobbyist kept four Rainbow Slender-Boas of a plain brown subspecies (one male and three females) together at 32°C,

90°F (at night around 20°C, 68°F) in the summer and 28°C, 82°F (about 15°C, 59°F, at night) in winter at constant day lengths of 14 hours. During the mating season, which under these conditions lasted from mid-September to late November, the male was very restless and ate very little. The increasing body weight of the female indicated pregnancy. Finally the abdomen of this animal was so distended that skin was visible between the scales 30-40 cm (12-16 in) in front of the cloaca. Females in late stages of pregnancy displayed an increased need for warmth and often rested supine with open mouth, gasping for breath. Births usually took place from late March to late April, always in the morning hours, and lasted about 20 minutes. The otherwise very peaceful mothers were very aggressive at this time. The young snakes usually broke through the thin, elastic chorion immediately after birth but occasionally after an hour. Remnants of the umbilical cord disappeared within a day. The litter sizes of 8 to 21 youngsters correlated with the length and body weight of the mother. On the other hand, the length and weight of the young Rainbow Boas varied little: they were about 35 cm (14 in) long and weighed about 30 grams (1 oz). Over 11 years, the breeding group mentioned earlier produced 12 litters with a total of 165 young. It is noteworthy that there was only one stillbirth and two infertile eggs during this period. Under the conditions described, each of the females gave birth at intervals of two years despite yearly copulations.

Rearing: The young boas molt after six to ten days. Some of them have already swallowed their first nestling mice before molting. The further rearing was unproblematic. At first two to eight baby mice were fed. Starting at a body length of about 40 cm (16 in), 14-day-old mice were fed. At a length of 50 to 60 cm (20-24 in) the youngsters, which at first were speckled, took on the uniform brown coloration of their parents. In the second year of life males clearly lagged behind their female siblings of the same age in weight and length. Sexual maturity can occur at an age of two and a half years. Because of the risk of interrupting growth after the first litter, however, females should not be mated until they are four years old and are about 1.5 meters (5 ft) long; males can be mated at three years of age.

OTHER SPECIES

The Fischer's Slender-Boa (*Epicrates striatus*) from Haiti and the Bahamas needs a tall terrarium with a sturdy, branched climbing tree. Daytime temperatures of 24 to 30°C (75-86°F) are adequate. Because this species hibernates from December to January in its homeland, the temperature in the terrarium should be lowered by 5 to 6°C (9-11°F) during this period to stimulate the readiness to breed. Matings took place from December to May. Fifteen to 20 youngsters were the rule in captive breedings. Often, however, unfertilized eggs and eggs that had died in early stages of development were also deposited, so that 40 or more youngsters could be expected in successful litters. Newborn Fischer's Slender-Boas were 27 to 50 cm (10.8-20 in) long and weighed 7 to 14 grams (0.25-0.5 oz) or more. With these Slender-Boas, as well as with the Boa Constricor (*Boa constrictor*), the Garden Tree-Boa (*Corallus enydris*), and anacondas (*Eunectes*), females ate unfertilized eggs during birth or shortly thereafter.

The Cuban Slender-Boa (*Epicrates angulifer*) is strictly protected in its homeland. At a maximum length of 4.5 meters (14.9 ft), this is the largest slender-boa species. This snake has been bred repeatedly in the terrarium. Copulations in the period from January to May sometimes lasted a whole day. In a litter of six live young and one dead youngster produced in mid-October, the newborns were on average 72 cm (28 in) long and weighed 175 grams (6.1 oz). Seven young Cuban Slender-Boas from a litter produced in mid-September were 58 to 63 cm (23.2-25.2 in) long, weighed 185 to 200 grams (6.5-7 oz) the day after birth, molted after 16 to 20 days, and took the first food independently between the 20th and 31st day of life. A few hours after birth the initially very peaceful snakes became very aggressive and tried to bite any presumed enemy. In comparison, young Jamaican Slender-Boas (*Epicrates subflavus*) were only 49 cm (19.6 in) long and weighed 15 grams (0.52 oz).

GREEN ANACONDA (*EUNECTES MURINUS*)

Keeping: Living exclusively near and in water in their South American homeland, anacondas all need a large water bowl in the terrarium. They often lie in their bowl the whole day at water temperatures of 26 to 29°C (79-84°F). The Green Anaconda (*Eunectes murinus*) grows to a length of 7 to over 9 meters (23.1-29.7 ft) and is the largest living snake after the Reticulated Python (*Python reticulatus*). This species has been bred successfully over several generations in captivity and is quite interesting to keep in a special terrarium, as long as uniformly high daytime and nighttime temperatures of about 30°C (86°F) can be maintained. The Green Anaconda's excitability and tendency to bite demand caution, however.

Propagation: Matings of the Green Anaconda, which occurred from January to July in the northern hemisphere, usually took place in shallow water. After a gestation period of about seven months, the mother snake often gave birth to the young anacondas at five-minute intervals in the water basin. It was observed that the young immediately left the water and scattered in all directions after yawning repeatedly for about three seconds. The 8-cm (3.2 in) yolk sac usually broke off from the 30-40-cm (12-16 in) umbilical cord within the first hour of life; after ten days the remnants of the umbilical cord had disappeared completely. An egg tooth was not observed either in young anacondas or in most other species of boas. The number of live young ranged from 10 to 90, on average about 40; their length at birth was 50 to 95 cm (20-38 in) and they weighed between 190 and 450 grams (6.7-15.8 oz).

Rearing: The offspring of the Green Anaconda spent most of their time in the water, where the snakes also usually spent the night, ate (primarily mice—fish were rejected by some young anacondas), and defecated. Like the Ball Python, the Green Tree-Python, and members of the genera *Calabaria*, *Charina*, *Candoia*, *Lichanura*, and *Tropidophis*, young anacondas also assume a "ball" form. This is more likely to frighten predators by its unusual form than a concealing (cryptic) behavior pattern. With a

Colombian Rainbow Boa, *Epicrates cenchria maurus*. Photo by J. Vergner.

Cuban Slender-Boa, *Epicrates angulifer*. Photo by I. Vergner.

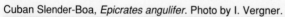

good diet, Green Anacondas grow very rapidly, as is shown by the median values cited for individuals of one litter:

At birth: 268 grams (9.4 oz), 74 cm (29 in);

At five months: 404 grams (14.1 oz), 96 cm (38.4 in);

At ten months: 1,067 grams (37.3 oz), 140

contrast to its large relative retains a very attractive coloration even in old age. It has been bred over several generations. Only 2 to 22 young were produced after a gestation period of six to nine months. The birth lengths were generally 40 to 70 cm (16-28 in) and the youngsters weighed

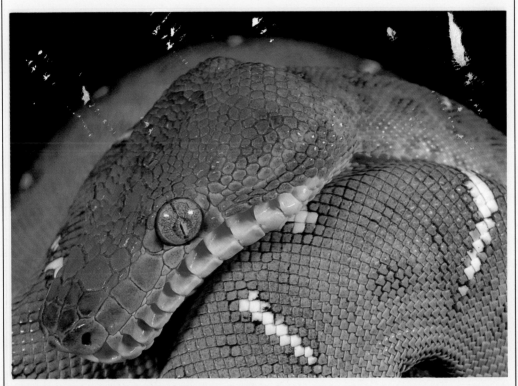

Emerald Tree Boa, *Corallus caninus*. Photo by Jim Merli.

cm (56 in);

At 14 months: 1,767 grams (61.8 oz), 152 cm (61 in). The largest specimen of the litter by this time weighed 2,800 grams (98 oz or 6.13 pounds) and was 170 cm (68 in) long.

YELLOW ANACONDA (*EUNECTES NOTAEUS*)

Like the Green Anaconda, this species is very partial to water, but it also inhabits clearings in the rainforests of northern Argentina, southern Brazil, Bolivia, and Paraguay.

Propagation: This species is ready to breed at 2 meters (6.6 ft) in length, and in

between 95 and about 150 grams (3.3-5.3 oz).

Rearing: Getting the young to take their first meal often presented problems. For example, among other things, hairless and hairy young mice, fish, and frogs were refused, but chicks of Japanese Quail and later also chicks of domestic chickens were accepted immediately. Later the young anacondas took mice, young rats, and hamsters. Their interest in fish varied—some snakes did not eat fish or ate them only in exceptional cases, while others feed exclusively on fish.

EMERALD TREE-BOA (*CORALLUS CANINUS*)

Among the Central and South American boas of the genus *Corallus*, the Emerald Tree-Boa (2-3 meters, 6.6-9.9 ft) is the New World counterpart to the Green Tree-Python *(Chondropython viridis)*. Though it usually is quite difficult to acclimate because of its sometimes pronounced individual food preferences, it is doubtless one of the most beautiful giant snakes.

Keeping: A roomy, well-planted rainforest terrarium with a large water bowl and daytime temperatures between 25 and 35°C (77-95°F), 20 to 25°C (68-77°F) at night, as well as high humidity, is necessary for the well-being of this snake. Stuffy air must be avoided. Emerald Tree-Boas often are already damaged when they reach captivity. Probably the most common transport injury is excessively high water loss (dehydration) that cannot be balanced out by drinking. Older snakes often suffer from constipation, enteritis, and intestinal torsion as a result of too low humidity. Younger Emerald Tree-Boas do not always adapt to eating rodents in the terrarium; although rodents are convenient to feed, they do not necessarily correspond to the natural prey. Undigested remnants of bone and hair can cause volvulus (intestinal torsion and obstruction), which can be minimized with a diet of Zebra Finches, parts of one-day-old chicks, and the like.

Propagation: Copulations of Emerald Tree-Boas were observed from December to March. The births of the up to ten young that are bright red on the back took place primarily from August to early October after a gestation period of about seven months. Birth often occurred high in the branches of the climbing tree. The small snakes crawled actively from the cloaca by means of strong serpentine motion and found a hold in the branches or fell to the floor. Average lengths at birth of 40 to 50 cm (16-20 in) with a body weight of 27 to 45 grams (1-1.6 oz) were reported. As food they voluntarily accepted, among other things, dead mice from forceps. The young started to change color at 19 weeks of age; this process took six to eight weeks. The intense green color of the parents was attained after the seventh molt at an age of about 15 months.

OTHER SPECIES

Garden Tree-Boas (*Corallus enydris*), both the nominate form and the subspecies *C. e. cooki*, Cook's Tree-Boa, are less troublesome and have been bred over several generations in the terrarium. After copulations from February to April and a gestation period of about seven months, 3 to 30 young, usually 5 to 20, were produced. They were 30 to 53 cm (12-21 in) long and weighed 8 (0.28 oz)—in large litters—to 30 grams (1.05 oz). Although some of the youngsters voluntarily accepted fuzzy young mice or Zebra Finches, others had to be force-fed at first with small aquarium fishes or pinkie mice.

MADAGASCAR TREE-BOA (*SANZINIA MADAGASCARIENSIS*)

The Old World counterpart to the Garden Tree-Boa is the Madagascar Tree-Boa (up to 2.5 meters, 8.25 ft, long), which also makes similar demands with respect to the terrarium and the temperature regime, but which manages with lower humidity. These boas are said to differ in aggressiveness according to their collecting locality on Madagascar. In their homeland they estivate from late May to August.

Propagation: A rest period at temperatures of about 17 to 20°C (63-68°F) with low light levels could be a decisive prerequisite for breeding in the terrarium. The gestation period lasts about five months. The young were 34 to 42 cm (13.6-16.8 in) long and weighed 22 to 35 grams (0.8-1.2 oz) at birth. In terrarium births, even those of imported, pregnant wild-caught females, deformities have frequently been observed, above all curvature of the spine. Whether sudden changes in temperature or genetic abnormalities were responsible has not been determined. Healthy young snakes were reared without much trouble on mice of appropriate size.

ROSY BOA (*LICHANURA TRIVIRGATA*)

The Rosy Boas (80-90 cm, 32-36 in) come from arid habitats of western North America and have become quite popular over the last few years. The taxonomy is quite confused at the moment, but most herpetologists recognize a single species with three subspecies (*L.*

t. trivirgata, L. t. roseofusca—sometimes considered a full species, and *L. t. gracia*), but other subspecies names commonly are applied to captive-bred animals. There are several color patterns being bred for the market today.

Propagation: Corresponding to the climatic conditions in its homeland, it is recommended to observe a three- to four-month hibernation at 10 to 15°C (50-59°F). In this way, particularly in the United States, *L. t. roseofusca* has been bred repeatedly. After a four-month gestation period the mother snake gave birth to 4 to 12 young. They were already 25 to 30 cm (10-12 in) long and were reared on pinkie mice and small chicks. Within a year the best feeders had grown to a length of over 70 cm (28 in); they were sexually mature at two years of age. *L. trivirgata* was kept from late November to late February at daytime temperatures of 24°C (75°F), 21°C (70°F) at night, and day lengths of ten hours. Then the day lengths were increased by half an hour a week to 16 hours and the terrarium temperature raised to 30°C (86°F), 27°C (81°F) at night. In July several copulations up to 40 minutes long were observed, and in mid-November four young snakes 30 cm (12 in) long came into the world. Only one day after birth, well before the first molt at the age of 8-12 days, the first little *Lichanura trivirgata* ate a five-day-old mouse.

CUBAN DWARF-BOA (*TROPIDOPHIS MELANURUS*)

Several species of the meter-long (or less) dwarf-boas of the genus *Tropidophis* have been bred in moderately warm tropical terraria with deep substrates and climbing facilities. Dwarf-boas often feed on frogs and toads in the wild and cannot always be acclimated to small mammals in the terrarium. The Cuban Dwarf-Boa probably is the most common species of the approximately 16 species from the Antilles and northern South America. Its scientific specific name refers to the deep black tip of the tail of most adults. Juveniles, in contrast, have a bright light green tail tip.

Propagation: A 47-cm (18.8 in), 76-gram (2.7 oz) Cuban Dwarf-Boa gave birth in late November to two youngsters 15.2 and 14.3 cm (6 and 5.7 in) long and weighing 2.0 and

1.6 grams (0.07 and 0.06 oz). With other breeders, after about 70 days of pregnancy up to 21 young were produced that weighed between 3.2 and 4 grams (0.11-0.14 oz) and were about 18 cm (7.2 in) long.

Rearing: The young snakes are very hard to rear. Sometimes they must be force-fed with mouse parts. An example gives evidence of the rate of growth of this snake: A Dwarf-Boa weighing 3.2 grams (0.11 oz) at birth ate small frogs and weighed 32.8 grams (1.15 oz) after one year and 62 grams (2.2 oz) after two years at a body length of 50.2 cm (20 in). At an age of one and a half years it started to feed on mice. Among the other *Tropidophis* species, breedings of the Bahaman Dwarf-Boa (*T. canus*) as well as the birth of four young (1.5 grams—0.05 oz, 16 cm—6.4 in) by a wild-caught female of the Two-Spot Dwarf-Boa (*T. semicinctus*) from Cuba are known. All of the young presented problems in rearing.

SAND-BOAS (*ERYX*)

Sand-boas are small (50-100 cm, 20-40 in) snakes from relatively dry, open habitats such as steppes and the edges of deserts. They are kept relatively frequently because they are satisfied with small terraria with deep substrates, a few hiding places, and small mammals of appropriate size as food. The Rough-Scaled Sand-Boa (*E. conicus*), the Brown Sand-Boa (*E. johni*), the Central Asian Sand-Boa (*E. miliaris*), and the Kenyan Sand-Boa (*E. colubrinus*)—all inhabitants of warm regions—have been bred time and again in the terrarium. Rough-Scaled Sand-Boas, for example, gave birth 1 to 11 young with lengths of 19 to 22.5 cm (7.6-9 in). This colorful species, which ranges from Pakistan through India to Sri Lanka, has been reported (probably incorrectly) to lay eggs in some regions. Brown Sand-Boas, following a gestation period of about four months, repeatedly gave birth to 25-28-cm (10-11-in), approximately 20-gram (0.7-oz) banded young, not all of which immediately accepted nestling mice.

The Central Asian Sand-Boa, also called the Dwarf Sand-Boa because of its length of only 50 cm (20 in), has a species-typical adaptation of the eyes: they are directed diagonally upward, which makes its life in

Garden Boa, *Corallus enydris*. Photo by J. Vergner.

loose sand easier (it is the only *Eryx* to normally live in loose sand). Terrarium temperatures between 25 and 35°C (77-95°F) with nightly cooling as low as 10°C (50°F) suit this species quite well. A two- to three-month hibernation at 8 to 10°C (46-50°F) stimulates the reproductive activity of this species, which probably does not reach sexual maturity until its fourth year of life. Usually in June, 6 to 12 young about 12 to 14 cm (5-5.6 in) long are produced. Young Central Asian Sand-Boas prey on large insects but are most easily reared with pinkie mice.

The Tartar Sand-Boa (*Eryx tataricus*) also has been overwintered at cool temperatures and has been bred often in captivity. Litters of 10 to 20 youngsters (length 12 to 20 cm, 5-8 in) produced in August to September were reared with baby mice. A terrarium hybrid with a male Central Asian Sand-Boa also is known.

Several breeding reports exist for *Eryx colubrinus loveridgei*, the most commonly seen form of the Kenyan Sand-Boa. Several weeks of dryness and separation of the sexes proved to be beneficial for the stimulation of copulation in summer. Litter sizes were 4 to 17 live young. The typical body lengths of the newborns were between 16.5 and 20 cm (6.6-8 in) and their birth weights ranged from 5 and 9 grams (0.18-0.32 oz). It proved practical to rear the young sand-boas individually in small terraria; most took their first mice independently. Stuffing them with pink mice was very difficult when force-feeding became necessary. Therefore, dead pink mice were stuffed into a syringe with a rounded tip with a diameter of 4.5 millimeters (0.2 in) and crushed; the mouse pap could now easily be pressed into the gullets of the little sand-boas.

The Javelin Sand-Boa (*Eryx jaculus*), distributed from the Balkan Peninsula through Asia Minor to North Africa, is one of the most frequently kept sand-boas in the terrarium. Breeding was successful after hibernation at 5°C (41°F) in the usual overwintering box. After the temperatures were gradually raised again to 32°C (90°F), 20°C (68°F) at night, in late February, the first copulations took place in mid-March. After 107 days, in mid-June, after vigorous body contractions by the fe-

Above: The Madagascar Tree-Boa, *Sanzinia madagascariensis*. Photo by J. Vergner. **Below:** Cuban Dwarf-Boa, *Tropidophis melanurus*. Photo by I. Vergner.

male, one young 20 cm (8 in) long weighing 8 grams (0.28 oz) was born. Its rearing with pinkie mice in a refrigerator container presented no problems.

ADVANCED SNAKES

The largest superfamily of snakes is the relatively advanced Caenophidia, usually said to contain five families:
1) colubrids (Colubridae) with about 14 subfamilies and about 300 genera;
2) elapids or cobras (Elapidae) with about 50 genera;
3) sea snakes (Hydrophiidae) with two subfamilies and 15 genera;
4) vipers (Viperidae) with three subfamilies and 11 genera; and
5) pitvipers (Crotalidae) with 12 genera.

This family arrangement, though familiar, has been challenged repeatedly of late. Colubridae is though to consist of several perhaps unrelated lines of snakes, while the Elapidae and Hydrophiidae are intimately related and difficult to separate in traditional fashion. Few herpetologists in North America accept the Crotalidae as a valid family, preferring to think of the pitvipers as a subfamily of Viperidae. There also are several small and relatively obscure groups of snakes that fall variously between the colubrids and the venomous snakes and have been accorded separate family status by some workers.

The extraordinary variety of the Caenophidia with respect to morphology as well as ecology and habits makes an exact systematic classification very difficult. Particularly with the colubrids, as knowledge of the phylogenetic relationships continues to be gained, the hobbyist will have to reckon on inconvenient but necessary systematic reclassifications. From the most species-rich family, the Colubridae, the following subfamilies include important representatives among terrarium animals:
1) water snakes (Natricinae) with about 37 genera;
2) true colubrids (Colubrinae) with about 50 genera;
3) American hognoses (Xenodontinae) with 27 genera;
4) wolf snakes (Lycodontinae) with about 52 genera;

5) African egg-eating snakes (Dasypeltinae) with one genus;
6) rear-fangs (Boiginae) with 73 genera.

The group of the rear-fangs (Boiginae) probably is not a closely related unit in the modern sense, but rather a stage that various genera have reached independently of one another.

I've included data on the various venomous snakes because many hobbyists are interested in these, though the actual keeping of venomous snakes is filled with legal problems and the constant chance of a deadly bite. Sea snakes are scarcely suitable for private snake keeping and are not discussed; all but one genus (*Laticauda*) give live birth.

WATER SNAKES

Many snakes from the subfamily Natricinae are among the species that are particularly suited for keeping in the terrarium—even for the beginner in the terrarium hobby—and are easy to breed. The frequently kept species of the numerous water snakes and garter snakes can be classified in groups based on their ecological requirements. Thus, the species that live more or less amphibiously, are tied to open water, and feed on fishes and amphibians in the wild can be dealt with as a group. The genera *Natrix* and *Nerodia* are typical representatives of this group. Keeping these water-loving species in a roomy aquaterrarium, which is recommended everywhere in the hobby literature, is doubtless correct, as is the advice that even the most aquatic species must have an absolutely dry basking site if they are to avoid various bacterial and fungal "blister" diseases. Pasty excrement deposited in the water bowl, however, makes frequent water changes necessary. The keeping of water snakes for many years by the author shows that fairly large removable water bowls in otherwise dry terraria can offer the snakes good environmental conditions. Moss and a few pieces of root complete the furnishings of the cage.

Many of these water-loving snakes are satisfied with an exclusively fish diet in the terrarium. Live and dead fishes of appropriate size, pieces of fish with bones and entrails, and also strips of fish fillet fortified with calcium and vitamin preparations (especially vitamins D and the B-complex) make up the basic diet. Depending on the species, age, and individual requirements, earthworms, slugs, pinkie mice, strips of beef heart, and so on are also eaten. Southeast Asian Fish Snakes, *Xenochrophis piscator*, kept by the author preferred newborn rats.

Typical representatives of the water snakes are the Eurasian grass snakes (*Natrix*), which formerly included a very broad range of species but which today are limited to species found in Europe and Asia, including *N. natrix*, the Ringed Snake; *N. tessellata*, the Dice Snake; *N. maura*, the Viperine Water Snake; and *N. megalocephala*, which was described in 1987.

RINGED SNAKE (*NATRIX NATRIX*)

The most common snake in central Europe is the Ringed Snake. With the exception of Ireland and a few Mediterranean islands, it is found throughout Europe. To the east its range extends beyond Lake Baikal. The larger females reach a median length of 85 cm (34 in) in central Europe; males, in contrast, grow only to 68 cm (27 in). Specimens over 1 meter long (40 in) are rare; the record length is 2.05 meters (6.77 ft). Of the eight subspecies of the Ringed Snake, the pretty *Natrix natrix persa* from southeastern Europe and western Asia is the most common in European terraria.

Propagation: Overwintering the Ringed Snake from October to March at temperatures of about 5°C (41°F) induces the snakes to copulate in about late April to May. Wild female Ringed Snakes prefer to lay their clutches from early July to mid-August in piles of reeds, leaves, compost, or sawdust; this preference should be addressed in the terrarium by supplying a suitable laying container. In the wild, especially favorable sites are used for years by many females, leading to mass layings of hundreds or even thousands of eggs. The number of eggs per clutch varies with the size and age of the female. Six and 105 eggs are the extreme values. The average is eight to ten for first clutches, about 30 eggs with older females. There are two characteristic egg forms: an elongated-oval type and a shorter, rounder type. The pure white eggs usually are about 23-40 mm long by 12-20 mm in diameter (0.92-1.6 X 0.48-0.8 in) and weigh 3 to 5 grams (0.1-0.18 oz).

The incubation of Ringed Snake eggs at 25 to 28°C (77-82°F) presents no difficulties. Depending on the incubation temperature and its fluctuations, the developmental period ranges from 30 days (constant 28 to 30°C, 82-86°F) to about 75 days (under conditions in the wild). Freshly hatched Ringed Snake resemble their parents in coloration and are 14 and 22 cm (5.6-8.8 in) long; the average value of 600 specimens was 18.8 cm (7.52 in). They weigh 2.7 grams (0.95 oz) on average. Allowing for different temperature requirements for subspecies from warmer regions, what was said about reproduction applies fundamentally for all subspecies.

Noteworthy with Ringed Snakes are several descriptions of hatching of twins, as well as the laying of two giant eggs by a specimen of *N. n. schweizeri*. The giant eggs were 6.7 and 6.1 cm (2.7 and 2.4 in) long, 1.5 cm (0.6 in) wide, and weighed 6 and 5.5 grams (0.21 and 0.19 oz), respectively. After 45 days of incubation, one male and one female youngster 23 and 24 cm (9.2 and 9.6 in) long, respectively, hatched from them. Subspecific hybrids are also known.

DICE SNAKE (*NATRIX TESSELLATA*)

Dice Snakes are kept and bred under conditions very similar to those for the Ringed Snake, which is not surprising because the ranges of the two snakes are in part identical: The Dice Snake ranges from eastern Germany, the Czech and Slovak Republics, and Italy to central Asia.

Propagation: Dice Snakes have been bred over several generations. In one case, an 85-cm (34-in) male mated in late May with a 103-cm (41.2-in) female that laid seven eggs 46 days later. The normal clutch size of the Dice Snake is between 5 and 25 eggs. Six young snakes, 18 to 20 cm (7.2-8 in) long, hatched from the eggs 42 days after they were laid. They took guppies after a week as the first food. At an age of 18 months a captive-bred female mated and laid 14 eggs (weighing 7 to 9 grams, 0.25-0.32 oz) after 59 days. A second clutch (16 eggs including five unfertilized eggs) was laid 43 days later, and a third clutch of 13 eggs was laid after another 36

Above: Dice Snake, *Natrix tessellata*. Photo by J. Vergner. **Below:** Florida Water Snake, *Natrix fasciata pictiventris*. Photo by D. Schmidt.

Above: Red-tailed Rat Snake, *Gonyosoma oxycephalum*. Photo by F. Golder. **Below:** Common Garter Snake, *Thamnophis sirtalis*. Photo by L. Sassenburg.

days, from which, however, only two young-sters hatched. The incubation times of these three clutches ranged from 38 to 42 days. Repeated egg-laying within a year certainly is not unusual under good terrarium conditions.

SIMILAR SPECIES

For Viperine Water Snakes (*Natrix maura*) of western Europe and northwest Africa, two to three clutches a year in the terrarium is not out of the ordinary. With one Viperine, which laid four times in one year, the interval between the clutches was 34 to 41 days. The number of eggs normally ranged from 4 to 20 and the incubation periods (temperature 25 to 28°C, 77-82°F) were between 40 and 53 days. The youngsters usually were 15 to 18 cm (6-7.2 in) long.

The rearing of the young of all *Natrix* species presents few problems because aquarium fishes, earthworms, and pieces of fish are readily taken.

AMERICAN WATER SNAKES (*NERODIA*)

The genus *Nerodia*, which includes some ten species, is distributed from Canada to Mexico but is absent from western North America (where largely replaced by species of garter snakes, *Thamnophis*). With certain differences in temperature corresponding to their more northern or southern ranges, all species and their many subspecies can be kept under similar conditions. The American water snakes make the same demands with respect to keeping in the terrarium as the representatives of the genus *Natrix*, but all are livebearing and usually grow longer and heavier than the Ringed Snake.

Propagation: A cool overwintering at 8 to 12°C (46-54°F) for two to three months (5 to 8°C, 41 to 46°F, with northern forms) is recommended. Hibernations lasting five to six months are not harmful with northern species such as *Nerodia sipedon* and even some *N. erythrogaster*, but a period of this length is not necessary for reproductive stimulation.

The size of the litters produced from May (southern forms) to October varies greatly and averages about 20 to 40 young. There is considerable variation in the body lengths of the newborns: 12 cm (4.8 in) in some *N. sipedon* to 32 cm (12.8 in) in *N. rhombifer*. Large numbers of young are common—-of the Green Water Snake (*Nerodia cyclopion*) a record litter of 101 young is known, and the Northern Water Snake (*N. sipedon*) with 99 is not far behind.

I will use the Florida Water Snake (*N. fasciata pictiventris*) as an example of breeding these snakes because I bred them over several generations. In one instance, a pair was observed copulating repeatedly in late February, only a few days after warming following hibernation, which had lasted for ten weeks at 8°C (46°F) in a terrarium without artificial lighting. The female was about 90 cm (36 in) long and weighed 620 grams (21.7 oz); the male, on the other hand, was only 75 cm (30 in) long and weighed 200 grams (7 oz). Similar sex-specific differences in size are typical of many water snakes. The snakes were kept at temperatures of 22 to 28°C (72-82°F), 18 to 22°C (65-72°F) at night. They were fed mostly dead food fishes. Starting on June 13 the female refused food, visibly increased in girth, and gave birth to young on July 7.

Rearing: All young of the Florida Water Snake molted on the first or second day of life and were on average 27 cm (10.8 in) long. With no problems at all, they took from a dish small strips of fish starting on the second or third day of life and grew rapidly. Their rate of growth was dependent on the keeping temperature and the appetite associated with it. At temperatures of about 28°C (82°F) the animals fed almost daily and grew very quickly. Lower temperatures delayed digestion. Two to three feedings a week then were sufficient. Only a few days after giving birth the parents copulated again, and on October 28 a second litter with 19 young was produced. No deformities or stillbirths occurred in any of the litters. Because the youngsters had developed well, they were overwintered at cool temperatures in the first year of life. At an age of one year they were between 40 and 50 cm (16-20 in) long; they reproduced at two years of age.

FISH SNAKE (*XENOCHROPHIS PISCATOR*)

Asian water snakes should be kept at temperatures of about 24 to 30°C (75-86°F) with slight nighttime cooling. One common member of the genus *Xenochrophis* is the Fish Snake, which ranges from Pakistan to southern China and south to the Indo-Australian Archipelago. Adults are up to 1.2 meters (4 ft) long. Fish Snakes, typical snakes of rice fields, are extremely pugnacious and produce bites that bleed heavily. Specimens do not necessarily become less aggressive after acclimation.

Propagation: Depending on the climatic conditions in their large range, Fish Snakes may estivate or hibernate, and simulating these conditions can help to stimulate reproduction. Fish Snakes have been propagated repeatedly. The reported record clutch consisted of 88 eggs, and the 17-21-cm (6.8-8.4-in) young hatched after a 62-89-day incubation period. They molted several days after hatching and soon caught small fishes, the principal prey of the Fish Snake. Like most water snakes, the youngsters also took tadpoles and small frogs.

SIMILAR SPECIES

Another genus from southern and Southeast Asia is *Amphiesma*. This genus contains about 39 species and like *Xenochrophis* was formerly classified in the genus *Natrix*. The most familiar species is the Rufous-naped Keelback (*A. stolata*), a very adaptable snake that feeds on young mice, earthworms, and beef heart in addition to fish and fish fillets in the terrarium. In certain regions of its homeland it estivates during the dry season and hibernates in the cooler north. Other species of *Amphiesma* and closely related genera occasionally appear on the market.

In the terrarium the snakes bred readily from January to April when exposed to sunlight. After a gestation period of 58 and 60 days, four to six eggs only 1 X 2 cm (0.4 X 0.8 in) were laid; clutch sizes of up to 14 have been reported in the wild. After incubation periods of 50 to 62 days at 25 to 30°C (77-86°F), the young hatched at lengths of 20-24 cm (8-9.6 in). They proved to be easy to feed with fish fillets and strips of beef heart, later with small fishes and pinkie mice. The Australian *Amphiesma mairi* (now in the genus *Tropidonophis*), which is said to be able to exhibit autotomy of the tail, lays 5 to 12 eggs; its young are 13-18 cm (5.2-7.2 in) long and are supposed to prefer tadpoles and the smallest frogs as the first foods, which makes sense because the adults eat frogs and fishes.

Despite its peacefulness, *Amphiesma stolata* has been reputed to have a venomous bite, but this may be due to confusion with different but superficially similar species. Several genera of the Natricinae are known to be mildly venomous even though they lack fangs and true venom glands. At least two cases of bites by the handsome black, green, and red Tiger Keelback, *Rhabdophis tigrinus*, proved to be fatal to the human victims. In the care of *Rhabdophis* species, several of which are available occasionally and have been bred, the most important rules for keeping venomous snakes must be observed, all the more so because no antiserum is available and the effect of any particular bite is unpredictable.

RED-TAILED RAT SNAKE (*GONYOSOMA OXYCEPHALUM*)

Based on osetological characters (particularly of the vertebral column), the Red-tailed Rat Snake occupies an uncertain position in the subfamily Natricinae, though some authors still classify them with the rat snakes (*Elaphe*). Two green rat snakes from the India-Burma area (*E. prasina*, *E. frenata*) sometimes are placed in *Gonyosoma*, so obviously the taxonomy of these snakes is far from being settled. Extensively distributed over southern Asia, the Red-tailed Rat Snake grows to a length of 2 meters (6.6 ft) and usually is difficult to acclimate, particularly since freshly imported snakes often arrive in poor physical condition. They are strongly arboreal snakes that are native to mangrove forests and bamboo thickets and which prey on birds and small mammals. Well-acclimated specimens, however, can be quite hardy and may breed in the terrarium.

Propagation: Keeping the sexes separately is a prerequisite for mating. The clutch sizes in the terrarium usually ranged from six to eight pure-white eggs, from which the young

Above: Corn Snake, *Elaphe guttata*, laying eggs. **Below:** Yellow Rat Snake, *Elaphe obsoleta quadrivittata*, with eggs. Both photos by K. Dedekind.

Above: Gray Rat Snake, *Elaphe obsoleta spiloides*, just hatched. Photo by D. Schmidt. **Below:** Fox Snakes, *Elaphe vulpina*. Photo by V. Nagele.

hatched after 84 to 91 days at 28 to 29°C (82-84°F). The egg dimensions at the time of laying were 5.2 to 6.0 X 2.6 to 2.8 cm (2-2.4 X 1-1.1 in); they weighed on average about 27 grams (0.95 oz). The newborn snakes were 38 to 54 cm (15.2-21.6 in) long. Three specimens of the F1 generation, among them one female, became sexually mature after about four years and also reproduced.

GARTER SNAKES (*THAMNOPHIS*)

The genus *Thamnophis* embraces over 20 species and numerous subspecies. They have an undivided anal scale, which distinguishes them from the species of *Nerodia*. As a rule, the identification of species and subspecies is quite difficult for the hobbyist, and even for the experts. In general, garter snakes usually range from 50 to 80 cm (20-32 in) in length and are rather slender. *Thamnophis gigas*, the Giant Garter Snake, grows to 1.5 meters (5 ft) in length.

The various species of garter snakes are ecologically quite adaptable and are found from Canada to Central America, from the coast to altitudes of 2,400 to 2,800 meter though usually in the vicinity of water or at least damp meadows.

Keeping: Unlike other more water-loving Natricinae, garter snakes mainly live on land. They prefer moist habitats, but also colonize forested and mountainous sites. In the terrarium, dry keeping conditions are preferable to those that are constantly moist. Climbing facilities and hiding places as well as a water bowl are adequate prerequisites for healthy care. Wild garter snakes feed on a diverse list of foods, but in the terrarium they can be fed relatively easily with fishes of appropriate size (live or dead), strips of fish, lean meat, pinkie mice, slugs, and earthworms. Vitamin supplements should not be neglected. Garter snakes are sensitive to vitamin B deficiency. The flesh of saltwater fishes and minnows contains the enzyme thiaminase, which breaks down vitamin B1. Garter snakes with vitamin B deficiency exhibit poorly coordinated jerky movements and fall on their sides or their backs.

Overwintering at cool temperatures is the most important reproductive stimulus. In nature, garter snakes hibernate for various periods of time depending on their locale; this applies even to snakes from subtropical Florida. Only the Central American species from warm lowland regions probably do not need to hibernate (those from the higher, cooler mountains may need hibernation). I have found it beneficial to leave all snakes in their terraria to hibernate. The temperature should be lowered gradually over a period of two weeks to 8°C (46°F) in December and the terrarium lights turned off. After eight weeks the room temperature is slowly increased to 18°C (65°F) and heat from the lighting raises the temperature in the terraria to the required 22 to 30°C (72-86°F). Hibernation can of course also take place in a suitable box filled with moss and leaves. It is better to keep juveniles at warm temperatures and to continue feeding them in the first winter of their lives. This results in stronger animals.

Propagation: The mating season begins a few weeks after the end of hibernation, after copious feeding and the first molt. Under favorable conditions in the terrarium, a second period of mating activity was observed, which led to a second litter. Several males in mating condition often followed one female, crawled with undulating movements over the female's back, and tried, while embracing the female's tail, to insert a hemipene into her cloaca. In several species the males have been seen to bite the necks of the females as a component of mating behavior. Copulation was terminated after 10 to 20 minutes.

All *Thamnophis* species give birth to live young, which leave the thin chorion during or shortly after birth. The gestation period of garter snakes seems to depend on the ambient temperature as well as genetics. For *T. sirtalis*, 87 to 116 days are reported; a Butler's Garter Snake (*T. butleri*) carried young for 90 days; and for *T. elegans*, 120 to 150 days are reported. During pregnancy most females continue to feed with normal appetites; individual snakes even feed until a few days before giving birth. The female gives birth to all the young of the litter within one to two hours. In addition, particularly with young females, stillbirths and infertile eggs are not unusual. Typically the number of young produced ranges from 4 to 35. For *T. sirtalis* a record litter of 85 young is reported in the literature. Depending on species, litter size, and the size of the mother, young garter snakes usually are 11 to 24 cm (4.4-9.6 in) long and weigh 2 to 4 grams (0.07-0.14 oz).

Rearing: The newborns molt in the first hours after birth. The occurrence of a birth usually is detected by the presence of shed skins scattered through the terrarium, the youngsters having long since crawled to hiding places. The young grow rapidly with generous feedings of the smallest fishes, pieces of fish, and earthworms every two or three days. Under certain circumstances they already reach sexual maturity by one year of age. It is beneficial, however, to delay breeding young *Thamnophis* until they are at least two years old.

Of the numerous species and subspecies, the most widespread in terraria probably is the typical or eastern subspecies of the Common Garter Snake (*T. sirtalis sirtalis*), greenish black with yellow stripes; a black phase is commonly available. More colorful is *T. s. parietalis*, the Red-sided Garter Snake, which exhibits the usual three yellow longitudinal bands but has red spots on the flanks on an olive-brown to black ground color. Also commonly available are the Bluestriped Ribbon Snake (*T. sauritus nitae*) of Florida; Butler's Garter Snake (*T. butleri*), which is very restricted in distribution and threatened, so it should only be purchased as captive-bred specimens; and seasonally the Plains Garter Snake (*T. radix*).

Probably all garter snakes can be bred with success in the terrarium, but problems with identification and availability of the species from the Pacific Coast of the United States and Canada, plus the rarity of tropical American species in captivity, makes it impossible to test this statement at the moment. A Western Ribbon Snake, *T. proximus*, following a gestation period of about four months, repeatedly gave birth to seven or eight young. They were 19 to 21 cm (7.6-8.4 in) long and grew to a length of 44 to 66 cm (17.6-26.4 in) after 14 months. Without any external stimulus, *T. radix* mated in January and gave birth in May to six young, 6 cm (2.4 in) long, that took earthworms after a week.

The following interspecific cross, typical of several known, reflects the taxonomic problems existing within the genus *Thamnophis*. In late January, two males of *T. sirtalis parietalis* mated with a female *T. butleri*. In late April, in addition to two 0.6 X 1.2 cm (0.02-0.5 in) unfertilized eggs, the female also gave birth to three young 17 cm (6.8 in) long. They basically looked like *T. butleri*, but exhibited the bands and red spots of the paternal species. The tropical species *T. melanogaster* has given birth to 4 to 13 young, 17 to 19 cm (6.8-7.6 in) long. The more northern garter snakes, such as *T. butleri* and some subspecies and varieties of *T. sirtalis*, can be kept in outdoor terraria for months at a time or even the whole year and also may breed there, though there will be a reduction in annual reproduction because of the less favorable and more irregular climatic conditions.

OTHER SPECIES

The handsomely colored Ringnecked Snake, *Diadophis punctatus*, presents some feeding problems in the terrarium because, in addition to earthworms and small insects, it mainly feeds on small amphibians (especially salamanders) and reptiles. Females caught while pregnant have frequently laid eggs, but there are no reports of true captive breeding. The Brown Snakes, *Storeria dekayi*, kept by the author exclusively and voraciously ate earthworms, but rejected insects, snails, and pieces of fish; they also are reported to eat small slugs. After barely four months of pregnancy, they gave birth to young 7 to 10 cm (2.8-4 in) long. The young snakes can be fed with small earthworms and fruitflies (*Drosophila*).

TYPICAL COLUBRIDS

The subfamily Colubrinae exhibits a great diversity of species, the phylogenetic relationships of which have not yet been studied sufficiently. A large number of familiar terrarium animals come from this group, exemplified by the species-rich genera of the rat snakes (*Elaphe*), the racers (*Coluber*), and the kingsnakes (*Lampropeltis*).

RAT SNAKES (*ELAPHE*)

Keeping: With about 40 species from Europe, North America, and Asia, the rat snakes

Corn Snake, *Elaphe guttata guttata*. Photo by B. Kahl.

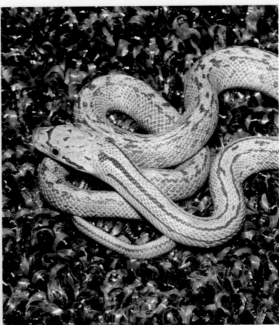

Three newborn examples of rat snakes. **Top right,** a leucistic Texas Rat Snake, *Elaphe obsoleta lindheimeri*. **Top left,** a "Gulf Hammock Rat Snake," *Elaphe obsoleta "williamsi,"* (no longer recognized by most taxonomists). **Below,** an albino Corn Snake, *Elaphe guttata guttata*, of the "creamsickle" variety. All photos by W. P. Mara.

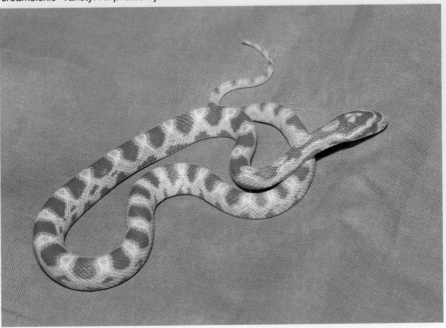

contribute numerous easy-to-keep and easy-to-breed representatives to the terrarium hobby. Most *Elaphe* species are not particularly demanding with respect to keeping conditions. A tall terrarium that is not too small and has fairly large raised basking sites and many climbing facilities as well as a water bowl is sufficient. Temperatures of 25 to 30°C (77-86°F), 22 to 25°C (72-77°F) at night, usually are fine, with winter non-hibernating temperatures generally 5 to 8°C (9-14°F) lower. Most rat snakes are easy to feed with small mammals (mice, rats, hamsters) and birds (chicks, sparrows). Overwintering at cool temperatures for two to three months in the time from November to March—most easily right in the terrarium—promotes breeding. Even for snakes from subtropical southern North America, a rest period of several weeks at 8 to 10°C (46-50°F) has a positive effect. Shortening the day length to six to eight hours in the light-poor months of December and January stimulates reproduction. Tropical American and Southeast Asian rat snakes in general should be kept at warmer temperatures and without hibernation.

CORN SNAKE (*ELAPHE GUTTATA*)

The natural range of the colorful Corn Snake, one of the most popular and most common colubrids kept in the terrarium, extends from the southeastern and central United States to northeastern Mexico. Its record length is 182 cm (72.8 in), but it usually reaches a length of just 80 to 120 cm (42-48 in).

Propagation: This species is bred so frequently in terraria that its stocks are ensured and wild-caught animals are needed at most for genetic diversity and vitality. In recent years Corn Snakes have been bred in several pure strains; albinos lacking the black (amelanistic) or the red (anerythristic) pigment are very much in favor with many hobbyists. For breeding it is advisable to keep together groups of one or two males and one to four females. With several females, however, mutual obstruction during egg-laying can occur, so an egg-laying container for each female is indicated. Sometimes the ritual fights of several males disturb copulation.

In the interest of long-term and high reproductive rates, females should not be bred too early the first time. The onset of sexual maturity at one year of age is not rare, but these 70-80-cm (28-32-in) snakes are of course not yet fully grown, and pregnancy stops the further growth process. One female Corn Snake was just nine months old when she laid five fertile eggs. Female Corn Snakes should be over 1 meter (40 in) long before they are mated for the first time.

In two reports, Corn Snakes laid their eggs 51 and 69 days after observed copulations. The clutch size was very small in very young females, only five to seven eggs. Older females laid 12 to 32 (on average about 18) eggs that, depending on the size of the female and the number of eggs, were 3.0 to 4.6 cm (1.2-1.8 in) long, 1.3 to 2.8 cm (0.5-1.1 in) wide, and as a rule weighed 4 to 7 grams (0.14-0.25 oz). As long as the conditions in the terrarium were dry, the containers provided for egg-laying were used. After egg-laying the females should be given the opportunity to regain their strength by means of an ample supply of food fortified with vitamin and calcium supplements. Well-fed older females often lay a second, although usually smaller, clutch two months after laying the first.

The clutches were transferred to an incubator as soon as possible for maturation. The eggs tolerated a broad temperature spectrum of 18 to 32°C (65-90°F) as long as the temperature did not change too rapidly. The preferred incubation temperature is 27 to 30°C (81-86°F) with a decrease at night of 5 to 8°C (9-14°F). The first eggs usually hatch in about 70 days. This incubation period was observed at an average temperature of 27°C (81°F). At average values of 32°C (90°F) maturation was shortened to 53 days, at 30°C (86°F) to 60 to 65 days, and at 25°C (77°F) it was increased to as long as 90 days. In addition, nocturnal temperatures of course play a role. Consequently, the incubation of the second clutches in the fall always took several more days because of the lower nighttime temperatures. Depending on egg size, the length of freshly hatched Corn Snakes varied from 20 to 32 cm (8-12.8 in), on average from about 25 to 27 cm (10-10.8 in).

Rearing: The young snakes first molted

between the fourth and fourteenth days. Unfortunately, in many cases barely half of all youngsters voluntarily accepted food in the form of pinkie mice. Very small terraria stimulated the feeding reflex; in almost all cases putting one Corn Snake in a plastic container with a baby mouse broke the spell. Snakes that stubbornly refuse to feed must be force-fed with pinkie mice. It is advisable to keep Corn Snakes that eat voluntarily separate from those that must be force-fed, because self-feeding snakes develop better than force-fed ones. Youngsters with good appetites grow fast. The propagation and rearing of the more rarely kept subspecies *Elaphe guttata emoryi*, the Great Plains Rat Snake, do not differ from that of the nominate form.

Noteworthy is the successful mating of a male Corn Snake with a Yellow Rat Snake (*Elaphe obsoleta quadrivittata*). From 11 eggs (4.2 X 1.8 cm, 1.7 X 0.7 in) laid, one viable 25-cm (10-in) hybrid exhibiting the markings of both parents hatched after 57 days. At an age of three years, this snake was backcrossed with a male Corn Snake and laid 12 eggs, from which nine young hatched; they looked very much like Corn Snakes, but were larger and more robust than pure-bred snakes of the same age.

AMERICAN RAT SNAKE (*ELAPHE OBSOLETA*)

Elaphe obsoleta is native to central and eastern North America and is broken into some five subspecies that are notoriously variable in markings and coloration. The subspecies all are kept in the terrarium: Yellow Rat Snake (*E. o. quadrivittata*), Gray Rat Snake (*E. o. spiloides*), Everglades Rat Snake (*E. o. rossalleni*), Texas Rat Snake (*E. o. lindheimeri*), and Black Rat Snake (*E. o. obsoleta*). All subspecies are over 1.5 meters (5 ft) long, powerful, and quite adaptable snakes.

Propagation: The frequently quite stormy matings began following hibernation and—depending on the time regime—eggs were laid in the period from May to June; second clutches were laid from late July to August. The clutch sizes of the author's snakes ranged from 6 to 22 eggs (3.2-5.5 X 2.0-2.7 cm, 1.3-

2.2 X 0.8-1.1 in) in different subspecies; clutches of 40 or more eggs have also been reported. The incubation periods were 62 to 73 days. Whether different clutch sizes, egg sizes, and birth weights or lengths of the freshly hatched young—according to data in the literature, the weights were between 4.5 and 12 grams (0.16-0.4 oz) and the lengths ranged from 12.5 to 40 cm (5-16 in)—are dependent more on the mother's constitution or on the subspecies in question could only be determined statistically with more extensive breeding material.

Feeding problems occasionally turned up with a few of the author's young *E. o. rossalleni*; otherwise almost all youngsters of *E. obsoleta* took food without problems after the first molt.

When the subspecies of *E. obsoleta* are kept together, it should be kept in mind that they are fertile with one another and that hybridization should be prevented.

SIMILAR SPECIES

The Fox Snake (*E. vulpina*) does well under the same terrarium conditions as Corn Snakes. Although this species has been bred a number of times in the terrarium, it still is far from common. The Trans-Pecos Rat Snake (*E. subocularis*, now often put in the genus *Bogertophis*) is bred even more rarely. This nocturnal species grows to a length of 1.5 meters (5 ft) and is a typical inhabitant of the Chihuahuan desert in western Texas, adjacent New Mexico, and northeastern Mexico. One captive-bred female laid four eggs (5.6 X 2.7 cm, 2.2 X 1.1 in) in July. At incubation temperatures of 22 to 28°C (72-82°F), the young snakes, 10-11 grams (0.35-0.39 oz) and 29-31 cm (11.6-12.4 in) long and with an almost transparent appearance, hatched after 96 days. The head in particular looked almost transparent. All young took pinkie mice after the molt. Subsequent difficulties in molting could probably be traced to keeping conditions that were too dry.

FOUR-LINED RAT SNAKE (*ELAPHE QUATUORLINEATA*)

The Four-lined Rat Snake is a peaceful, hardy species that makes no special demands with respect to temperature and can

Above: Chinese King Rat Snake, *Elaphe carinata*. Photo by W. P. Mara. **Below:** Aesculapian Rat Snake, *Elaphe longissima*. Photo by R. D. Bartlett.

Above: Radiated Rat Snake, *Elaphe radiata*. Photo by D. Schmidt. **Below:** Amur Rat Snake, *Elaphe schrencki*. Photo by L. Sassenburg.

be fed exclusively with mice and chicks. The eastern subspecies, *E. q. sauromates*, which largely retains its blotched or saddled juvenile markings, probably is kept more often than the other subspecies. *E. q. sauromates* ranges from southeastern Europe through the Caucus to Iran. Three more or less distinctly longitudinally striped subspecies live in Italy, in the western Balkan Peninsula, and on the Aegean Islands. Four-lined Rat Snakes rarely grow longer than 2 meters (6.6 ft).

Propagation: After a two- to three-month hibernation, *E. quatuorlineata* often copulated for four to six hours following intensive pursuits. Clutches of about 8 to 17 eggs (4.9-6.5 X 2.8-3.4 cm, 2-2.6 X 1.1-1.4 in; 26 to 48 grams, 0.9-1.7 oz) were laid after 54 to 63 days. After 53 to 60 days of incubation (27°C, 81°F), 28 41-cm (16.4-in), 20-30-gram (0l7-1 oz) young hatched. They were reared without trouble. At an age of one year, one was 85 cm (34 in) long and weighed 220 grams (7.7 oz); at barely three years of age it was 140 cm (56 in) long, weighed 1,100 grams (38.5 oz), and was sexually mature.

OTHER SPECIES

One of the most elegant (though not particularly colorful) rat snakes is the Aesculapian Rat Snake (*E. longissima*), which ranges over large parts of central and southern Europe to western Asia. During copulation, as in a number of other snake species, biting is a relatively common component of mating behavior. From the 5 to 11 eggs per clutch (3.5-5.3 X 1.5-2.6 cm, 1.4-2.1 X 0.6-1 in), the young snakes (average birth weight 7.6 grams, 0.27 oz) hatched after about 60 days. Because of their head markings they closely resembled Ringed Snakes. The yellow head spots disappear with age, as does the juvenile blotches. After raising the incubation temperature to 31 to 32°C (88-90°F) for three weeks, the author's Aesculapian Rat Snakes hatched after 48 and 49 days.

The most beautiful and most coveted European snake of all, the colorful Leopard Rat Snake (*E. situla*), is threatened even more than is the Aesculapian Rat Snake because of biotope destruction, killing, and excessive collecting. It has proved difficult to meet the demand for this snake through systematic breeding, because care and long-term keeping alone are not without their problems. When breeding was successful, the captive-bred animals were much easier to keep. The course of the yearly cycle of Leopard Rat Snakes is similar to that of other southern European snakes. From the two to eight, as a rule four, eggs of a clutch (egg size: 3.8-6.0 X 1.5-2.2 cm, 1.5-2.4 X 0.6-0.9 in; 14 to 24 grams, 0.5-0.8 oz), the young snakes hatched at 23 to 29°C (73-84°F) after 42 to 73 days. Newly hatched Leopard Rat Snakes were 29 to 36 cm (11.6-14.4 in) long and weighed about 15 grams (0.53 oz). At an annual growth rate of about 10 cm (4 in), the captive-bred snakes were sexually mature at about three and a half years of age.

Few breeding reports exist on the Ladder Rat Snake (*E. scalaris*), which is native to southern France and the Iberian Peninsula. In a documented captive breeding, six youngsters hatched from eight eggs (5 X 2 cm, 2 X 0.8 in). They were reared with pinkie mice and were about 70 cm (28 in) long after a year.

STEPPES RAT SNAKE (*ELAPHE DIONE*)

The Steppes Rat Snake, which ranges from the Ukraine to China and Korea, is easy to keep and hardly ever bites. It usually grows to a maximum length of 1 meter (40 in) and lives in the plains as well in higher sites in both dry and moist biotopes.

Propagation: After cool overwintering and separation of the sexes, captive snakes mated in March and April; after fall matings in the wild, the eggs are not laid until the following spring. In the terrarium, after a fall mating, four eggs (6.1-6.2 X 2-2.2 cm, 2.4-2.5 X 0.8-0.9 in) were laid in mid-December. Clutch sizes range from 4 to 17. It is notable that even under favorable terrarium conditions female Steppes Rat Snakes retain their clutches for a long time, so incubation times of only 13 to 28 days have been registered. These short incubation times raise the possibility that the Steppes Rat is livebearing under unfavorable climatic conditions in its huge range. The young snakes are 17 to 25 cm (6.8-10 in) long and took a quite diverse assortment of food in different breedings. In some cases they fed on young mice—slightly hairy rather than hairless—two days after the molt, and in others they had to be force-fed.

OTHER SPECIES

E. bimaculata, the Twin-spotted Rat Snake from central China, has much in common with the Steppes Rat Snake. In each case three to four elongated eggs were laid by the 60-70-cm (24-28-in) snakes. The approximately 30-day incubation period and the reproductive biology of these snakes, which occur in several color varieties, are very similar to those of the Steppes Rat. The majority of the young snakes, 20 to 25 cm (8-10 in) long, caught pinkie mice with no difficulty.

Transcaucasian Rat Snakes, *E. hohenackeri*, occasionally reach the terrarium. Despite a long history of keeping, virtually nothing is known of breeding in the terrarium.

AMUR RAT SNAKE (*ELAPHE SCHRENCKI*)

The shiny black and yellow-banded typical subspecies of the Amur Rat Snake has frequently been imported from the Far East in recent years. Its very sociable and peaceful behavior, its willingness to accept food, and not least its attractive appearance as well as its length of about 1.5 meters (5 ft) make the Amur Rat Snake a hardy, recommended terrarium charge.

Propagation: A hibernation lasting several months—at least two months with switched off terrarium lighting and heating, preferably at fairly low temperatures—is recommended for regular breeding. A pair kept by the author for years at room temperature produced almost exclusively infertile clutches of 8 to 13 eggs—the number can be as high as 30—the average dimensions of which varied between 4.1-6.1 X 2.4-2.8 cm (1.6-2.4 X 1-1.1 in) with weights of about 26 grams (0.9 oz). Though the female always fed regularly under these conditions, the male stopped feeding annually from August to about December for a maximum of 186 days.

After incubation times of 36 to more than 50 days, the 25-30-cm (10-12-in) young snakes with richly colored, contrasting mark-

ings hatched. They usually were reared without difficulty with pinkie mice. Three-month-old snakes ate canary eggs. Individual adults, like other rat snakes, take eggs of appropriate size, the shells of which—unlike the regurgitation of the African egg-eating snakes, *Dasypeltis*—are also swallowed and digested. With good feeding, the young Amur Rat Snakes take on the coloration of their parents at eight to ten months of age.

JAPANESE RAT SNAKE (*ELAPHE CLIMACOPHORA*)

This Japanese snake, body length up to 1.6 meters (5.3 ft), is one of the species that is rarely kept in our terraria. On account of its occurrence on several Japanese islands as well as on Kunasir in the Soviet Kurile Islands, this species sometimes is called the Island Rat Snake. An isolated albino population is found in Japan.

Propagation: Albinos bred in Japan always laid 9 to 14 eggs (5.2 X 2.6 cm, 2.1 X 1 in) 37 to 51 days after mating, from which after 61 to 65 days (26°C, 79°F) on average 43.4-cm (17.4) and 16.5-gram (0.6 oz) youngsters hatched. In the breeding of normal-colored snakes outside Japan, four eggs (6.2-6.5 X 2.5-2.7 cm, 2.5-2.6 X 1-1.1 in) usually were laid. They had to be incubated for up to 99 days. In a cooperative breeding in which I participated, Japanese Rat Snakes were overwintered for four to six weeks every year in darkness at 4 to 8°C (39-46°F). This regularly brought the males into breeding condition in February and March. This was indicated by restlessness and later by sometimes fierce ritual fights as well as pursuit and biting of the body. In early May a desiccated clutch of four eggs was found unexpectedly. A copulation lasting 30 hours took place in late August. It resulted 49 days later in a clutch of four cylindrical, pure-white eggs from which two young snakes (28 and 29 cm, 11.2 and 11.6 in, long) hatched after an incubation period of 75 days. The embryos in both remaining eggs had died at a length of about 15 cm (6 in). In comparison to other rat snakes, the young snakes ate proportionately little and grew slowly.

Russian hobbyists subjected Japanese Rat Snakes as well as a pair of frog-eating Japa-

Two products of hybridization between genera. **Above:** A Corn Snake, *Elaphe guttata guttata*, crossed with a Bullsnake, *Pituophis sayi*. **Below:** A Gray-banded Kingsnake, *Lampropeltis alterna*, crossed with a Corn Snake, *Elaphe guttata guttata*. Both photos by W. P. Mara.

Above: "Hurricane" Corn Snake (variety), *Elaphe guttata guttata*. Juvenile specimen. Photo by W. P. Mara. **Below:** Cross between a Yellow Rat Snake, *Elaphe obsoleta quadrivittata* and a Texas Rat Snake, *Elaphe obsoleta lindheimeri*. Mother shown with eggs. Photo by R. T. Zappalorti.

nese Four-lined Rat Snakes ((*E. quadrivirgata*) from the same region to the following stimulative regime. Until December the snakes lived separated by sex at temperatures of 28 to 30°C (82-86°F) during the day and 24 to 25°C (75-77°F) at night. Then the day length was shortened from 12 to 6 hours and the temperature was reduced to 18°C (65°F) at first and later to 12 to 13°C (54-55°F). The snakes spent all of January in darkness at a temperature of 7 to 8°C (45-46°F). Starting in February, the day length was slowly increased from 6 to 15 hours again and the temperature was raised. Starting in March, the snakes received several minutes of ultraviolet radiation every other day. The 100% hatching rate of four young *E. climacophora* and eight *E. quadrivirgata* confirmed the success of this reproductive stimulation. Another hobbyist fed his *E. quadrivirgata* on mice. From nine eggs laid in early July, six youngsters weighing 7 to 8 grams (0.25-0.28 oz) and 30 cm (12 in) long hatched after 49 to 50 days of incubation at constant temperatures of 28 to 29°C (82-84°F). The young snakes had to be force-fed with pinkie mice for the first two months.

OTHER ASIATIC SPECIES

The only *Elaphe* species that has been confirmed to be livebearing is the aquatic, small *E. rufodorsata*, often called the Chinese Gartersnake. In Germany it is called the Red-bellied Rat Snake, but this is not always applicable as the coloration is very variable and not all specimens have a red belly. Its range extends from China and Korea to eastern Amur. In the terrarium, 16 young snakes were produced after a gestation period of 109 days. Their average length was 17 to 20 cm (6.8-8 in) and they weighed about 2.4 grams (0.08 oz). In a second breeding in the fall of the same year, the gestation period was 100 days and 12 young were born. Fishes of appropriate size were favored as the rearing food. Later an attempt can be made to accustom the young snakes to pinkie mice.

China and Taiwan are the homelands of the Stinking Goddess (*E. carinata*), which grows to a length of over 2 meters (6.6 ft). This impressive rat snake gets its common name from the habit of emptying large postanal

glands to release an acrid, smelly secretion when threatened. Little is known about the habits in the wild. The snake probably prefers to feed on snakes and lizards, but acclimated snakes also willingly accepted mice and finally even one-day-old chicks disguised with mouse scent. From seven rather severely desiccated eggs found in the terrarium, three young snakes, which had to be force-fed at first, hatched after 44 to 47 days (28°C, 82°F). From a further clutch of seven eggs, four youngsters hatched after 52 days. They were 30 to 35 cm (12-14 in) long and weighed 18 to 20 grams (0.6-0.7 oz).

Another handsome Chinese rat snake is *E. moellendorffi*, the Red-headed Rat Snake, which generally is considered to be quite delicate. In a zoo breeding in the United States, one female laid six elliptical eggs from which the young hatched after 80 to 83 days at an incubation temperature of 27°C (81°F); they strongly resembled their parents.

Of the Southeast Asian rat snakes, *E. helena* and *E. radiata* have been bred sporadically. The 1 to 1.3 meters (3.3-4.3 ft) brown Common Trinket Snake (*E. helena*) likes to climb, although it is not a truly arboreal snake. A female kept in the terrarium laid a total of 11 clutches in three years. In each case one to five eggs were laid, 35 in total, from which, however, only 11 young hatched (egg size: 4.5 X 1.5 cm, 1.8 X 0.6 in) after a 63-68-day incubation period. After about a year and a half the captive-bred snakes were sexually mature and reproduced readily. From four clutches of a captive-bred female, each with three to seven eggs (1.6-2 X 3.4-4.1 cm, 0.6-0.8 X 1.4-1.6 in, weighing 7 to 9.5 grams, 0.25-0.33 oz), after the same incubation period this time about two-thirds of all youngsters hatched.

A pair of Radiated Rat Snakes (*E. radiata*) from Thailand owned by the author unexpectedly produced in late December seven pure-white, smooth eggs (4.3-5.4 X 2.2-2.5 cm, 1.7-2.2 X 0.9-1 in) that were not discovered until they had already dried out. Nine eggs were laid 63 days later, of which six proved to be infertile. After 85 days of incubation, one 24-cm (9.6 in) youngster hatched that had markings identical to its parents. This Radiated hatchling suffered from an eye deformity and had to be force-fed. It finally died at an age of five months, by which time it had grown to a length of 38 cm (15.2 in).

Little was known until recently of the care and propagation of the handsome Stripe-tailed Rat Snake (*E. taeniura*) from Southeast Asia. This snake grows over 2 meters (6.6 ft) long. From five white, elongated eggs (6.5-7.2 X 2.5-3 cm, 2.6-2.9 X 1-1.2 in) laid in the terrarium, all of the young (35 to 38 cm, 14-15.2 in long) hatched after 70 to 73 days. After their first molt they took pinkie mice independently. From a second clutch of four eggs, surprisingly five youngsters hatched—including one set of twins. Today the species is being bred more frequently and soon it should be possible to obtain captive-bred stock.

RACERS AND WHIPSNAKES (*COLUBER*)

The racers and whipsnakes of the genus *Coluber* (and its close ally *Masticophis*) are diurnal terrestrial snakes of generally arid biotopes. They are considerably more active and (even after fairly long stays in the terrarium) more aggressive than the rat snakes. In a revision of the nonuniform genus *Coluber* in 1943, many species were assigned to the genera *Coluber*, *Masticophis*, *Zamenis*, *Platyceps*, and *Haemorrhois*—the genus *Haemorrhois* at times has even included European, African, and Asiatic *Coluber* species. Not all herpetologists, however, follow this classification. The genus *Coluber* in its broad sense has approximately 30 species, including small species barely 60 cm (24 in) long as well as species 2.5 meters (8.3 ft) long.

Keeping: The Caspian Racer (*C. jugularis*), which is found as far west as the Balkan Peninsula and is especially popular in the form of the trans-Caucasian red subspecies *C. j. schmidti*; the Checkered Racer (*C. ravergieri*) of western Asia; the Yellow-green Racer (*C. viridiflavus*) of southwestern Europe; the Horseshoe Snake (*C. hippocrepis*) from the Iberian Peninsula and northwest Africa; and the American Racer (*C. constrictor*) frequently are kept in the terrarium.

All of these species usually accepted small mammals without difficulty, which was not always the case with the smaller, more slender species, like the Slender Whipsnake (*C.*

najadum, confused until recently on the Black Sea coast of southern Bulgaria with *C. rubriceps*, which is rare in Europe), *C. karelini*, *C. rhodorhachis*, and *C. algirus*. Youngsters often preferred lizards and insects such as crickets.

In sunny, heated dry terraria that offer sufficient room to move, racers can be hardy pets.

Propagation: Though the American Racer does not seem to be especially hard to breed (after overwintering the adults, eggs were laid repeatedly, from which the young snakes hatched after 51 to 63 days), little is known of true captive breedings of the other *Coluber* species. Imported pregnant Caspian Racers laid eggs, and the young—strongly blotched in contrast to the parents—were reared successfully. It was possible to feed them pinkie mice.

KINGSNAKES (*LAMPROPELTIS*)

The approximately eight species of kingsnakes are found from southern Canada to northwestern South America in habitats that range from desert to deciduous forest and plains to rainforest. Some species are only 35 cm (14 in) long; others grow to almost 2 meters (6.6 ft).

COMMON KINGSNAKE (*LAMPROPELTIS GETULA*)

The *Lampropeltis* species kept most often is the black or dark brown, yellow-speckled, ringed, or striped Common Kingsnake, of which several variable and often confusing subspecies are recognized. The subspecies differ primarily in their markings. There are, however, numerous transitional forms in coloration and markings, especially since the subspecies interbreed where their ranges meet and do so in the terrarium as well.

Keeping: In the terrarium, Common Kingsnakes prove to be undemanding charges. I kept the Eastern Kingsnake (*L. g. getula*), the Florida Kingsnake (*L. g. floridana*), hybrids of these subspecies, the Speckled Kingsnake (*L. g. holbrooki*), and the Desert Kingsnake (*L. g. splendida*) under the same conditions in dry terraria with large water bowls at daytime temperatures of about 25 to 30°C (77-86°F), 18 to 22°C (65-72°F) at night.

Above: Common Kingsnake, *Lampropeltis getula*, hatching. Photo by D. Schmidt. **Below:** California Kingsnake, *Lampropeltis getula californiae*. Photo by W. P. Mara.

Above: Scarlet Kingsnake, *Lampropeltis triangulum elapsoides*. Below: Gray-banded Kingsnake, *Lampropeltis alterna*. Both photos by L. Trutnau.

Basically, only snakes of the same size can be kept in a terrarium; keeping each individual separately seems even safer because of the tendency to cannibalism. Even freshly caught specimens feed well and soon take live or dead food animals (mice, young rats, chicks) from forceps. When catching prey, kingsnakes are rather voracious, but often they just bite the prey, sometimes only on the tail, and come up empty. When several kingsnakes in the same terrarium hunt for food they often bite one another, so they can never be fed without supervision.

Propagation: The author's snakes spent eight weeks in hibernation at a temperature of 8 to 10°C (46-50°F) and with the terrarium lighting switched off. During copulation in late March to April, males often bit the female in the neck region, which, however, did not cause injury. The clutch sizes were nine or ten eggs, in second clutches as well, from which young 25 to 29 cm (10-11.6 in) long hatched after 59 to 61 days. Second clutches needed 70 to 73 days to hatch as a result of nighttime temperatures that had dropped to 18 to 20°C (65-20°F) in the fall months. Extensive statistical studies by Zweifel of the reproductive biology of kingsnakes yielded the following data:

Copulation period: 4.3 hours (2 to 6.5 hours), 25 observations; Gestation period: 52.2 days (37 to 73 days), 58 clutches; Maturation period: 65.7 days (51 to 78 days), 51 clutches.

Rearing: Most of the author's captive-bred snakes took their first mice shortly after molting at an age of 8 to 12 days, some even before that, and did not reject dead, thawed frozen baby mice either. Individual snakes had to be force-fed for several weeks before they fed independently. Forced-feeding was more difficult than with, for example, young rat snakes, because the young kingsnakes did not open their mouths willingly and exhibited vigorous defensive reactions. Strips of beef heart sprinkled with vitamins and calcium were easier to force-feed, but are not as nutritious as nestling mice. All of the author's young kingsnakes molted exactly ten times in the first year of life. By then they had grown to a length of 52 to 70 cm (20.8-28 in) and in each case had eaten between 72

and 85 nestling mice, later also newborn rats. The juveniles were not overwintered at cool temperatures in the first year of life.

The diverse subspecies of the Common Kingsnake have all been bred in a similar manner. Particularly worth mentioning are breedings of the attractive California Kingsnake (*L. g. californiae*), which with a total length of 70 to 80 cm (28-32 in) is one of the smallest subspecies. It exhibits white to yellow rings or a yellow dorsal band on a dark brown to blackish brown ground color. Both color varieties can occur in the same clutch. Albinos of both patterns, plus many strange mutations, have been produced and sold recently.

OTHER SPECIES

The numerous subspecies of the Milksnake (*Lampropeltis triangulum*)—at least 20, perhaps 25—differ greatly in coloration and markings, and also in body length and build. The typical subspecies usually exhibits brown, black-edged spots on the back; on the other hand, subspecies like *annulata, amaura, syspila,* and *sinaloae* have red, black, and yellow (or white) rings. An overwintering period lasting several months at 10 to 15°C (50-59°F) is necessary. Four to nine eggs were ready to hatch after, for example, about 55 days. Because of the lack of the lizard diet preferred by most members of the species, young Milksnakes usually had to be force-fed for several months, at first with strips of heart, later with pinkie mice and mouse parts.

The colorful Gray-banded Kingsnake (*Lampropeltis alterna*), a rocky desert dweller, lays four to six elongated eggs. Forty-one young snakes from 11 clutches required about 70 to 91 days for incubation at 22 to 28°C (72-82°F). The young snakes, 21 to 23 cm (8.4-9.2 in), at first recognized only small lizards as prey and therefore had to be force-fed.

Much less often available and seldom bred is the Sonoran Mountain Kingsnake (*L. pyromelana*). In terraria, three or four eggs were laid that measured 5.0 to 6.0 X 1.5 to 2.0 cm (2-2.4 X 0.6-0.8 in). After 68 to 92 days, the 22-26-cm (8.8-10.4-in), 4.9-5.9-gram (0.17-0.21-oz) young snakes saw the light of day; the majority of them would only take young lizards and were therefore force-fed. The very similar but more commonly seen California Mountain Kingsnake (*L. zonata*) also is not bred often. From clutches of three or four eggs, youngsters about 23 cm (9.2 in) long hatched. They spent the day in a system of tunnels they excavated themselves in the substrate and preyed on young lizards and pinkie mice.

OTHER COLUBRIDS

The range of the Smooth Snake (*Coronella austriaca*), a protected species in parts of Europe, extends from central Europe to Asia Minor and Transcaucasia. This diurnal, barely 70-cm (28-in) snake gives birth to up to 15 live young in August to September. After late mating and an eight-week hibernation, in early May the female gave birth to young 15 cm (6 in) long within three hours in the terrarium. They broke through the transparent chorion immediately after birth by means of wriggling movements; a few snakes, however, at first appeared to be lifeless for five minutes before finally freeing themselves with vigorous head movements. Because newborn lizards and lizard tails are seldom available for feeding, young Smooth Snakes usually have to be force-fed at first and imprinted on mice as a food source. The Gironde Smooth Snake (*Coronella girondica*) surprisingly is an egg-laying species. Probably only females caught while pregnant have laid eggs so far in the terrarium.

The dwarf snakes of the genus *Eirenis* occasionally are imported from the Middle East and western Asia. Some of the species that turn up in terraria include *E. modestus*, *E. collaris*, and *E. punctatolineatus*. These snakes are only 30-60 cm (12-24 in) long, and they are easy to keep in the heated dry terrarium. They are dietary specialists but are easy to feed with crickets and grasshoppers. Caution is advised, however, because they also are known to prey on small lizards. They are ideal snakes for the smallest terraria and do not destroy plants. Although wild-caught specimens have occasionally laid four to eight tiny eggs—the youngsters were barely 10 cm (4 in) long—nothing is known to me about a true terrarium breeding. With these

snakes, fanciers of small terrarium animals could find an interesting field of activity.

At 3.6 meters (11.9 ft), the Dhaman (*Ptyas mucosus*) of India and southern Asia is a giant among the colubrids. At temperatures of about 25 to 30°C (77-86°F) and with local bottom heating, the Dhaman can be very hardy and most specimens also become tame. They have been bred in the terrarium, laying up to 20 eggs producing young 40 cm (16 in) long at hatching. These babies were sexually mature after 20 months.

The African Green Bushsnake (*Philothamnus irregularis*), has been bred in captivity. Unfortunately, these attractive natives of the rainforest and gallery forest only occasionally took mice; frogs and lizards were preferred. From the clutches of 6 to 16 eggs, the young snakes (22-26 cm, 8.8-10.4 in) hatched after 65 days.

On the other hand, the Black Treesnake (*Thrasops jacksoni*) from East Africa and the Congo basin seems to be a grateful charge: It is not fussy with respect to diet and readily eats mice, young rats, and chicks. Of nine eggs laid in the terrarium in December, five were fertile and all hatched after 84 to 86 days. In contrast to their enamel-black parents, the freshly hatched specimens were blackish brown with light brown spots at first and became shiny black with yellow and blue-green markings after the third molt. Propagation also was successful in the second generation.

A common snake in southern Africa is the Mole Snake (*Pseudaspis cana*), which has also been bred in heated dry terraria without cool overwintering. Thirty to 50 live young are probably the norm, but 84 and 95 young Mole Snakes in a litter also have been recorded.

The snake-rich New World contributes not only many *Elaphe* species, several types of *Coluber*, and all the *Lampropeltis* species, but also numerous other snakes of interest in the terrarium hobby. For example, the Rough Greensnake (*Opheodrys aestivus*), which is particularly abundant in the Everglades, is a dietary specialist that can be fed in the terrarium with insects (crickets, grasshoppers) and insect larvae (caterpillars) as well as spiders and snails. Forty-two days after copu-

Above: African Green Bushsnake, *Philothamnus irregularis*. Photo by D. Schmidt. **Below:** Smooth Snake, *Coronella austriaca*. Photo by J. Vergner.

Above: Long-nosed Bushsnake, *Philodryas baroni*. Photo by F. Golder. **Below:** Mud Snake, *Farancia abacura*. Photo by D. Schmidt.

lation, 3 to 12 sticky, smooth, cream-colored eggs (2.6 to 3.4 X 1.0 to 1.2 cm, 1-1.4 X 0.4-0.5 in) were laid in the terrarium in a substrate of soil, peat, and granulated charcoal (1:2:1) 15 cm (6 in) deep and were left there to mature. The first young snake appeared after 51 days; the youngsters were 17.0 to 21.2 cm (6.8-8.4 in) long and weighed 1.3 to 1.6 grams (0.05-0 6 oz). The initially gray-green young subsequently turned olive-green, until after several molts they had finally taken on the grass-green color of the parents. Rearing them with live insects was uncomplicated. The extremely short incubation period of its close relative, the Smooth Greensnake (*Opheodrys vernalis*) of only 4 to 34 days is noteworthy.

Although the impressive, over 2-meter-long (6.6-ft) Indigo Snake (*Drymarchon corais*) formerly was frequently kept in the terrarium because of its beautiful blue-black, gleaming scales and its only slight aggressiveness, detailed breeding reports in the literature are rare. Stimulation of reproductive activity was achieved only through a change in day length, low winter temperatures, and separate keeping of the sexes. Copulations occurred from November to February and several clutches of 5 to 11 eggs were laid in late May. Eight young snakes about 44 cm (17.6 in) long hatched; others had died before hatching. The youngsters of two other breedings with nine and ten eggs, respectively, hatched at 27°C (81°F) after 45 days and at 29°C (84°F) after only 28 to 29 days (egg size: 5.4 to 6.4 X 3.8 to 4.0 cm, 2.2-2.6 X 1.5-1.6 in; 56 to 63 grams, 2-2.2 oz). The parents were 218 cm (87.2 in), male, and 179 cm (71.6 in), female, long and weighed 4.6 and 2.0 kilograms (10.1 and 4.4 pounds), respectively; the freshly hatched young attained a length of 34 to 45 cm (13.6-18 in) and a birth weight of 26 to 50 grams (0.9-1.75 oz). The young Indigos as a rule fed independently.

The Coachwhip (*Masticophis flagellum*), which ranges through much of the eastern and southwestern United States southward into northern Mexico, is rather closely related both morphologically and biologically to the racers, *Coluber*. It has been bred in captivity, young 30 to 40 cm (12-16 in) long hatching after an incubation period of 76 to 79 days.

The Pine Snake (*Pituophis melanoleucus*) has been bred repeatedly in the terrarium. This robust snake, which is divided into a dozen or more subspecies or even three or four full species, is kept and cared for like the North American rat snakes. The incubation periods reported varied from 46 to 100 days; the hatchlings were 30 to 40 cm (12-16 in) long and took pinkie mice as the first food.

Of the very racer-like patchnosed snakes of the genus *Salvadora*, the Mountain Patchnose (*S. grahamiae*) from the southwestern United States and Mexico occasionally is kept. In a warm, dry terrarium these slender, nocturnal snakes feed on mice—in my experience, frozen, thawed ones as well as live ones. No reports exist on captive breeding. Young snakes are supposed to have hatched after 125 to 131 days from ten eggs laid by a female that was pregnant when she was collected.

At a length of about 2.5 meters (8.3 ft), the Chicken Snake (*Spilotes pullatus*) is one of the largest snakes of Central and South America, but claims of lengths of up to 4 meters (13.2 ft) hardly seem credible. In a large, heated "rat snake terrarium," Chicken Snakes accepted mice, rats, and of course chicks. They laid an average of 15 to 25 eggs, but up to now they have been bred only rarely in captivity. The incubation period ranged from to 54 to 56 days.

AMERICAN HOGNOSES AND ALLIES (XENODONTINAE)

This subfamily contains some 27 genera, all of which are found in the Americas. A number of species of xenodontines have been propagated successfully in the terrarium. Many of the species are specialized to feed on frogs and toads, and many or most are reported to have mildly toxic saliva that may cause relatively severe signs in allergic humans. Caution is advised with all snakes of this group.

The South American False Water Cobra (*Cyclagras gigas*) is a large, powerful snake that needs a roomy terrarium with a large water bowl. As a rule, small mammals and chicks are taken readily. False Water Cobras mated in August in the terrarium and in October and November laid 14 to 42 milk-white, 5.2 to 5.8 X 3 cm (2.1-2.3 X 1.2 in) eggs; however, the eggs were not successfully hatched.

Wagler's False Viper (*Xenodon merremi*) is a native of the tropical forests of South America. It is essential to guard against being bitten by your pet, because a mildly toxic saliva is produced. *Xenodon merremi* needs very high humidity in the terrarium. It lays 15 to 25 eggs. Young snakes hatched after about 110 days from eggs laid by imported pregnant females. Like the adults, they preferred a diet of toads and frogs.

The Gold-speckled Water Snake (*Liophis miliaris*) of the Amazon basin, on the other hand, is primarily a fish eater. This species has laid up to eight eggs in the terrarium. The young snakes grew very rapidly and at an age of seven months had already reached the size of their 60-80-cm (24-32-in) parents.

The Argentine Speckled Water Snake (*Liophis poecilogyrus*) has a range similar to that of the Gold-speckled Water Snake. This diurnal, moisture-loving snake eats fish and sometimes mice as well. Following mating in the terrarium, seven eggs were laid from which young hatched after 43 days at 28 to 29°C (82-84°F).

The South American bushsnakes of the genus *Philodryas* have been bred in well-planted rainforest terraria. Interestingly, the Long-nosed Bushsnake (*P. baroni*) occurs in both a green and a brown color variety. A male 1.3 meters (4.3 ft) long and a female 1.8 meters (5.9 ft) long were kept in a tall, heavily planted terrarium and spent most of their time on the floor. In late November, 12 cylindrical, pure-white eggs (size: 4.9 to 6.0 X 2.4 to 2.7 cm, 2-2.4 X 1-1.1 in; weight: 21.5 to 33 grams, 0.75-1.2 oz) were laid. The entire clutch weighed 305.5 grams (10.7 oz); the female weighed 343 grams (12 oz) after laying the eggs. The young snakes (average length of 37.5 cm, 15 in) hatched after 83 days of incubation. Both pure brown and pure green individuals were present without any intermediate forms. The Argentine Green Snake (*P. olfersi*) is considerably smaller. A captured pregnant female laid eight cylindrical eggs (3.9 X 1.7 cm, 1.6 X 0.7 in; 7.9 grams, 0.28 oz) in mid-October, from which young 28 cm (11.2 in) hatched after exactly 89 days.

The shy and fast Cuban Racer (*Alsophis cantherigerus*) needs a roomy terrarium. It has been bred repeatedly in captivity. Ten to 14 eggs are laid usually from June to August. They were 2.8 to 3.6 X 1.4 to 1.8 cm (1.1-1.4 X 0.6-0.7 in) and weighed 2.9 to 5.2 grams (0.1-0.18 oz) at laying. Depending on temperature, incubation took 60 to 97 days. The young snakes were 21 to 25 cm (8.4-10 in) long and weighed only 1.5 to 3 grams (0.05-0.1 oz). The young snakes proved to be quite difficult to rear because they refused all food at first and had to be force-fed every four days with 2-cm (0.8-in) aquarium fishes, later with freshwater fish fillets and strips of horse meat. Eventually earthworms, young Cuban Treefrogs, and lizards were taken. At an age of ten months, they finally ate pinkie mice smeared with fish on their own for the first time.

Virtually nothing was known about the reproductive biology of the nocturnal and almost exclusively aquatic Cuban Water Snake (*Tretanorhinus variabilis*) until it was bred for the first time in the terrarium in the late 1960's. Oviparity was demonstrated when a female approximately 80 cm (32 in) long laid eight eggs from which four youngsters, each 14 cm (5.6 in) long and weighing 4.8 grams (0.17 oz), hatched after 35 days. The young water snakes molted after seven to nine days and began to catch live guppies and small frogs at an age of three weeks. At 18 months of age, a 60-cm (24-in), 80-gram (2.8 oz) captive-bred female laid for the first time, although the eggs were infertile.

The North American hognosed snakes of the genus *Heterodon* are the last group of xenodontines that will be discussed here. They prey on frogs and toads, although the Western Hognose (*H. nasicus*) also takes lizards in the wild and will feed on small mice in the terrarium. This makes the Western Hognose relatively easy to keep, and it is fairly commonly bred in captivity. The Eastern Hognose (*H. platirhinos*) feeds almost exclusively on toads and frogs and is almost impossible to adapt to any other diet, making it a poor terrarium choice. The Southern Hognose (*H. simus*) is uncommon and seldom available, but is said to be somewhat adaptable to a terrarium diet.

Green Tree Snake, *Ahaetulla prasina*. Photo by F. Golder.

WOLFSNAKES (LYCODONTINAE)

MUD SNAKE (*FARANCIA ABACURA*)

Most of the approximately 50 genera assigned to the Lycodontinae are Asian and African in origin, but at least one North American genus, *Farancia*, is assigned here, rightly or wrongly. The genus contains two iridescent black and red, heavy-bodied burrowing snakes from the southern United States, the Mud and the Rainbow Snakes. The Mud Snake is bluish black above and bright red on the belly with large black checks. At 1.4 meters (4.6 ft), it makes a most impressive terrarium animal.

Keeping: Mud Snakes can be very hardy in the terrarium if the right food can be acquired—a big if for most keepers. In nature they feed mostly on large elongated salamanders such as amphiumas and sirens, sometimes taking fishes such as eels and also the occasional earthworm. Unless you can duplicate this diet and provide them the attention they need when feeding, you should not try to keep Mud Snakes. The author acquired a pregnant female that refused the most diverse sorts of food and had to be force-fed with fish. She died after only two months,

though without having shown any signs of emaciation.

Propagation: A few days after she was obtained, the snake laid 26 white eggs (3.1 to 3.4 X 1.9 to 2.0 cm, 1.2-1.4 X 0.8 in) in mid-August. With a record clutch of 104 eggs, the Mud Snake is one of the most productive snakes of all. (Natural clutch sizes may be somewhat exaggerated because this species is known to indulge in group nests.) The eggs were successfully incubated at 27 to 30°C (81-86°F), 20 to 23°C (68-73°F) at night, and 100% relative humidity on pieces of foam rubber. Twenty-four young snakes hatched between the 55th and 57th day of incubation. Many of the egg shells looked like wet parchment, and even the red bellies of the young snakes were visible through the shells. The soft shells disintegrated after the young hatched.

Rearing: The youngsters were 22 to 24 cm (8.8-9.6 in), gray, and displayed the same color pattern as the mother. After the first molt on about the fifteenth day of life they became shiny red and black. All of the food (guppies, pieces of fish, earthworms, crickets) offered was refused, so forced-feeding finally had to be undertaken. It proved impossible to force open the mouths of the youngsters to push in a piece of food. Finally a pap was prepared from fish, a calcium preparation, and occasionally vitamins, of which at first about 1 milliliter and later several milliliters were squirted into the gullet with a plastic syringe. The author kept six young snakes at 25 to 28°C (77-82°F) during the winter and force-fed them about once a week. In the following year, the young snakes finally caught and ate a few salamander larvae and freshly transformed frogs. They had grown to only about 30 cm (12 in) and had molted six to seven times. Dead young frogs and parts of larger frogs were not taken; for this reason I started force-feeding with fish pap again. Unfortunately, the young Mud Snakes died at an age of 16 months during their first hibernation at 10°C (50°F). Apparently the forced-feeding had not been able to build up enough fat reserves for them to survive hibernation.

BROWN HOUSESNAKE (*BOAEDON FULIGINOSUS*)

The Brown Housesnake is very common from East Africa to the Cape of Good Hope. A mouse-eating snake, it is an undemanding charge in the terrarium. It sometimes is placed in the genus *Lamprophis*. This nocturnal snake is about a meter (40 in) long and is satisfied with a medium-sized, dry terrarium with moderate bottom heating.

Propagation: Brown Housesnakes have been bred frequently in recent years. Wild-caught specimens from Ethiopia laid clutches in June and July; the young snakes hatched after 77 to 87 days at 23 to 30°C (73-86°F). Clutches from terrarium breedings consisted of 5 to 10 eggs 3.3 to 5 X 1.9 to 2 cm (1.3-2 X 0.8 in) in size. The sexes were separated in some cases to stimulate mating. The incubation periods were between 56 and 75 days. Usually all of the 18 to 25 cm (7.2-10 in) long and 3 to 6 grams (0.1-0.2 oz) young housesnakes took pinkie mice immediately.

EGG-EATING SNAKES (DASYPELTINAE)

AFRICAN EGG-EATING SNAKE (*DASYPELTIS SCABRA*)

The only genus of the subfamily Dasypeltinae is the African *Dasypeltis*, of which about six species, especially *D. scabra*,

Flying Snakes, *Chrysopelea ornata ornatissima*. Photo by F. Golder.

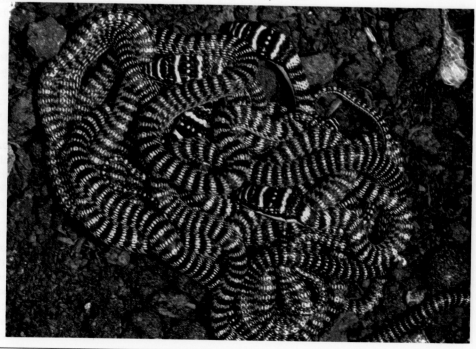

have been kept and also propagated somewhat regularly in the terrarium. The ecology and habits of the Indian Egg-eating Snake (*Elachistodon westermanni*)—classified in its own subfamily—are largely unknown because of its rarity. It is not even known if it is as specialized an egg-eater as the African species; probably only five specimens exist in the museums of the world.

Dasypeltis scabra inhabits, in addition to true deserts, dense lowland rainforests and very high elevations, essentially all habitats of East Africa from Egypt south. Females reach a length of about 1 meter (40 in); males grow to about 70 cm (28 in).

Propagation: African Egg-eaters mated in the warm, dry terrarium without special external stimulation in June and July. The males bit the nape or back of the female and copulated for up to 22 hours. After about 43 days of pregnancy, an average of 13 (6 to 23) eggs per clutch were laid (egg sizes: 3.2 to 4.2 X 1.6 to 2.0 cm, 1.3-1.7 X 0.6-0.8 in; egg weights: 4.6 grams, 0.16 oz, or more).

Incubation lasted 52 to 65 days; the young snakes, which were easy to tell apart on the basis of their individual head markings, were 20 to 28 cm (8-11.2 in) long and weighed 5.2 to 6.1 grams (0.18-0.2 oz).

Rearing: Only a few days after hatching, the young egg-eaters took eggs of Zebra Finches and other finches, but only after they were placed singly in small plastic terraria. Food acquisition for a species that specializes in bird eggs is a problem for most hobbyists. Only large specimens can manage chicken eggs. The claim that egg-eaters also eat insects, snails, or snail eggs was not verified. Voluntary pauses in feeding of up to 11 months probably indicate a survival strategy of the wild snakes, which even in their tropical homeland cannot find bird eggs the whole year. Many terrarium specimens, however, were kept successfully and even bred for years with forced-feeding. The administration of chicken egg yolk through a tube inserted in the gullet is a good substitute diet. Egg-eaters normally regurgitate the egg shells, but shell fragments often are found in the droppings as well. For this reason a calcium preparation should be added to the substitute food.

REAR-FANGS (BOIGINAE)

The representatives of the genus-rich, phylogenetically nonuniform subfamily Boiginae are characterized by grooved (usually) enlarged teeth that are located in the back of the mouth. Although the toxic effects of rear-fang bites are quite variable and often are not dangerous to people, accidental bites with fatal results are known with the Boomslang (*Dispholidus*), the Birdsnake (*Thelotornis*), and perhaps the mangrove snakes (*Boiga*). The fierce snakes (*Malpolon*) and the sandsnakes (*Psammophis*) have potent toxins. Perhaps rear-fang bites generally are harmless mostly because the poison fangs are located far back on the jaw and do not come in contact with the site of the average bite. In the care of rear-fangs in the terrarium, all of the most important basic principles of venomous snake care should be heeded, even if this seems overly cautious.

Many rear-fangs are hard to keep because they are reptile eaters, preying on lizards and snakes, or they have specialized on frogs.

EUROPEAN FIERCE SNAKE (*MALPOLON MONSPESSULANUS*)

At a length of over 2 meters (6.6 ft), the European Fierce Snake (also known as the Montpellier Snake) is one of Europe's largest snakes. The typical subspecies inhabits the area from North Africa across the Iberian Peninsula to Italy, while the subspecies *M. m. insignus* occurs from the Balkan Peninsula to Transcaucasia. Dry slopes and forest edges are the preferred biotope.

This often quite active snake is one of the rear-fangs that should be kept in a roomy, well-heated—25 to 32°C (77-90°F), dropping to room temperature at night—dry terrarium. It can be fed with small mammals and birds. Because the fangs are located fairly far forward in the jaw, it can be dangerous to humans.

Propagation: Wild-caught pregnant females laid 8 to 12 pure-white eggs that were 3.1 cm (1.2 in) long and weighed 8 grams (0.3 oz). After 63 to 65 days at 25°C (77°F), 20°C (68°F) at night, the young snakes hatched and molted within three days. They averaged 21.6 cm (8.6 in) long and weighed 5.7 grams (0.2 oz). Only one youngster took pinkie mice;

others willingly ate only young lizards. Grasshoppers should also be on the menu of young fierce snakes.

TREE SNAKES (*AHAETULLA*)

The tree snakes of the genus *Ahaetulla* (formerly known as *Dryophis*) inhabit the forests of tropical Southeast Asia. At almost 2 meters (6.6 ft) in length, *A. nasuta* and *A. prasina* are the longest and most common species. *A. nasuta* has been propagated in the moist, warm rainforest terrarium. Ten young snakes of one clutch were on average 44 cm (17.6 in) long and weighed 2.4 grams (0.08 oz) each. They accepted young frogs as food. Because the young snakes refused strips of fish disguised with frog scent, they were force-fed every four to five days with heart, fish, and mouse parts. Larger stuffed pieces were regurgitated after two to three days; some snakes died in the process, suffering from cramps. At three months of age the first young snake, which was now 55 cm (22 in) long, ate pinkie mice for the first time.

SIMILAR SPECIES

Central and South American counterparts of the tree snakes (*Ahaetulla*) are the vine snakes, including *Oxybelis fulgidus*. Primarily lizard and frog eaters, vine snakes can be accustomed to small birds and mice. After copulations in December, the female was unable to lay the entire clutch in early March and died after 13 days. From the remaining pure-white eggs (4.8 to 5.1 X 2.0 to 2.2 cm, 1.9-2 X 0.8-0.9 in), one youngster 43.5 cm (17.4 in) hatched after 83 days at 24 to 26°C (75-79°F). With its green coloration and the white longitudinal lines on the flanks it looked the same as its parents. It had to be force-fed with nestling mice.

FLYING SNAKES (*CHRYSOPELEA*)

Flying snakes are kept under the same terrarium conditions as the tree snakes. A single wild-caught specimen of *C. ornata* kept by the author took offered nestling mice without problems. Later it bit on the tail of a tree snake (*A. prasina*) that was kept in the same terrarium. A few minutes later the tree snake died from the effect of the venomous bite. A flying snake (*C. ornata*) approximately 1.3 meters (4.3 ft) long laid 8 to 14 cylindrical eggs in the terrarium. The eggs were 2.8 to 3.6 X 1.4 to 1.6 cm (1.1-1.4 X 0.6 in) and weighed 4.0 to 4.9 grams (0.14-0.17 oz). During incubation at 25 to 26°C (77-79°F) the eggs increased in weight by more than a third. After 70 to 92 days the eggs hatched, the young snakes interestingly always cutting through the shell at the poles. The youngsters, 18.7 to 20.5 cm (7.5-8.2 in) long, exhibited a pale green ground color and had dark rings. They had to be force-fed with small fishes at first.

CAT SNAKES (*BOIGA*)

The cat snakes or mangrove snakes inhabit the most diverse biotopes of tropical Asia and Africa. The Southeast Asian Mangrove Tree Snake (*B. dendrophila*), called the Ularburong in Malay, is handsomely colored and grows up to 2 meters (6.6 ft) long. The blackish blue dorsal side is crossed by bright yellow rings. The bite of this powerful snake is poisonous and reputedly can be fatal. Ularburongs are nocturnal and eat chicks, chicken eggs, mice, and rats, as well as their terrarium mates. To stimulate reproduction, lowering the keeping temperatures of about 28 to 35°C (82-95°F) by about 6°C (10°F) in the winter and mimicking the summer monsoon have been recommended. Terrarium animals laid 5 to 13 eggs; the incubation periods were 122 to 129 days at 25 to 27°C (77-81°F), 93 to 95 days at 27°C (81°F), and 92 to 93 days at 30°C (86°F). A captive-bred female mated at barely two years of age in late April and laid five eggs 51 days later, another five eggs after an additional 120 days, and four more in March of the following year. All eggs of the last clutch, however, were infertile. The young snakes were 28 to 40 centimeters (11.2-16 in) long, weighed 12 grams (0.4 oz), and did not molt until they were four to six weeks old. Some had to be force-fed for two to four months with pinkie mice. Later they usually took two mice weighing 15 grams (0.5 oz) each per week and grew rapidly; one young snake grew from 33 to 72 cm (13.2 to 28.8 in) in five months.

The barely meter-long (3.3-ft) Steppes Cat Snake (*Boiga trigonata*), which ranges from central India to central Asia, rarely reaches the market. In its Indian homeland this snake feeds primarily on agamid lizards of the genus *Calotes*, but in the terrarium it can be fed exclusively with nestling to half-grown mice. A female that lived with two males in a terrarium with dimensions of only 75 X 70 X 80 cm (30 X 30 X 32 in) produced five clutches of seven to ten eggs in three years. From the total of 41 eggs produced, 40 young snakes hatched after incubation in moist peat. They proved to be hard to rear. Mice were not accepted, so forced-feeding with strips of vitamin-enriched beef heart and mouse legs and tails had to be carried out. The independent intake of mice was not observed until the specimens were two and a half years old.

SANDSNAKES (*PSAMMOPHIS*)

The approximately 16 species of sandsnakes are widely distributed mostly in the steppes and savannahs of Asia and Africa. The literature contains numerous reports on their "cleaning" head movements; this is a rare comfort behavior for snakes that also occurs with species of the fierce snakes (*Malpolon*). With a body length of 1.2 to 1.5 meters (4-5 ft), the African *Psammophis sibilans* probably is the most frequently kept species in the terrarium. It feeds on mice. From clutches of ten and four eggs 3.5 cm (1.4 in) long, weighing about 4 grams (0.14 oz), young snakes 20 to 25 cm (8-10 in) long hatched after 91 and 64 days, respectively. A Red-striped Sandsnake (*P. subtaeniatus*) scattered a total of 12 eggs throughout the terrarium one day in August. Without external assistance, none of the youngsters hatched even after more than 77 days. From a second clutch of 11 eggs, deposited in a protected corner in mid-October, ten young snakes hatched after about 64 days of incubation in moist sand. The youngsters from this second clutch, at a length of about 30 cm (12 in), were larger than those of the first clutch. After the young sandsnakes had refused earthworms, crickets, and pinkie mice, they were stuffed with raw chicken and horse meat as well as strips of beef heart dipped in egg yolk; at times they were also force-fed a lactose-free dietetic food through a tube. The young sandsnakes developed well on this diet.

Cat-eyed Snake, *Leptodeira nigrofasciata*. Photo by F. Golder.

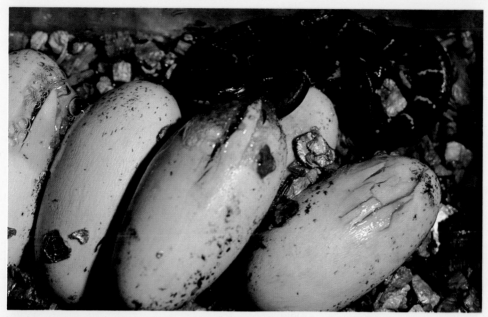

Mangrove Tree Snake, *Boiga dendrophila melanota*, hatching. Photo by V. Nagele.

SIMILAR SPECIES

The Shaapsteker (*Psammophylax rhombeatus*) from South Africa closely resembles the sandsnakes. Wild-caught specimens soon became tame in the terrarium and ate mice. Two of them laid five and six eggs in late October. The young snakes hatched after an incubation period of 44 to 45 days and molted two to three weeks later. They had to be force-fed with heart, but digested this food well and grew fast.

BOOMSLANG (*DISPHOLIDUS TYPUS*)

The Boomslang is an arboreal snake of equatorial and southern Africa that is about 1.5 meters (5 ft) long. This snake is very variable in coloration and needs a heated tropical terrarium with numerous climbing branches. As a rule, brown Boomslangs are supposed to be females, whereas the ones of a different color tend to be males. Boomslangs should be kept only by experienced venomous snake keepers who have a supply of the specific antiserum available—the only one effective against rear-fang toxins. Boomslangs become very tame and seldom bite, but precisely this fact has led to serious bites. Caution also is advised in the forced-feeding even of young snakes. Boomslangs have been propagated repeatedly in the terrarium. They lay 8 to 20 or more cylindrical eggs 3.4 to 4.0 X 1.6 to 2.6 cm (1.4-1.6 X 0.6-1 in) that weigh 11.1 to 14.5 grams (0.4-0.5 oz). Maturation took 84 to 94 days at about 28°C (82°F); however, reports of over 120 to even 210 days also exist. Immediately after hatching, when disturbed the 40-cm (16-in) young snakes displayed the species-typical threat behavior, vertical distension of the neck region and the front of the body, and immediately struck at the intruder. When newborn mice and rats, lizards, frogs, and crickets were not accepted, forced-feeding had to be used. Because the natural diet of Boomslangs consists primarily of chameleons, adults often are difficult to acclimate to mice.

HERALD SNAKE (*CROTAPHOPELTIS HOTAMBOEIA*)

The Herald or White-lipped Snake, a nocturnal inhabitant of arid areas, grows to a length of about 70 cm (28 in) and is distributed through eastern and southern Africa. Although this species prefers frogs and toads, it can also be fed with small mice. This rear-fang laid 6 to 12 eggs 2.7 to 3.5 X 0.8 to 1.2 cm (1.1-1.4 X 0.3-0.5 in). The incubation of the eggs of a wild-caught specimen from Ethiopia, which were laid in mid-May, took 73 days. The young snakes were only about 8 cm (3.2 in) long.

CAT-EYED SNAKES (*LEPTODEIRA*)

The cat-eyed snakes are found from South America to southern Texas and seldom grow longer than 1 meter (3.3 ft). The Banana Snake (*L. annulata*), which is mostly terrestrial and lives from Mexico to Argentina, has entered the literature because of long-term amphigonia retardata. Frogs and lizards are the natural foods of the cat-eyed snakes. Noteworthy is the captive breeding of a barely 80-cm (32-in) pair that had been force-fed for five years exclusively with mice. The nocturnal snakes spent the day under a foam-rubber cover. Two to three times a year the female laid six to nine pure-white eggs, 2.3 to 3.0 X 1.0 to 1.3 cm (0.9-1.2 X 0.4-0.5 in). At 24 to 28°C (75-82°F) and 100% relative humidity, the incubation period was 62 to 65 days. The young snakes were 15 cm (6 in) long at hatching and were initially force-fed up to a size of about 21 cm (8.4 in) with guppies, later with nestling mice. At an age of six months they were 30 to 38.5 cm (12-15.4 in) long.

THE VENOMOUS SNAKES: ELAPIDS, VIPERS, PITVIPERS

Keeping venomous snakes in the terrarium is a controversial practice. Although they scarcely differ in their requirements from nonvenomous snakes, a lot of special provisions are required for keeping venomous snakes that are intended to ensure the safety of the hobbyist and his environment. Every hobbyist who wants to keep venomous snakes must become familiar with these provisions.

Keeping these snakes should not, however, be rejected out of hand. The venomous snake genera are just as interesting as the nonvenomous snakes; they need to have their requirements and habits studied and also need protection for their survival in the wild.

Although the author cannot contribute any of his own experiences on keeping and propagating poisonous snakes in the following sections, the examples of published breed-

ing successes should prove valuable as a review of the literature.

COBRAS AND ALLIES (ELAPIDAE)

Most of the approximately 200 species of the family Elapidae are colubridlike and relatively slender. With the King Cobra (*Ophiophagus hannah*)—record length of over 5.5 meters (18.2 ft)—and the Australian Taipan (*Oxyuranus scutellatus*)—a generous 4 meters (13.2 ft) long—this family contains two of the three largest species of venomous snakes. Many species, however, barely reach a length of 1 meter (3.3 ft).

COBRAS (*NAJA*)

The eight or more cobra species (their taxonomy currently is being disputed) are terrestrial snakes of the most diverse biotopes, from the thorn-bush steppes to the margins of tropical rainforests, from Africa to Southeast Asia. Their maximum lengths are between 1.4 and 2.5 meters (4.6-8.3 ft). Because of the hood most species spread when excited, they are also called the hooded cobras.

Propagation: Some species of cobras are bred regularly. For example, the Asian *Naja naja*—frequently kept in the subspecies or full species *N. n. naja*, *N. n. kaouthia*, and *N. n. atra*—usually mated in the terrarium in November and December and laid 9 to 32, on average about 16, eggs after a gestation period of 38 to 103 days. More often than not second clutches of up to 21 eggs were laid within a month. The eggs measured 4.5 to 5.5 X 2.2 to 2.6 cm (1.8-2.2 X 0.9-1 in) and weighed about 20 grams (0.7 oz). At incubation temperatures ranging from 21 to over 30°C (70-86°F), the young cobras hatched after 43 to 93 days in three to six hours. The presence of an egg tooth is disputed. Even when disturbed during hatching, the excitable youngsters exhibited their species-typical threat behavior. The length of the hatched cobras, perhaps also somewhat species-dependent, was between 22.5 and 36 cm (9-14.4 in). The first molt took place after 15 to 27 days; by then some of the youngsters had already independently taken 2-3.5-gram (0.07-0.12-oz) white mice and grass frogs. At first the youngsters are gray-green with contrasting, variable markings, but the coloration fades at three to four months of age (juvenile coloration again perhaps varying with species or subspecies). One-year-old captive-bred snakes weighed between 73 and 253 grams (2.6-8.9 oz).

Unlike the Southeast Asian Cobra, *N. naja*, the Black and White Cobra (*N. melanoleuca*) comes from Africa. It can be very long-lived in the terrarium. After ritual fights between the males and extended courtship, 11 to 13 eggs were laid in October and May. The young cobras hatched after 78 to 104 days and were 35 to 40 cm (14-16 in) long. In one case twins that hatched were clearly smaller than their siblings. After the molt at an age of eight to ten days, the young cobras first took frogs, later small mice. When frogs were not available, the snakes had to be force-fed three or four times with pinkie mice before they fed independently.

A group of Cape Cobras (*N. nivea*) took shelter at winter temperatures of about 15 to 22°C (59-72°F), but matings began in mid-March. Eight to 12 eggs, some of which were infertile, were laid in each case in May and June. The young snakes hatched after 59 to 60 days at 29 to 30°C (84-86°F); some of them ate pinkie mice on their own, while others had to be force-fed.

Captive breedings have also been reported with the Egyptian Cobra (*N. haje*), the Mozambique Spitting Cobra (*N. mossambica*), and the Black-necked Spitting Cobra (*N. nigricollis*).

OTHER SPECIES

The largest living poisonous snake, the King Cobra (*Ophiophagus hannah*) of southern and southeastern Asia, also displays a hood; this snake is very closely related systematically to the genus *Naja*. Because it preys almost exclusively on snakes, its feeding in the terrarium is problematic. In some cases King Cobras accepted dead rats and strips of meat disguised with snake scent; in others they were acclimated to freshwater fishes, particularly eels. A female in a zoo terrarium repeatedly built a nest of leaves and twigs in which it laid 41 and 51 eggs. After an incubation period of 10 to 11 weeks, the young snakes hatched. The youngsters

exhibited the characteristic juvenile coloration of a blackish background color with pale bands.

The Black Forest Cobra (*Pseudohaje goldi*) seldom is imported but has been bred in its African homeland. Eleven and 17 eggs of 5.1 to 6.4 X 2.5 cm (2-2.6 X 1 in) were laid in two clutches; they were matured successfully at 29 to 30°C (84-86°F) through an incubation period of 88 to 94 days.

MAMBAS (*DENDROASPIS*)

Mambas are slender and very agile tree dwellers in tropical savannahs and forests of central and southern Africa. The Black Mamba (*D. polylepis*) at 4 meters (13.2 ft) is the largest species. All species are very dangerous and extremely aggressive, especially before they have become acclimated.

Propagation: Eastern Green Mambas (*D. angusticeps*) as well as Black Mambas have been bred over several generations in captivity. Green Mambas copulated for 15 to 17 hours in the terrarium in mid-April and laid five normal eggs 6.8 to 8.7 X 2.8 to 3.0 cm (2.7-3.5 X 1.1-1.2 in) as well as three smaller, infertile eggs after 99 days. After 85 to 88 days of incubation, two baby mambas 40 cm (16 in) long hatched. They accepted pinkie mice after five days. In contrast to their pale leaf-green parents, the young snakes were a gleaming metallic turquoise color.

OTHER ELAPIDS

The Taipan (*Oxyuranus scutellatus*), one of the most poisonous snakes of the Australian continent, was bred regularly over several generations in an Australian zoo. In eight years, 83 young snakes were produced. True captive breedings also have been achieved, although mostly in Australia, with the Death Adder (*Acanthophis antarcticus*) native to that continent. Three young males reared in Europe were kept together in very close quarters because of misidentification of the sex. In stressful situations the snakes struck at and bit their cagemates instead of the offered prey animals. The remaining snake, which survived in captivity for almost 16 years, reached 392 grams (13.7 oz) and a length of 77 cm (30.8 in).

The Water Cobra (*Boulengerina annulata*), belonging to the only aquatic genus of the family (if you exclude the *Laticauda* sea snakes, often considered to be elapids), has been bred. It feeds primarily on fishes and amphibians. After 78 to 84 days, 15 young snakes from 31 to 43 cm (12.4-17.2 in) long and weighing up to 20.3 grams (0.7 oz) hatched from 22 eggs that were 5.2 to 6.4 X 3.1 to 3.5 cm (2-2.7 X 1.2-1.4 in) long and weighed 3.2 to 3.8 grams (0.1 oz). They fed on small fishes (*Gambusia*) and pinkie mice.

TRUE VIPERS (VIPERIDAE)

NORTHERN ADDER (*VIPERA BERUS*)

The Northern or Common Adder has a huge range across the whole Palearctic from however, only take frogs. Field mouse and deer mice, occasionally house mice (remember the chance of serious intestinal worm problems), often are preferred to laboratory mice. A hibernation period lasting several months and a roomy terrarium with local bottom heating provide the conditions for their breeding.

Propagation: During the mating period that starts soon after hibernation, ritual fights, especially between freshly molted males, are not uncommon. The copulations in May can last up to two and a half hours. In observations in the wild it was determined that the gestation period of Northern Adders lasts 2.5 to 4.5 months depending on weather conditions. In the terrarium one female Northern Adder gave birth to nine

Caucasus Viper, *Vipera kaznakovi*. Photo by L. Trutnau.

Spain to Siberia and is the best known representative of its genus. It is closely related to the Caucasus Viper (*V. kaznakovi*), which formerly was classified as a subspecies of the Northern Adder, and the Iberian Viper (*V. seoanei*), which some taxonomists still classify as a subspecies of the Northern Adder, as well as the Meadow Viper (*V. ursini*).

Keeping: Imported Northern Adders can be good mouse eaters and live for many years in the terrarium; many individuals, live young 82 days after an observed copulation, with five- to eight-minute pauses between the individual births. After a few seconds of total stillness the young snakes moved vigorously and penetrated the chorions with their heads. Remnants of the yolk sac still clung to them for some time. The litter sizes were generally between 4 and 20 young, with seven to ten youngsters considered average. At a body length of about 14 to 21 cm (5.6-8.4 in), the young snakes weighed about 4 grams (0.14 oz).

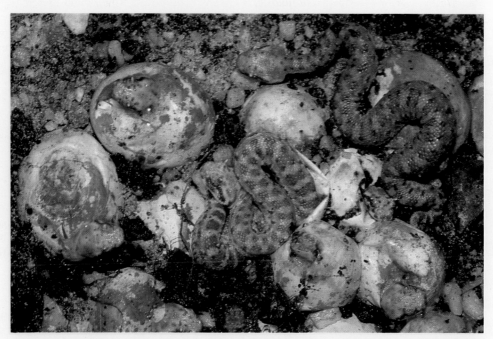

Above: Desert Horned-Vipers, *Cerastes cerastes*. Photo by L. Trutnau. **Below:** Common Puff-Adder, *Bitis arietans*. Photo by J. Vergner.

Rearing: At 28 to 30°C (82-86°F) the young Northern Adders usually fed independently after four to ten days. They preferred tiny frogs and frog parts; newborn mice had to be cut up because of their size. Pieces of beef heart also were accepted, especially when the young snakes bit into them first.

SIMILAR SPECIES

Caucasus Vipers (*V. kaznakovi*) have been bred repeatedly in the terrarium. The young adders fed on crickets, grasshoppers, pinkie mice, and of course small frogs and lizards. Their brown juvenile coloration changed into the attractive markings of the parents after several molts.

The Meadow Viper (*V. ursini*) also has been propagated. Its small (12 to 13 cm, 4.8-5.2 in) young preferred crickets and small grasshoppers and also took cockroaches and mouse parts.

LONG-NOSED VIPERS (*VIPERA AMMODYTES*)

A turned-up tip of the snout—the nasal horn—characterizes the southeastern Europe Asp Viper (*V. aspis*), the Long-nosed Viper (*V. ammodytes*) of southwestern Asia and adjacent Europe, and the Snub-nosed Viper (*V. latastei*) from the Iberian Peninsula and northwestern Africa.

The most highly recommended and easy-to-keep species of the genus *Vipera* for the terrarium hobby is doubtless the Long-nosed Viper (*V. ammodytes*). Because of misconceptions about its native biotope, it is still often called the Sand Viper. It usually grows to 60 to 70 cm (24-28 in), rarely about 1 meter (40 in) long, and prefers arid slopes overgrown with shrubs as well as rock piles along arid meadows and fields.

Keeping: Daytime temperatures between 24 and 28°C (75-82°F), at night below 20°C (68°F); mice, sparrows, and chicks as the dietary basis; a roomy terrarium; and above all a four- to five-month dry overwintering at 4 to 6°C (39-43°F) are among the conditions necessary for propagation. Uncontrolled feeding must be avoided, because as a result of their big appetites many specimens become extremely obese and unsuitable for breeding.

Propagation: The prospects of successful propagation improve when groups including several males are used. Ritual fights usually are initiated when several males in breeding condition encounter a sexually mature female of their species. Copulations usually took place in the terrarium in April and May, depending on the timing of hibernation. Gestation periods seldom are precisely known; 80 to 85 days as well as 113 days have been documented with captive snakes. Long-nosed Vipers usually give birth to their young in late October. Three to 20 young snakes per litter are possible, but five to nine young usually are produced in the terrarium, as a rule during the day. With boring head movements the young vipers free themselves from the elongated birth membrane and then quickly move along the terrarium glass and seek out shelter. The horn on the tip of the snout lies flat for days before it is first erected in the most robust young snakes. Sexes can be distinguished externally even in the young snakes: males usually are gray with prominent markings, while females have a brownish ground color and duller markings. The lengths given for newborn Long-nosed Vipers are between 14 and 26 cm (5.6-10.4 in); reported birth weights vary between 4.5 and 10.5 grams (0.16-0.37 oz).

Rearing: The interest young vipers displayed in the food offered to them was very variable. Because young lizards could not be offered as the first food, the best results were achieved with dry (!) live young frogs and the legs of slightly hairy gray mice. Prey reflexes were triggered only with quick movements of the young mice, which died one to five minutes after being bitten. Young snakes that refused to feed independently were fed with variable success with a food paste given through a tube; they exhibited hardly any appetite and lacked the initiative to capture prey. The initial aggressiveness of the young snakes soon subsided. At six to eight months they were already 50 cm (20 in) long; they became sexually mature at two years of age in the terrarium.

SIMILAR SPECIES

Regular breedings of the Asp Viper (*Vipera aspis*) refute the claim that this species is less suitable for terrarium keeping than other species of the genus. In the terrarium, hybrids with the Long-nosed Viper were produced. The Asp Vipers were quite easy to rear with pinkie mice.

The Snub-nosed Viper (*Vipera latastei*) readily took live and dead mice. This species has been propagated on numerous occasions in captivity. The young snakes apparently are quite easy to rear with small lizards, grasshoppers, and hairless mice.

ORIENTAL VIPERS (*DABOIA*)

Formerly classified in the genus *Vipera*, today the Oriental Vipers often are placed in the genus *Daboia*. Interestingly, the majority of the subspecies of the Levantine Viper (*D. lebetina*) lay eggs, but *D. l. obtusa* and the nominate subspecies generally are livebearing in some regions. Levantine Vipers are in general quite hardy in the terrarium and present no problems in feeding. Breeding them is not as easy, although it has occurred. The young snakes should be reared with pinkie mice, if necessary force-fed. The Atlas Viper (*D. mauretanica*), like the Levantine Viper, likes warmth. A clutch of 21 eggs laid by a pregnant wild-caught female has been reported. The young snakes (25 to 28 cm, 10-11.2 in) took mice independently following their first molt after nine or ten days.

The Ottoman Viper (*D. xanthina*) is an inhabitant of higher elevations of Turkey that are subject to cold conditions. Cool overwintering at 4 to 10°C (39-50°F) is an essential stimulus for the reproduction of this species. Two weeks after hibernation and rewarming to 26 to 30°C (79-86°F), the first copulations were observed. Ten young snakes were produced after 84 days. They left their membranes after a few minutes, but molted only after seven to eight days. They were on average 20 cm (8 in) long and usually fed immediately after molting.

Palestine Vipers (*D. palaestinae*) have been propagated repeatedly in the terrarium. They laid their eggs about 35 days after mating. The young snakes, which hatched after about two months, readily fed on pinkie mice. Russell's Viper (*D. russelli*), which is widely distributed over southern Asia and because of its beautiful markings and its hardiness is very popular with fanciers of venomous snakes, needs higher temperatures, 27 to 32°C (81-90°F) during the day, 22 to 24°C (72-75°F) at night, with local bottom heating at 28 to 35°C (82-95°F). Russell's Vipers like to be sprayed regularly with lukewarm water. This snake has been propagated on many occasions. For example, 27 and 29 young snakes were born in June and July; they molted and took nestling mice immediately. They fed extremely well and were already 90 to 110 cm (36-44 in) long at one year of age.

CARPET- OR SAW-SCALED VIPERS (*ECHIS*)

The carpet-vipers have a huge area of distribution from Africa to central and southern Asia. Their toxin is considered to be the most potent viper toxin; despite quick treatment with serum, bites by *Echis* still were fatal. Both the Saw-scaled Carpet-Viper (*E. carinatus*) and the Painted Carpet-Viper (*E. coloratus*) have been propagated repeatedly. When the two species were crossed, the mates copulated repeatedly in early May during a period of five days and the female laid 14 eggs after four months. The maturation of the clutch on sphagnum moss at 26 to 32°C (79-90°F) and 80-90% humidity took 39 to 43 days. The nine healthy hybrids that hatched were about 15 cm (6 in) long and weighed only 1.1 grams (0.04 oz) each. After the first molt, seven to nine days after hatching, when they ignored crickets, grasshoppers, and wax moths, they were force-fed with strips of beef heart. Pure-bred *E. carinatus* offspring bred by other hobbyists have in some cases taken pinkie mice, crickets, and especially lizards.

COMMON PUFF-ADDER (*BITIS ARIETANS*)

Arid regions from North Africa and Arabia to South Africa are the homeland of the 90-120-cm (36-48-in), sometimes over 180 cm (72 in) , Common Puff-Adder.

Keeping: The Puff-Adder usually becomes well acclimated to terrarium keeping. Many specimens often lie about sluggishly the whole day in the terrarium, but others bite without warning and with unexpected speed. Bottom heating, which provides local warming to 28 to 32°C (82-90°F), contributes to the well-being of the snakes.

Cascabels, *Crotalus durissus terrificus*. Photo by L. Trutnau.

Propagation: The Puff-Adder is propagated frequently, often too frequently. Its usually quite large litters—with 157 young they probably hold the record among snakes—can hardly even be given away free to qualified hobbyists. This has led to the curious circumstance that some Puff-Adder keepers want to have their snakes surgically sterilized.

When they are kept in groups, impressive ritual fights often are observed. Puff-Adders reach sexual maturity relatively early. For example, 14-month-old snakes mated in June, and in January and February of the following year, besides a few unfertilized eggs, gave birth to plump young 12 to 19 cm (4.8-7.6 in) long and weighing 5 to 15 grams (0.18-0.5 oz); births occurred at intervals of 2 to 20 minutes. Immediately after they freed themselves from the chorions, the newborn Puff-Adders burrowed into the substrate and molted without problems.

Rearing: At an age of two days, the first young mice (weighing up to 4 grams, 0.14 oz) were eaten. Even the smallest specimens only 12 cm (4.8 in) in length managed such mice effortlessly.

In another litter, a 10-kilogram (22 pounds), almost 2-meters (6.6-ft) female gave birth to 20 young 21 cm (8.4 in) long and 9.8 grams (0.3 oz) that molted within the first hours of life; most fed the first evening.

SIMILAR SPECIES

Young Gaboon Vipers (*Bitis gabonica*) were predominantly born in March in the terrarium. Two small members of the genus, the 40-cm (16-in) Horned Puff-Adder (*B. caudalis*) and the Berg Puff-Adder (*B. atropos*) of South Africa, occasionally have been propagated. The tiny young (8 to 9 cm, 3.2-3.6 in) of the Horned Puff-Adder had to be force-fed for six months with thin strips of beef heart before they took pinkie mice at a length of 22 cm (8.8 in). Young Berg Puff-Adders soon ate pinkie mice and mouse parts, particularly when they were kept individually.

OTHER VIPERS

North African Desert Horned-Vipers (*Cerastes cerastes*) are hardy and attractive charges in the heated desert terrarium with a thick layer of sand. An overwintering of several months at 10 to 15°C (50-59°F) with the terrarium lighting turned off is necessary to promote readiness to breed. Usually in July and August, 13 to 16 oval, soft-shelled eggs are laid that must be kept quite moist during incubation. The 16-18-cm (6.4-7.2-in) young hatched after 45 to 48 days and usually had to be force-fed at first with pinkie mice.

The Persian Horned-Viper (*Pseudocerastes persicus*) also has been bred. Before it could be bred, however, information on its natural habits had to be collected. Gradually lowering the temperature from 30°C (October) to 25°C (December) (86 to 77°F) while simultaneously shortening the day length (December: five hours; 20°C, 68°F, in the dark phase, 15°C, 59°F, at night), and then increasing the amount of daylight up to ten hours and raising the temperature to 27 to 30°C (81-86°F) from January to March led to mating. Fifteen eggs were laid after a gestation period of 107 days (April to July). After only 17 days, six young snakes 15 to 16 cm (6-6.4 in) long hatched. The crickets and nestling mice offered after the first molt were not taken, so the young snakes had to be force-fed once a week with strips of beef heart.

The predominantly green Rough-scaled Bush Viper (*Atheris squamiger*), a species from western central Africa, has been bred successfully on a number of occasions. The snakes mated in August at an age of 16 months and gave birth the following March and April to quite variably colored youngsters about 23 cm (9.2 in) long weighing 5 grams (0.18 oz). As a rule, the young could be reared without any particular problems with mice and small fishes.

The African Night-Adders (*Causus*) feed principally on frogs and toads and could scarcely be accustomed to other prey animals. The Rhombic Night-Adder (*C. rhombeatus*) is quite productive. Its eggs have been brought to maturity on several occasions. This species is very adaptable and hardy.

PITVIPERS (CROTALIDAE)

About a dozen genera belong to the pitvipers, a family named for the pit-shaped temperature sensory organ between the snout and eyes that is used by the predominantly crepuscular and nocturnal snakes to orient themselves and to search for warm-blooded prey. Many herpetologists consider the pitvipers to be just a subfamily of the Viperidae.

RATTLESNAKES (*CROTALUS*)

The majority of rattlesnake species are native to the southwestern United States and Mexico. Only the Cascabel Rattlesnake (*C. durissus*, including the distinctively marked Uracoan Rattlesnake, *C. d. vegrandis* of Venezuela) has advanced as far as South America. With the exception of the Santa Catalina Rattlesnake (*C. catalinensis*), all have the characteristic tail rattle that they use to produce the typical buzzing warning sound. The large species in particular are very dangerous because of the long poison fangs and the amounts of toxin they inject.

Gaboon Viper, *Bitis gabonica*. Photo by Jim Merli.

SPECIES OF RATTLESNAKE (*CROTALUS*) THAT HAVE BEEN CAPTIVE-BRED MORE THAN ONCE

Species	Type of terrarium	Keeping temperature daytime (nighttime) (°C)	Overwintering Duration (months)	Overwintering temperature (°C)
Eastern Diamondback Rattlesnake (*C. adamanteus*)	arid terrarium	25 to 27 (18 to 20)	2 to 3	10 to 15
Western Diamondback Rattlesnake (*C. atrox*)	arid terrarium	25 to 32 (18 to 20)	2 to 3	10 to 15
West Coast Rattlesnake (*C. basiliscus*)	arid terrarium	25 to 30 (20 to 22)	not applicable	
Sidewinder (*C. cerastes*)	desert terrarium	25 to 32 (18 to 20)	3 to 4	15 to 18
Cascabel Rattlesnake (*C. durissus*)	arid terrarium	24 to 30 (24 to 30)	not applicable	
Timber Rattlesnake (*C. horridus*)	forest terrarium	23 to 28 (18 to 20)	4	10
Rock Rattlesnake (*C. lepidus*)	forest terrarium	24 to 28 32 (in localized areas) (18 to 22)	4	8 to 12
Speckled Rattlesnake (*C. mitchelli*)	desert terrarium	25 to 32 (18 to 22)	3 to 5	8 to 12
Red Diamond Rattlesnake (*C. ruber*)	desert terrarium	25 to 32 (18 to 20)	3 to 4	8 to 12
Mojave Rattlesnake (*C. scutulatus*)	forest terrarium	18 to 28 depending on provenance (18 to 22)	3 to 4	10 to 15
Western Rattlesnake (*C. viridis*)	arid terrarium	22 to 28 (18 to 28)	4 to 5	less than 10
Ridgenose Rattlesnake (*C. willardi*)	forest terrarium (moist)	18 to 25 (less than 18)	4 to 5	less than 10

Keeping: A number of rattlesnake species have been bred in terraria both in the United States and Europe. Frequently available and often kept for many years and propagated in the terrarium are the Western Diamondback Rattlesnake (*C. atrox*); the very even-tempered Red Diamond Rattlesnake (*C. ruber*), which is kept under similar conditions; the Western Rattlesnake (*C. viridis*) and the Timber Rattlesnake (*C. horridus*). These species are fed with small mammals and birds of suitable size. Youngsters of the Eastern Diamondback Rattlesnake (*C. adamanteus*)—with a record length of over 2.5 meters (8.25 ft) and a body weight of 10 kilograms (22 pounds) the largest rattlesnake—became acclimated more readily to terrarium conditions than did wild-caught adults. The interesting Sidewinder (*C. cerastes*), like its Old World counterpart the Desert Horned-Viper (*Cerastes cerastes*), should have a layer of sand at least 10 cm (4 in) deep. Some snakes, however, absolutely refused to eat mice and starved if they were not given lizards.

Propagation: Impressive ritual fights can be observed with most species after hibernation; they are followed by copulation. All rattlesnakes are livebearing and give birth, depending on size, to 6 to 60 young that usually can be reared without problems with pinkie mice. Young Eastern Diamondback Rattlesnakes, for example, ate medium-sized mice only a few days after birth.

The tropical Cascabel (*C. durissus*) is known to have extraordinarily long gestation periods of 240 to 270 days. The subspecies *C. d. terrificus* has been bred frequently. One-day-old Cascabels were 20 to 35 cm (8-14 in) long; at three years of age one captive-bred snake was sexually mature and measured 127 cm (51 in). Not infrequently hybrids occur between various *Crotalus* species and their subspecies when they are kept together.

PYGMY-RATTLESNAKES (*SISTRURUS*)

These small relatives of the rattlesnakes from the United States and Mexico have considerably smaller rattles than *Crotalus* and have nine plates covering the head (greatly fragmented plates are present in *Crotalus*).

All three species, of which the Mexican Pygmy-Rattlesnake (*S. ravus*) at 50 to 70 cm (20-28 in) in length is the largest and most dangerous, have been bred repeatedly in the terrarium. They are livebearing but they almost never give birth to more than ten young. The Massasauga (*S. catenatus*) took mice and young rats in the terrarium and reacted to several months of cool overwintering with increased readiness to breed. The Mexican Pygmy-Rattlesnake should be kept at daytime temperatures of 20 to 30°C (68-86°F) and hibernated at somewhat lower temperatures. The Lowland Pygmy-Rattlesnake (*S. miliarius*) also was propagated under these conditions. Newborn rattlesnakes of all species were 15 to 24 cm (6-9.6 in) long and took nestling mice without further ceremony after the first molt.

COPPERHEADS (*AGKISTRODON*)

The copperheads are native to North America and also to Asia. Recently the Asian species were divided among the genera *Deinagkistrodon*, *Hypnale*, and *Calloselasma*, with those remaining in *Agkistrodon* placed in the genus or subgenus *Gloydius*.

COTTONMOUTH (*AGKISTRODON PISCIVORUS*)

The Cottonmouth or Water Moccasin is a thick-bodied pitviper that is vaguely similar to and often confused with some of the *Nerodia* species. It is highly aquatic. It grows to a length of about 75 to 120 cm (30-48 in) (record length 188 cm, 75 in) and prefers standing bodies of water in the southern United States.

Keeping: This snake has a large natural spectrum of prey and should be fed with fishes and small mammals. A fairly cool hibernation is advised, because it makes the male's attempts to mate all the more active. At the same time, an interesting defensive behavior of the female toward the ready-to-mate male has been observed: she suddenly turns around and positions herself with head raised high in threat posture.

Propagation: Cottonmouths have been bred frequently and over several generations. After a gestation period of four to six months (reports of more than 11 months also exist),

Southern Copperhead, *Agkistrodon contortrix contortrix*. Neonatal specimen (note brightly colored tail). Photo by Mella Panzella.

five to eight or more young are produced. In contrast to their dull brown to nearly black parents, they have yellow-brown cross bars. Typically they are 25 to 30 cm (10-12 in) long. After the molt at eight days, occasionally before, small fishes, nestling mice, and young frogs (especially the latter) are taken. Sometimes, how-ever, rearing takes a lot of effort in the first weeks.

AMERICAN COPPERHEAD (*AGKISTRODON CONTORTRIX*)

The American Copperhead is a crepuscular and nocturnal inhabitant of forests, meadows, and pastures of most of the eastern and

Above: Golden Lancehead, *Bothrops insularis*. Photo by Dr. Sherman A. Minton. **Below:** Pope's Green-Pitviper, *Trimeresurus popeorum*. Photo by H. Dedekind.

central United States that generally is 60 to 90 cm (24-36 in) long, occasionally reaching 130 cm (52 in). It is a popular venomous snake in the terrarium because of its exquisite markings, its ease of keeping, and not least because it is not all that dangerous. It is urgently recommended to keep this snake singly, because not only does it readily take mice, young rats, sparrows, or chicks, but conspecifics as well. Continuously high temperatures lead to a suspension of feeding.

Propagation: American Copperheads mated after several months of hibernation at 3 to 8°C (37-46°F). Males were very aggressive during this time. After a gestation period of 105 to 110 days, usually four to six, but as many as 17, young snakes were produced. At first they were motionless, coiled two or three times in their transparent chorion for several minutes up to as long as a few hours before they freed themselves with jerky movements of the head and body. Average lengths were 20 to 22 cm (8-8.8 in). Only a few accepted pinkie mice right away. If frogs were not available as food, many of them had to be force-fed two or three times.

OTHER SPECIES

The Plain-scale Pitviper (*A. [Gloydius] halys*), native to Siberia and eastern Asia, has seldom been bred so far. In the dry terrarium with a water bowl and with cool overwintering, copulations took place in late March to April. In late August and early September, three to ten young snakes 13 to 19 cm (5.2-7.6 in) long and weighing about 5 grams (0.18 oz) were born. Because crickets were ignored and lizards were not available, often several months of forced-feeding were necessary before the young snakes took mice and mouse parts.

The most warmth-loving copperhead is the Malayan Pitviper (*Calloselasma rhodostoma*). This snake and the Hundred-Pace Pitviper (*Deinagkistrodon acutus*) are the only egg-laying species of the *Agkistrodon* group, the litters averaging some 10 to 35 eggs. The young snakes hatched after 35 to 60 days at 28 to 32°C (82-90°F). Owing to a lack of frogs, they had to be force-fed with nestling mice before they caught their own mice.

AMERICAN LANCEHEADS (*BOTHROPS*)

The approximately 50 species of this genus represent the most diverse ecological and morphological types; all species are livebearing. Their body lengths range from 60 cm to 2 meters (24-40 in). Recently the genus has been split into about six smaller genera or subgenera, including *Bothriechis, Porthidium*, and smaller groups.

EYELASH PALM-PITVIPER (*BOTHROPS SCHLEGELI*)

A typical inhabitant of the moist and warm rainforest terrarium is the Eyelash Palm-Pitviper, which is found from southern Mexico to Venezuela and Ecuador. This nocturnal and arboreal pitviper preys on frogs and birds, but does not reject mice in the terrarium. Body lengths of more than 80 cm (32 in) are rarely recorded.

Propagation and Rearing: After a temperature regime of 18 to 29°C from April to November and 18 to 24°C from November to March, one pair of this species copulated in February and gave birth to 20 live young snakes and four infertile eggs 164 days later. In another litter of 20 young, which were only 10 to 15 cm (4-6 in) long and weighed 1 to 1.5 grams (0.035-0.05 oz), some were yellow and others were greenish. The young snakes molted after five to seven days and captured young treefrogs (*Hyla cinerea*). In the following months they fed on frogs and lizards, which they occasionally lured within striking range with the yellow tip of the tail.

In another group of Eyelash Palm-Pitvipers, matings took place in April to early May. After 250 to 253 days a total of 46 live young 15.5 to 17.7 cm (6.2-7 in) long and weighing on average 3.3 grams (0.16 oz) were born. After a good two weeks the first molt took place. All of the young pitvipers had to be force-fed at first with strips of meat before they took pinkie mice in the fourth month of life. Young snakes of another litter had grown large enough after about three months that day-old mice could be given. In order to accomplish this, in each case a nestling mouse was held with forceps before a snake and was tapped against the snout repeatedly until the snake bit the mouse. Then the mouse was placed in the snake's mouth and, so long as the snake was not disturbed, it was also swallowed. This feeding method was to be sure very time-consuming, but better than stressful forced-feeding.

OTHER SPECIES

The Jararacussu Lancehead (*B. jararacussu*) lives near water in the wild and therefore prefers a large water bowl in the rainforest terrarium. These snakes, which grow to 1.5 meters (5 ft) and more, feed on mice and rats. In two litters, 40 and 37 young snakes about 28 cm (11.2 in) long were produced. They were quite aggressive and at first took lizards, later slightly hairy young mice. They grew rather slowly and at an age of three years had only reached lengths of 64 to 75 cm (25.6-30 in).

Well-heated dry terraria with bathing facilities as well as small mammals—occasionally also chicks—for food are the keeping requirements of the occasionally bred, more terrestrial Urutu Lancehead (*B. alternatus*), Fer-de-Lance (*B. atrox*), Rainforest Hognosed-Pitviper (*B. nasutus*), and Neuwied's Lancehead or Jararaca Pintada (*B. neuwiedi*).

Twelve young Urutu Lanceheads were about 20 cm (8 in) long and weighed 15 grams (0.5 oz). Some of them refused lizards and frogs offered as an experiment and had to be force-fed. One Hognosed-Pitviper that had mated in April gave birth to 12 young about 15 cm (6 in) long; they were initially force-fed with the heads of day-old mice.

ASIAN PITVIPERS (*TRIMERESURUS*)

Counterparts of the American lanceheads of the genus *Bothrops* are the Asian *Trimeresurus*. The often green arboreal and shrub-dwelling species are also known by the collective term bamboo-pitviper. With over 40 species, this genus is quite diverse and includes several ecological groups. It also has been split recently, with three or four genera (*Trimeresurus, Ovophis, Protobothrops, Tropidolaemus*) recognized by some workers.

WHITE-LIPPED GREEN-PITVIPER (*TRIMERESURUS ALBOLABRIS*)

This usually plain green species grows to 60, rarely over 90, centimeters (24, 36 in) in length and lives in low trees and bushes in northern India, Nepal, Indochina, southern China, Taiwan, Hainan, and the Indo-Malayan area. Its toxin is not very potent but can confine victims to bed for a fairly long time. These pitvipers catch mice and nestling rats.

Propagation: Temperatures in summer of about 27°C (81°F), 22°C (72°F) at night, and cooling in winter to 20°C (68°F) led to breeding. Seventeen to 21 young were produced, not all of which wanted to leave their chorions voluntarily. They were about 12 cm (4.8 in) long, weighed 5 grams (0.18 oz), and were green like their parents. Rearing usually took place singly in plastic containers, because siblings were eaten. Pinkie mice held before the snakes with forceps were noticed and eaten sooner than those lying on the bottom. Forced-feeding was carried out with strips of beef heart enriched with vitamins and dusted with calcium.

OTHER SPECIES

A female of the light green to olive, arboreal Pope's Green-Pitviper (*T. popeorum*) gave birth to 17 young about 20 cm (8 in) long and weighing 6 grams (0.2 oz). The 80-cm (32-in) mother weighed 355 grams (12.4 oz) before pregnancy; she weighed 190 grams (6.7 oz) after giving birth to the young, although the snake had fed continually during pregnancy. At two weeks, after the first molt, all of the young snakes of this litter willingly took pinkie mice.

The Mangrove Pitviper (*T. purpureomaculatus*) prefers to live near the coast in mangrove thickets; in the terrarium it can be kept like *T. albolabris*. Without external stimulation, female Mangrove Pitvipers gave birth to 3 to 11 young 17 to 20 cm (6.8-8 in) long, not all of which, however, were viable. They usually had to be force-fed with pinkie mice. One snake, which willingly ate mice right away, doubled in length in one year.

The Okinawa Habu (*T. flavoviridis*) and the Himehabu (*T. okinavensis*) were bred in the terrarium in their Japanese homeland. It is noteworthy that the latter species both gives birth to live young and lays eggs that need only a few days of incubation.

TS-128, 592 pgs, 1400+ color photos

TS-144, 208 pgs, 200+ photos & illus.

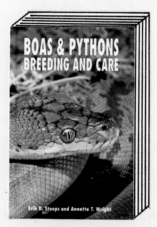

TS-194, 192 pgs, 175+photos

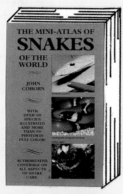

TS-193, 736 pgs, 1400+
color photos

TS-189, 224 pgs, 180+ color photos

KW-127, 96 pgs, 80
color photos

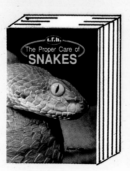

TW-111, 256 pgs, 180+
color photos

AP-925, 160 pgs, 120
photos